New Architecture and Technology

Gyula Sebestyen

Associate Editor: Chris Pollington

Architectural Press

OXFORD   AMSTERDAM   BOSTON   LONDON   NEW YORK   PARIS
SAN DIEGO   SAN FRANCISCO   SINGAPORE   SYDNEY   TOKYO

Architectural Press
An imprint of Elsevier Science
Linacre House, Jordan Hill, Oxford OX2 8DP
200 Wheeler Road, Burlington MA 01803

First published 2003

British Library Cataloguing in Publication Data
Sebestyen, Gyula
    New architecture and technology
    1. Architecture and technology 2. Architecture, Modern – 20th century
    I. Title
    720.1'05

Library of Congress Cataloguing in Publication Data
A catalogue record for this book is available from the Library of Congress

ISBN 0 7506 5164 4

For information on all Architectural Press publications
visit our website at www.architecturalpress.com

Composition by Scribe Design, Gillingham, Kent, UK
Printed and bound in Great Britain by MPG Books Ltd, Bodmin, Cornwall

Contents

Preface

The author of this book has spent most of his professional life actively engaged in building research and construction technology progress. He has immersed himself particularly in the international aspects. Many of his publications discuss topics in these fields. One of these has been his recent book *Construction: Craft to Industry*, published in 1998, which surveys achievements in building science and construction technology progress. Following its publication the author felt the need to go further with the objective of surveying trends in new architecture and the impacts of technological progress on new architecture.

This work, then, should be seen as the continuation of *Construction: Craft to Industry*. Whereas the earlier book surveyed building research and technological progress, this one reviews the impact of technological change on new architecture. Given its broad scope, the book does not aim to treat individual sub-fields in detail; it restricts itself to highlighting general trends. This also serves to explain why no attempt is made to cover all or at least many of the earlier publications about various subjects in the book.

It has been repeated almost ad infinitum that architecture is as much an art as it is an industry. Regrettably, most of the books about this form of human activity tend to focus on one or the other aspect and seldom on their interrelationship. If, however, one does come across a book on this relationship, it concentrates, with certain notable exceptions, on the past's historical styles. We may be enlightened about Brunelleschi's solution for the Dome (i.e. Santa Maria del Fiore) in Florence, or the new type of centring for the London Blackfriars masonry bridge devised by Robert Mylne. These cases are well documented to say nothing of many other similar events going back several hundred years, but where do we find literature concerning modern technology's impact on present-day architecture? But perhaps we are being unjust here. There are some eminent publications (see for example: T. Robbin, *Engineering a New Architecture*, 1996, Yale University Press and A. Holgate, *Aesthetics of Built Form*, 1992, Oxford University Press) but the interwoven development of recent technology and architecture certainly merits further analysis. This precisely is the intention of this book.

Architecture has always had two seemingly contradictory aspects: a local or domestic one and an international or global one. Both aspects have recently become even more pronounced. Local or domestic architecture has been cross-fertilized by international trends and international architecture has been fed inspiration by local traditions. Architectural and engineering consultancies, contractors and clients set up global and regional offices capable of simultaneously servicing the global and the local market. On the other hand, local designers and contractors increasingly affiliate themselves with large national or international practices. Identification of architectural trends has been rendered more complicated by the tremendous diversification of functional requirements and by the architects' ambition to design not only to satisfy various requirements but also to bring characteristics of the buildings' environment into harmony with the features of their projects. Finally, one should not forget that architects themselves undergo change over time so that their projects may reflect changing aspirations.

We commence our analysis by a survey of late twentieth-century architecture (Chapter 1).

Chapters 2 to 4 discuss various aspects of the impact on new architecture of technological progress: Chapter 2, building materials; Chapter 3, buildings and structures; Chapter 4, services. Then follows in Chapter 5 the impact of invisible technologies: research and science, information and telecommunications technology. Chapter 6 reviews the interrelationship of new architecture, urban development, economy, environment and sustainability. Chapter 7 deals with the new phenomenon of architectural aesthetics, while Chapter 8 outlines the price of progress: damages and failures. Finally, Chapter 9 provides a summary.

Technology basically influences architecture in three ways. Firstly, technical progress affects architectural design directly. Architects now make use of computers, achievements in natural science, management knowledge, and take advantage of assistance emanating from various engineering disciplines. Secondly, architects have to design buildings while taking into account the modern technologies of construction: prefabrication, mechanization, industrialization. Thirdly, architects design buildings in which activities with modern technologies take place, which means that requirements on the buildings are formulated. This book covers all three aspects of the interrelationship of architecture and technology. On the other hand, those problems of technological progress that have no direct impact on architecture, are not, or at least not at any length, discussed. The book does not contain detailed case studies but it lists a great number of realizations with examples of the various ways technology impacts on new architecture.

No distinction is made between References and Literature and both are included under the title 'Bibliography'. The Bibliography primarily covers the publications consulted by the author during his work on the book and, even so, have usually been restricted to the most recent publications. The Bibliography may be considered not only as the source of References but also as recommended further reading material.

The author had to limit the number of illustrations. Obviously, a book with such a broad scope could feature many more illustrations than it actually does and those that are included have been restricted to an illustration and visualization of the book's text. For many of the captions a particular method has been employed. The main text of the captions defines the illustration and following this are the technical details and features to which the author specifically wishes to draw the attention of readers. The illustrations are positioned within the framework of the corresponding subject matter as the illustrations within that chapter or section, but their number is not generally indicated in the text because in most cases there is no reference specific to an illustration; it is only the common subject area that links them to each other.

Acknowledgements

The author wishes to express his appreciation to all those who contributed in their different ways to the preparation of the book by information, illustrations or other means.

The author records his gratitude to Julius Rudnay who was kind enough to read the first draft of Chapter 1 and to make a number of useful suggestions.

The author wishes to thank Christopher Pollington for his exhaustive revision of the draft manuscript and for his substantial assistance in final editing. His notable contributions to Chapters 5, 6 and 8 are also gratefully acknowledged. Much of the final wording is attributable to him.

Highly valued editorial contributions were also received from Agnes Sebestyen, Judit Adorian and the team at Architectural Press.

Naturally, the author accepts sole responsibility for any remaining errors or other deficiencies.

1

Trends in architecture

1.1 An Overall Survey

Architectural styles and trends have been discerned and described ever since ancient times. The objective of this chapter is to build on this tradition by describing these trends while placing particular emphasis on the second half of the twentieth century. Whilst other chapters will be dealing with the technological aspects and diverse specific areas of architecture, this one will focus on the changes in architectural styles, but not at the expense of ignoring the corresponding technical, aesthetic, social and other influences. The intention is not to compile a comprehensive history of architecture, and the chapter is restricted to aspects relevant to the subject of the book: to the impact of technological progress on new architecture. For expediency, the discussion is divided into three 40-year periods: 1880–1920, 1920–60 and from 1960 to the present. As the subject of this book is contemporary architecture, the first period will be discussed only in perfunctory terms. More emphasis will be given to the second one, and still greater detail to the final and most recent period.

Whilst this book is devoted to the contacts between architecture and technology, one should not forget the other aspect of architecture as being also an art, indeed one of the fine arts. It has in particular a close affinity with sculpture. In some stylistic trends (for instance in the Baroque and in the Rococo) the division between these two branches of art was scarcely perceivable. In modern times architecture was more inclined to separate itself

from sculpture although certain (e.g. futurist) sculpture did receive inspiration from modern architecture. Later, during post-modern trends, sculpture again came close to architecture so that some architectural designs were conceived as a sculpture (Schulz-Dornburg, 2000). However, in all that follows in this book we focus attention on the interrelationship of (new) architecture and technology.

On the other hand, up-to-date (high-tech) technology may be directly used for new forms of architectural art. Such forms, as for example the application of computer-controlled contemporary illumination techniques, are part of the subject matter of this book and will be discussed at the appropriate place.

1.1.1 The period 1880–1920

It was this period that saw the end of ancient and historical architectural styles, such as Egyptian, Greek, Roman, Byzantine and the later Romanesque, Gothic, Renaissance, Baroque, thus paving the way for twentieth-century modernism. Independence was achieved by what were former colonies as, for example, in Latin America. The benefits of scientific revolution and industrial development were reaped mostly by the leading powers of the day: Great Britain, the United States, France, Germany and Japan. Their conflict resulted in the First World War of 1914–18. At the end of this war it seemed that society was being impelled by democracy and the ideas of liberal capitalism and rationalism, and it was hoped that scientific and economic progress would provide the means for solving the world's problems.

During this 40-year period the construction industry progressed enormously. Even earlier in the 1830s, railway construction was expanding at first in the industrialized countries, later extending to other parts of the world. The growing steel industry provided the new structural building material. A few decades later, the use of reinforced concrete began to compete with steel in this field.

The progress in construction during this period was perhaps best symbolized by the Eiffel Tower, designed by Gustave Eiffel (1832–1923) (Figure 1.1), a leading steel construction expert of his time. In fact, the Tower was built for the Paris World Exhibition in 1889 and the intention at the time was that it should be only a 'temporary' exhibit. Originally 300 metres high, it was taller than any previous man-made structure. More than a century later, during which it has become one of the best-loved buildings in the world, it is still standing intact.

A subsequent engineering feat was the Jahrhunderthalle in Breslau (now Wroclaw), designed by Max Berg (1870–1947) (Figure 1.2), and completed in 1913, a ribbed reinforced concrete dome, which, with its 65-metre diameter, was at its time of construction the largest spanning space yet put up in history. In this heroic period, such technical novelties as central heating, lifts, water and drainage services for buildings became extensively used.

In architecture and the applied arts, there were attempts to revive historical styles, such as the neo-Gothic and neo-Renaissance. Later, the mixture of these historical styles and their reinterpretation gave rise to the Art Nouveau or Jugendstil movements, collectively known as the 'Secession', which literally meant the abandonment of the clas-

Figure 1.1 The Eiffel Tower, Paris, France, 1887–89, structural design: Gustave Eiffel, 300 m high. One of the first spectacular results of technical progress in construction. © Sebestyen: *Construction: Craft to Industry*, E & FN Spon.

Figure 1.2 Jahrhunderthalle, Breslau (Wroclaw), Germany/Poland, 1913, architect: Max Berg. The first (ribbed) reinforced concrete dome whose span (65 m) exceeds all earlier masonry domes.
© Sebestyen: *Construction: Craft to Industry*, E & FN Spon.

sical stylistic conventions and restraints. A similar style was propagated in Britain by the designer William Morris (1834–96), and in America by his followers, in the Arts and Crafts movement, whose aim was to recapture the spirit of earlier craftsmanship, perhaps as a reaction to the banality of mass production engendered by the Industrial Revolution. Consequently, a schism occurred amongst artists, designers and the involved public, between those who advocated adherence to the old academic style and tradition and 'secessionists', who favoured the use of new techniques and materials and a more inventive 'free' style. Also during this period some architects, both in Europe and America, began to experiment with the use of natural, organic forms, such as the Spaniard Antoni Gaudí (1852–1926) in Barcelona and the American Frank Lloyd Wright (1869–1959) (Plates 1 and 2); the latter; in addition, drawing on local rural traditions and forms. Amongst European protomodernists, the Austrian Adolf Loos (1870–1933), the Dutchman Hendrik Petrus Berlage (1856–1934) and the German Peter Behrens (1868–1940) merit mention. Using exaggerated plasticity and extravagant shapes, the German Erich Mendelsohn (1887–1953) and Hans Poelzig (1869–1936) were important figures in the lead into modern architecture.

1.1.2 The period 1920–60

Early modernism

The period has been defined as the period of 'modernism', when architecture finally broke completely with tradition and the 'unnecessary' decoration. With the end of the First World War in 1918, the traditional authority and power of the ruling classes in Europe diminished considerably, and, indeed, in some cases was completely eliminated through revolutions. Even in the victorious nations, such as France and Britain, the loss of life and sacrifice on a vast scale amongst ordinary people fuelled resentment against the establishment.

Germany, having lost the war, was in turmoil and the Austro-Hungarian monarchy ceased to exist altogether. In consequence, the political and economic realities of the time in Europe and elsewhere were most conducive to breaking with tradition, and in this, architecture was no exception.

In Europe, the first focal point of the new aesthetics, modernism, was the school of design, architecture and applied art, known as the Bauhaus, founded by Walter Gropius (1883–1969) in 1919 in Weimar, Germany. Whilst adopting the British Arts and Crafts movement's attention to good design for objects of daily life, the Bauhaus advocated the ethos of functional, yet aesthetically coherent design for mass production, instead of focussing on luxury goods for the privileged elite. Gropius engaged many leading modern artists and architects as teachers, including Paul Klee, Adolf Meyer, Wassily Kandinski, Marcel Breuer and László Moholy-Nagy, just to mention a few.

The early Bauhaus style is perhaps best epitomized by its own school building at Dessau, designed by Walter Gropius in 1925, a building of a somewhat impersonal and machined appearance. Gropius was succeeded as Director by Ludwig Mies van der Rohe (1886–1969) in 1930. Perhaps his best works of the period were the German Pavilion for the International Exhibition at Barcelona and the Tugendhat House at Brno, Czech Republic in 1929 and 1930 respectively. Mies van der Rohe can be counted as one of those architects who genuinely exercised a tremendous influence on the development of architecture. His Tugendhat House influenced several glass houses (Whitney and Kipnis, 1996). We can also see his influence on the architecture of skyscrapers and other multi-storey buildings.

In the Netherlands, influenced by the Bauhaus, but also contributing to it, Theo van Doesburg, Gerrit Thomas Rietveld and Jacobus J. Oud were members of the 'De Stijl' movement, which itself was influenced by Cubism. Their 'Neoplastic' aesthetics used precision of line and form. The culmination of early Dutch modernism was perhaps Rietveld's (1888–1964) Schröder House, built in 1924 at Utrecht (Figure 1.6).

In France the most influential practitioner of modernism was the Swiss-French architect Charles Edouard Jeanneret, universally known as Le Corbusier (1887–1965). His early style can best be seen in the two villas: Les Terrasses at Garches (1927) and the Villa Savoye at Poissy (1930), where the floors were cantilevered off circular columns to permit the use of strip windows. Flowing, plastically-modelled spaces and curved partition walls augmenting long straight lines characterize both buildings. Le Corbusier also influenced the profession through his theoretical work *Towards a New Architecture* published in 1923 as well as through his activity abroad and in international professional organizations. The creation of the CIAM (Congrès Internationaux d'Architecture Moderne) in 1928 underpinned the movement towards modernism, industrialization and emergence of the 'International Style'.

A realization on an international scale of this trend was the residential complex in Stuttgart, Germany, in which seventeen architects participated. Gradually, in several European countries modernism became dominant. Some of the countries in which eminent representatives were to be found (e.g. France, Germany, Great Britain and the Netherlands) receive mention later; while other countries (e.g. Italy) although not cited directly had equally outstanding architects.

Along with the aesthetic transformation of architecture, technical progress was also remarkable, and nowhere more so than in the United States, where in the late 1920s, following the achievements and examples of the Chicago School some 25 years before, there was a further period of boom in the construction of skyscrapers. The Empire State Building in New York, designed by architects Shreve, Lamb and Harmon, completed in 1931, symbolizes what is best from this period. With its 102 storeys and a height of 381 metres, it remained for 40 years the tallest building in the world. Another construction of great symbolic value was the Golden Gate Bridge at San Francisco, California. This is a suspension bridge with a span of 1281 metres and was completed in 1937.

Meanwhile in Europe, wide-spanning roofs were constructed without internal support by a new type of structure: the reinforced concrete shell based on the membrane theory. The Planetarium in Jena, Germany (constructed between 1922 and 1927), with a span/thickness ratio of 420 to 1 is a prime example. Additionally, wide-spanning steel structures (space frames, domes and vaults) were developed.

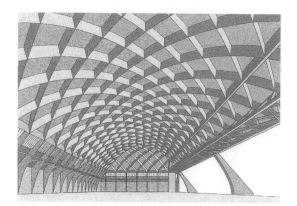

Figure 1.3 Airplane Hall, Italy, designer: Pier Luigi Nervi, 1939–41, floor surface 100 × 40 m, vault assembled from pre-cast reinforced concrete components. An early (pre-Second World War) example of prefabrication with reinforced concrete components. © Sebestyen: *Construction: Craft to Industry*, E & FN Spon.

The promising economic progress of the 1920s received a severe jolt in 1929 as a result of the worldwide economic crisis that was to last for about three years. Although by the early 1930s there was again an upswing in the economy, new political events affected the course of modern architecture. Germany, as had Italy several years earlier, became a fascist dictatorship in 1933. Modernism, however, was an anathema to Nazi ideology, on both aesthetic and ideological grounds. Consequently, the Bauhaus, the leading school of modern architecture in Europe, was forced to close its doors. Many of its teachers and pupils emigrated, mainly to the United States, where they continued to propagate the ethos of the school, thus transferring the ideals and aesthetics of European modernism to the United States, which for the next 25 years or so remained the leading country for modern architecture.

In Russia, after the October Revolution of 1917 the Bolsheviks took power, establishing the Soviet Union, where there was a period of innovative experimentation in the arts and architecture (structuralism, constructivism). Vladimir Tatlin's (1885–1953) Worker's Club (1929) constitutes a notable example. However, at the end of the 1920s, a totalitarian form of communism was consolidated under the leadership and terror of Stalin, which decreed the artistic superiority and imperative of socialist realism, a type of monumental classicism. In this style, intended to be an expression of power, both communism and fascism shared an aesthetic affinity, in spite of their manifestly different ideologies. Consequently, modern artists and architects found themselves isolated, and, as had been the case in Germany, many elected to leave the country.

1945–60. The post-Second World War sub-period

In Europe, the Second World War ended with the defeat of Nazi Germany. The United States markedly strengthened its economic and political position. The war itself had caused damage on an unprecedented scale in many countries. Consequently, the post-war reconstruction of housing, industrial stock, transport and infrastructure presented a monumental task, but with it came massive opportunities for the building industry, and particularly for the architects. The first industrialized reinforced concrete large-panel housing was built at Le Havre, in France (1949). Subsequently, variants of this system were developed all over Europe. Its use found particular favour in the planned economies of the Soviet Union and of Soviet-dominated Eastern Europe. It was the aspiration entertained by planners and politicians alike that industrialized architecture would resolve the housing shortage arising from war damage and the population increase, as well as from the burgeoning expectations of rising living standards in the post-war era.

The large-scale construction of new social multi-storey residential buildings contributed to reducing the housing shortage. Whilst the merits of housing factories can be debated in terms of economy and productivity, the aesthetic and social disadvantages of industrialized housing can seldom be in contention: numerous towns throughout Europe inherited the unwelcome legacy of large, impersonal, often unwanted and decaying housing estates. Nor did the prefabrication of family houses, applying the experience of shipbuilding, car manufacturing and the plastic industries, bring any general relief to

housing shortage. Nevertheless, in some countries (in Europe, Japan, USA) it did contribute positively – although in most cases only marginally – to the provision of new housing.

Many European town centres were severely damaged or entirely destroyed: London, Bristol, Rotterdam, Dresden and Warsaw, to mention just a few. These cities, especially in Western Europe, became the site of large-scale development and feverish property speculation. In spite of the many notable exceptions, the overall aesthetic effect was often mediocre, incongruous and soulless.

One of the more successful examples of post-war city centre development, which has stood the test of time, is the Lijnbaan (1953), a shopping quarter in war-ravaged downtown Rotterdam, designed by J.H.van den Broek and J.B. Bakema. The needs and opportunities of wholesale town development gave rise to the profession of town planning. It became an important profession and discipline, exerting its own significant influence on architectural theory and practice. Consequently, such novel concepts as the new towns and satellite town developments emerged or were revived on a worldwide scene also.

Perhaps the most innovative and monumental example of such projects of the period was the new capital. The most striking of these was Brasilia, the new administrative capital of Brazil, designed by Oscar Niemeyer and Lucio Costa in 1956, where town planning ideas went hand in hand with inspiring architectural style. Niemeyer's designs realized in Brazil, and also in France, served as an inspiration to many architects around the world.

The technology and structure of various types of buildings (skyscrapers, wide-spanning structures, etc.) developed in various ways. In Europe, the Italian Pier Luigi Nervi (1891–1979) and the Spaniard Eduardo Torroja (1899–1961), both structural engineers, refined the use of long-span reinforced concrete structures, which had begun in the 1930s, with aesthetic flair. This resulted after the Second World War in the design of a number of spectacular reinforced concrete or steel roof structures. The American Richard Buckminster Fuller invented and patented the geodesic dome and tensegrity structures in the 1950s. Metal lattice grids with ingenious nodes, fabrication and assembly methods were invented and introduced. One of the first in this category was the MERO system, originally introduced by Max Mengeringhausen in Germany in 1942. Large column-free spaces are characteristic of certain types of buildings. Some of which have specific aesthetic features, such as external masts, lightweight filigree suspended or tensile members, extreme articulation of ceilings eventually designed directly with a repetitive articulation of the structure or construction or in combination of the structure and lighting, etc.

As already noted, many of the teachers and pupils at the Bauhaus emigrated to the United States.

Undoubtedly, the most influential among these was Ludwig Mies van der Rohe, the last director of the Bauhaus. Soon after his arrival in America, Mies van der Rohe was appointed as director of the Armour (now Illinois) Institute of Technology, where he remained for the next 20 years. Probably his most important commission was the skyscraper office building in New York with a glass and bronze exterior, which he designed with Philip Johnson, known as the Seagram Building (1956–58) (Figure 1.4).

The rigorous simplicity and elegance of this building has inspired many contemporary architects, but, alas, has also given rise to many inferior imitations around the world. The style itself has become known as the 'International Style', a phrase first coined in the 1930s. According to them, in this style the columns serve as the basic vertical load-bearing structure, thereby providing uninterrupted space on each floor. The building, which is of simple configuration and geometry, is surrounded by an uninterrupted external envelope, in which the windows are an integral part. Such façades are now termed as 'curtain walls' (Khan, 1998).

An even earlier example of the International Style (following some less notable examples during the 1930s) and the use of curtain walls can be seen at Lever House, New York, designed by Skidmore,

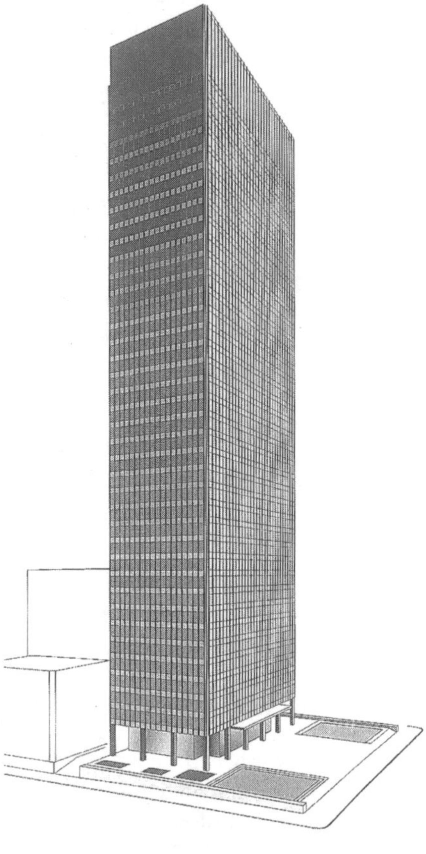

Figure 1.4 Seagram Building, New York, USA, 1958, architect: Mies van der Rohe in collaboration with Philip Johnson. Together with the Lever House building, a prototype of the International Style.

Figure 1.5 Cable-styled bridge, Pont de Normandie, France; main span: 856 m. *Source:* Freyssinet Photo Service.

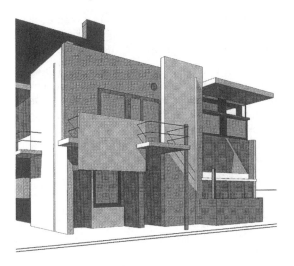

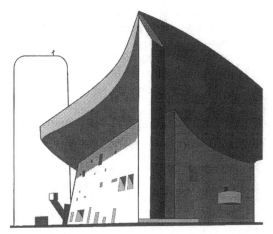

Figure 1.8 Chapel Notre-Dame-du Haut, Ronchamps, France,1950–55, architect: Le Corbusier. An organic design by the master of modernist architecture.

Figure 1.6 The Schröder Family House in Utrecht, The Netherlands, 1924, architect: Gerrit Rietveld. One of the first examples of modernist architecture during the 1920s.

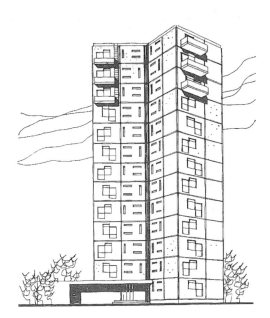

Figure 1.7 Large Panel Building, System Camus, Pantin near Paris, France. System building with room-sized large panels became a new form of industrialization in certain countries and for some time. © Sebestyen: *Large Panel Buildings*, Akadémiai Kiadó.

Owings and Merrill (1952) (Plate 3). The style itself had its adherents until many years after the Second World War. After 1960 it gradually came to lose its leading position, but is still alive as a part of the neo-modernist trend. Apart from housing, skyscrapers and wide-spanning structures, modernism and industrialization also left their mark on schools, commercial buildings, civil engineering structures and others.

1.1.3 The period 1960–2000. Post-modernism and after

This period was in general characterized by economic prosperity. The arms race between the superpowers extended into space, stimulating high-technology industries, such as electronics, communications, plastics and others, as well as the more traditional ones: the metal, glass and chemical industries. Innovations and inventions in armament and space research quickly found their way into everyday civilian use, and this applied to the building industry too. Economic prosperity was briefly interrupted by increased oil prices. The 1973–74 energy crisis spurred Western economies into devising new solutions for the reduction of energy use, for example by adopting higher standards of thermal insulation and by developing engines and motors with improved efficiency.

Gradually Western governments assumed responsibility for housing the 'masses' in addition to educating them, which by now took in all forms of higher education and cultural development. Public housing was elevated to mass production. Building and municipal services developed.

Architecture ceased to be restricted to a handful of building types. The increased variety and complexity of functions within and around buildings called for new structural and architectural solutions. Moreover, the construction of high-speed railways and the new facilities of air transport were of greater complexity than was traditionally the case. This, together with the general increase in the size of buildings and structures, led to the use of greatly increased spans. Therefore, any treatise on architecture must cover a much broader range than was the case in earlier periods.

The notion that buildings equipped with a multitude of modern services could serve as machines was first raised in the 1920s. It was Le Corbusier who famously said that a house is a machine for living in. This was a statement that did not find universal favour. Frank Lloyd Wright vented his sarcastic disagreement: 'Yeah, just like a human heart is a suction pump.' It was only later in the 'high-tech' post-modern period that the idea (i.e. that a building could be considered as a machine) actually materialized but then only in a limited sense. The early modern style was grounded on rationalism and it intended to break with the historical precedents. Fired by a new aesthetic vision, many architects became convinced of their ability to solve most social problems by architectural means. However, disappointment with modernism soon arose in the recognition of the failure to construct cities with an adequate quality of life (Jacobs, 1961). Many felt that a fresh start was required, which could contribute to urban renewal. Just to mention one of the similar statements about this development: 'The revolutionary ideal of solving societal problems through design that was so vehemently proclaimed by modernism's proponents in the heroic age of the 1930s was exposed as hollow'.

Gradually, from modernism and from its derivatives, such as brutalism, functionalism and structuralism, a new and different type of architecture

evolved with some practitioners and theoreticians accepting and others rejecting the post-modern label (Koolhaas, 1978, Jodidio, 1997).

Whilst some architects were prepared to see the post-modern style as a logical development of modernism, many considered that the new style was a reaction to the latter's impersonality. According to Jencks: 'the main motivation for Post-modern architecture is obviously the social failure of modern architecture' (Jencks, 1996) and

> Post-modern is a portmanteau concept covering several approaches to architecture which have evolved from modernism. As the hybrid term suggests, its architects are still influenced by modernism ... and yet they have added other languages to it. A Post-modern building is doubly coded – part Modern and part something else: vernacular, revivalist, local, commercial, metaphorical, or contextual. (Jencks, 1988)

Indeed the post-modernist style favoured the use of decoration, symbolism, humour and even mysticism. Unlike those favouring pastiche out of nostalgia for the past, the proponents of post-modernism were prepared to avail themselves of the use of up-to-date technology, as well as traditional materials. In this they recognized that technology affected architecture, both in form and function. The post-modern architecture is further set apart from the others and from late-modernism by Beedle in the following polemic:

> Jencks further distinguishes between Post-modernism in its inclusion of past historical style, which root[s] post-modern buildings in time and place, [and] late modernism, which disdains all historical imagery. Post-modern architecture is eclectic in its expression and employs ornament, symbolism, humor, and urban context as architectural devices. In contrast, late-modern architecture derives its principles almost exclusively from modernism and focuses on the abstract qualities of space, geometry and light. (Beedle,1995 and Jencks, 1986)

Developments in efficient heating and air-conditioning services opened up the possibilities of maintaining climatic comfort in large spaces, which were covered, or enclosed by a thin, often glazed envelope of minimal thermal inertia. Consequently, historical solutions, such as the tent or the atrium, could be revived in a new context and with the use of new materials and technology.

The atrium with glazed roof became a favourite feature of many office, hotel and shopping developments. Relatively recent concepts are sustainability, protection of the environment and energy conservation, all of which have influenced architectural thinking (Melet, 1999). Sustainability, in its most general meaning, refers to strategies in the present that do not harm or endanger future life. Various factors contribute to the design of sustainable buildings, which are also referred to as 'green buildings'. These factors, among others, include attention to energy-conservation and HVAC (heating, ventilation, air-conditioning) control, thermal storage and land conservation.

The 'new architecture' makes use of new geometric and amorphous shapes, new concepts and proportions, measure, colour, lighting and technological aspects. Some new non-technological factors, coming from the latest results of science and social development, also affect new architecture.

The original ideals of modernism were characterized by Jencks: 'Modern architecture is the overpowering faith in industrial progression and its translation into the pure, while International Style (or at least the Machine Aesthetics) [has] the goal of transforming society both in its sensibility and social make-up' (Jencks, 1996). Modernism, undoubtedly, achieved great technical progress in building but by the end of the modernist period (around the 1960s) disenchantment with it had set in strongly. This in turn led to post-modernism, which gradually spread throughout the world.

During the period 1960–2000 housing became a mass affair to the point when tens of millions of families could move into well-equipped homes. However, an improvement in world housing conditions and city life remains a task for the twenty-first century. At the same time one has to admit: 'One reason that the label post-modern has become accepted is the vagueness and ambiguity of the term' (Jencks, 1982).

The 1960s introduced new thinking, which gradually developed into the post-modern trend. The last 40 years of the century saw how post-modernism itself became spent and began to make way for new architecture, sometimes called super-modernism. New functions of buildings and the concentration of different functions in single versatile and flexible buildings required new building designs. New architecture does far more than simply retain and renew the achievements of the past's architecture; it also applies new principles.

These embrace new architectural and structural schemes, the satisfaction of new functional requirements and the use of modern construction and design technologies. Some of these are the new materials (reinforced concrete, metals, glass, plastics), tensioned structures (tents have been built since ancient times but their modern variants offer entirely new possibilities), long-span roofs over large spaces, retractable roofs, deployable structures, atria and many others. In certain types of buildings (hotels, offices) high atria have been introduced (Saxon, 1993).

What could we single out as symbolic of this period? Certainly one building alone would not match all criteria for such a symbol. Despite this, let us select some outstanding models. The Petronas Towers in Kuala Lumpur (completed in 1998, twin towers with a high-performance concrete core and cylindrical perimeter frame, 450 metres high, architect Cesar Pelli with associates) mark the very first occasion when the tallest building in the world has been constructed in a developing country.

The Akashi Bridge in Japan, completed also in 1998, has the longest span in the world (2022 metres). Great progress has been achieved in long-span building roofs: tensioned cable roofs, etc. From the imposing number of new cultural buildings, perhaps the Bilbao Guggenheim Museum (architect: Frank O. Gehry, completed in 1998) may best be characterized as containing the most up-to-date design features: a cladding made from thin titanium sheet, designed by computer program (Plate 6).

Many great masters of architecture have been identified and named in this chapter. In recent years new and talented architects have emerged and it can with justification be stated that a new generation has appeared on the scene (Thompson, 2000).

The speed with which functions, requirements and technology are changing has called for flexibility and adaptability in the design of buildings. This has also been expressed as strategies aimed at minimizing obsolescence (Iselin and Lemer, 1993).

Returning to the socio-political events, the most momentous of these in the late 1980s was the collapse of the communist system in Eastern Europe, and, with this, the end of the centrally planned economy and ideological constraints. However, from the point of view of architecture, the most far-reaching consequences of the event lay in economics. The event assisted the acceleration of the globalized economy, the penetration of multinational companies into new industries and, concomitantly, the rapid growth of commerce, technology, corporate identity and the aesthetics of consumerism. Globalization affects also architecture and construction, but globalization as an overall trend in society is still very much a matter of debate.

1.2 Stylistic Trends in New Architecture

Throughout history architectural styles, reflecting technological, social and aesthetic developments, have taken various directions, and the last 40 years have been no exception. As art historians, aesthetes, and indeed architects themselves, like to categorize architectural styles, they labelled this period as post-modern. However, as mentioned, the label brings together very different trends, and whilst many architects accept being classified as post-modern, there is no shortage of others who reject such categorization. The various ways to define styles and trends in new architecture are not discussed here. For our purpose we are making use of a simplified list of trends as follows:

- metabolic, metaphoric, anthropomorphic
- neo-classicist (neo-historic)
- late-modern, neo-modern, super-modern

- organic and regional modern
- deconstructivist.

The above is not a comprehensive list of accepted or widely used classifications. For example, Jencks (whose classifications are the most widespread and quoted) quite recently wrote about dynamic, melodramatic, beautiful and kitsch architecture (Jencks, 1999). Since that time, further trends have been identified. Indeed, there are countless other labels for different architectural styles, such as new expressionism, neo-vernacular, intuitive modernism, etc. We shall not attempt to make a full list of these labels, as often they would fail to define even a fraction of the oeuvre of a prolific architect.

1.2.1 Metabolic, metaphoric and anthropomorphic architecture

A metaphor is an artistic device, aimed at evoking certain feelings by creating some analogy between two dissimilar entities. Usually, therefore, in metaphoric architecture (sometimes also categorized as symbolic architecture, Jencks, 1985) the designer's aim is to derive some association or symbol from the function of the building or from its context, which then in some way is reflected in the appearance of the building. The use of the metaphor in architecture, in fact, is not new. For example, Gothic cathedrals often evinced mysticism and pious devotion. A similar purpose motivated Le Corbusier in the design of the Ronchamps Chapel. A notable example of metaphoric building in recent times is the Sydney Opera House (Figure 1.9), architect: Jorge Utzon; structural engineers: Ove Arup and Partners (Utzon, 1999).

The location of the building at Sydney Harbour inspired the architect to choose a roof system consisting of reinforced concrete shell segments, which resemble wind-stretched sails. The Sydney Opera House inspired Renzo Piano to design the new Aurora Place Office Tower, some 800 metres from the Opera, with fins and sails extending at the top of the 200-metres-high building beyond the façade. In the Bahia temple at New Delhi, the reinforced concrete shells bring to mind the petals of a flower. The roof of the Idlewild TWA terminal at New York Airport (architect: Eero Saarinen) reminds

Figure 1.9 Opera House, Sydney, Australia, architect: Jorn Utzon, structural design consultant: Peter Rice from Ove Arup. Metaphoric design with reinforced concrete shell roof, reminiscent of sails blown by wind.

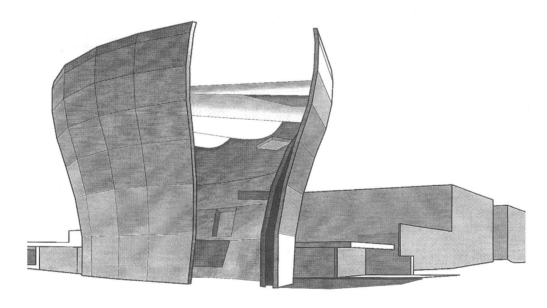

Figure 1.10 Hungarian Pavilion at Hanover, Germany, World Expo, 2000, architect: George Vadasz. Design based on metaphoric thinking: two hand palms? a petal?

the viewer of the wings of a bird or aeroplane, whilst the façade of the Institute of Science and Technology in Amsterdam (designed by Renzo Piano) recalls a boat. Santiago Calatrava's Lyon-Satalas TGV railway station building (1990–94) equally imposes on the spectator the impression of a bird's wings.

Some metaphoric examples by Japanese architects include:

- Shimosuwa Lake Suwa Museum, Japan (designer: Toyo Ito, 1990–93): from the exterior elevation this evinces the image of a reversed boat but, in plan, a fish.
- Museum of Fruit, Japan (designer: Itsuko Hasegawa, 1993–95): here the individual building volumes have been put under a cover of earth, which could be interpreted as representing the seeds of plants and fruits and so indirectly the power of life and productivity.
- Umeda Sky City, Japan (designer: Hiroshi Hara, 1988–93): here skyscrapers have been connected at high levels thus providing an association to future space structures.

Sometimes the metaphor is related to the human body or face, in which case we speak of an anthropomorphic approach. For example, Kazamatsu Yamashita's Face House in Kyoto, Japan, 1974, is designed to imitate a human face. Takeyama's Hotel Beverly resembles a human phallus. Some architects do not apply recognizable metaphors directly but deduce the building's form through metaphysical considerations. This approach also characterized the designs of some deconstructivist architects (see below). Daniel Libeskind projected the expansion of the Jewish Museum in Berlin in the form of a Star of David. This, however, is not immediately obvious to the casual visitor.

Metabolic architecture derives its name from the Greek word *metabole* meaning a living organism with biochemical functions. The term is applied, and not always appropriately, to non-living organizations or systems that react or adapt to external influences and are able to change their properties in response to various influences. The concept of 'metabolism' was affirmed at the international level at the Tokyo World Conference held in 1960 on industrial design by the Japanese Kisho Kurokawa,

Kiynori Kikutaka, Fumihiko Maki and Masato Otaka. By doing so, they wished to counteract aspects of modernism that sometimes adopted the approach of machine design in the context of architecture. At the same time this particular group of architects were also guided by the desire to diminish the impact of Western architecture on the Japanese traditions, without rejecting up-to-date technology in construction.

Subsequently, and influenced by American mobile home unit technology, Kurokawa introduced his

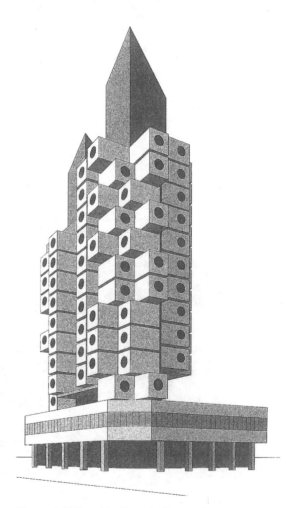

Figure 1.11 Nagakin Capsule Tower, Tokyo, Japan, architect: Akira Kurokawa. Metabolic (capsule) architecture.

'Capsule' theory, which was published in the March 1969 issue of the periodical *Space Design*. A cornerstone of this theory was the replaceability, or interchangeability, of the individual capsules. Kurokawa's first such building, which immediately succeeded in making him known worldwide, was the Nakagin Tower in Tokyo (Figure 1.11), built in 1972, in which capsules of a standard size were fixed to a reinforced concrete core. Whilst the core represented permanence, the capsules made possible functional adaptability and change. The Nakagin Tower was followed by further capsule buildings and unrealized projects of metabolic cities. Although metabolic architecture failed to gain wider acceptance, the idea of capsules was used in several forms, as for example in Moshe Safdie's residential complex at the Montreal Expo, which consisted of modular, pre-cast concrete boxes. Also, mobile home manufacturers in the USA, from whom the idea of capsule building originated in the first place, gained further inspiration from the architectural achievements of the concept. Kurokawa's later designs in the 1990s (the Ehme Prefectural Museum of General Science and the Osaka International Convention Centre, both in Japan, and the Kuala Lumpur airport, Malaysia, the last designed in association with the Malaysian Akitek Jururancang) do not follow the capsule theory; instead they are based on abstract simple geometric shapes made complex. The Kuala Lumpur airport's hyperbolic shell is reminiscent of traditional Islamic domes and thereby combines the modern with the traditional.

1.2.2 Neo-classicist architecture. Traditionalism. Historicism

In theory at least modernism negated all forms of the historical styles, while at the same time cultivating the idea of the building as a machine. It was this line of thought that later led to the idea of high-tech architecture, an early example of which is the Pompidou Centre in Paris, designed by Richard Rogers and Renzo Piano. By contrast, post-modernism took another route, by returning to the use of ornamentation and decoration, although usually not by simply copying historical details, but rather by applying the spirit and essence of historical styles.

Neo-classicist architecture used classical themes, principles and forms in loose associations, reminiscent of but not identical to historical patterns. Consequently, the style is quite diversified and its variants have been labelled as freestyle, canonic, metaphysical, narrative, allegoric, nostalgic, realist, revivalist, urbanist, eclectic, etc. (Jencks, 1987). The buildings of Ricardo Bofill in Montpellier, Marne-la-Vallée (Plate 4) and Saint Quentin en Yvelines, seem nearest to classicism in detail and composition (d'Huart, 1989). Although his designs reflect historical architecture, he prescribed construction by using prefabricated concrete components. The oeuvre of several other architects also belongs to this trend, even if the respective approaches may differ greatly. Robert A.M. Stern, Allan Greenberg, Demetri Porphyrios, James Stirling and Leon Krier and Robert Krier may be mentioned as outstanding representatives of the style. A questionable application of historical models, in the form of 'gated communities', appears in some countries, imitating the castle concept with a fence, moat and controlled entrance but applying the concept for the purpose of elitist dwellings.

Paradoxically, a nostalgic form of architectural historicism happened to emerge in some of the most advanced industrialized countries, sometimes appealing to popular taste. In the United Kingdom, the style found an influential and high-profile advocate in the person of the Prince of Wales, whose intervention led to the annulment of a competition for the extension of the National Gallery, London, in which the jury's preference for the modernist design by the firm Ahrends Burton and Koralek was set aside.

The Prince, reflecting a popular mood of the time, led his attack against modernism in defence of historicizing architecture at his 1984 Gala Address at the Royal Institute of British Architects with his question: 'Why has everything got to be vertical, straight, unbending, only at right angles and functional?' Under his influence, which found considerable public support in the UK, many buildings of contemporary function, such as supermarkets and shopping centres, which until then were designed to resemble barns, acquired a direct, even occasionally out of context, visual association with historical, vernacular architecture. In 1989 Prince

Charles formulated the ten principles upon which we can build as follows:

1. the place: respect for the land
2. hierarchy: the size of buildings in relation to their public importance and the relative significance of the different elements which make up a building
3. scale: relation to human proportions and respect for the scale of the buildings around them
4. harmony: the playing together of the parts
5. enclosure: the feeling of well-designed enclosure
6. materials: the revival and nurturing of local materials
7. decoration: reinstatement of the arts and crafts
8. art: study of nature and humans
9. signs and lights: effective street lighting, advertising and lettering
10. community: participation of people in their own surroundings.

The ideas of Prince Charles certainly encouraged traditionalists but they never became the sole inspiring force in architecture (Hutchinson, 1989). Charles's attack on the modernist projects submitted for the expansion of the London National Gallery resulted in a new project prepared by architects Venturi, Scott and Brown. The new design contains classicist but non-functional columns and it is only the architects' high-quality work that has saved the building from becoming pure kitsch.

In skilful hands, however, historicizing architecture could be quite subtle. For example, the new building of the Stuttgart New State Gallery, designed by James Stirling, Michael Wilford and Partners (1977–84), alludes to Schinkel's museum designs from over a century before with considerable flair, showing that old motifs can be brought back and meaningfully transformed in harmony with modern application. In another example, the façade of the administrative building in Portland, Oregon, by Michael Graves (1980–82) makes a neo-classicist impression, without using any authentic historical detailing (Graves, 1982). Neo-classicism, therefore, may appear with different features. Some further outstanding examples in this category are the buildings designed by the American Robert A.M. Stern,

the Californian Getty Museum designed by Richard Meier, the New York AT&T building designed by Philip Johnson and John Burgee. Papadakis treats in one of his books (Papadakis, 1997) the designs of twenty architectural practices and five projects of urbanism, all inspired by 'modern classicism'.

1.2.3 Late-modern, neo-modern, super-modern architecture

In spite of the popularity and success of the neo-classical and historicizing architecture, the modernist style has never been abandoned, as many architects continued to be led by its principles. Following the 1960s, these architects were sometimes labelled 'late-modernists' and, later, as 'neo-modernists' and 'super-modernists'. However, in time and under new influences, modernism acquired new characteristics and therefore the modernist design began to differ more and more from the pre-1960s' architecture.

Other labels, such as neo-minimalism, also appeared (Jodidio, 1998), in which the clear and simple lines of early modernism were evoked.

'High-tech' is recognized (by some) as having a style of its own. However, its elements can be present in all categories of new architecture. High-tech features are common in neo-modernism and deconstructivism, as for example at the Paris Pompidou Centre by Richard Rogers and Renzo Piano (Plate 5) mentioned above. The use of high-tech elements is even more characteristic of the British Norman Foster and the Japanese Fumihiko Maki. Indeed, the conspicuous use of these elements may impart the appearance of an industrial product to a building. The buildings as industrial products become apparent in the aggressive, metallic coated 'Dead Tech' buildings of the Japanese Shin Takamatsu or Kazuo Shinohara's more peaceful 'zero-machines' with a pure graphic architecture.

Modernism was characterized by an elimination of decoration and ornamentation. This resulted in the idea of 'minimalism' or 'plainness' (Zabalbeascoa and Marcos, 2000). This trend was preserved only to some extent in neo-modernism, which combined modernism with post-modernism, i.e. it did not altogether reject decoration and ornamentation although it did reject the historical forms.

1.2.4 Organic and regional modern architecture

The forms created by organic architecture, or to cite a French expression 'architecture vitaliste' (Zipper and Bekas, 1986), resemble those found in nature. As mentioned, some of its early masters were Frank Lloyd Wright who combined early modernism with organic elements, and Antoni Gaudí who made use of the art and traditions of Iberian brick-masonry (Van der Ree, 2000).

Frank Lloyd Wright often referred to his design methodology as organic and to nature as a source of inspiration to him. However, he did not define the meaning of the above. It is fair to state that whilst his designs were inspired by nature and indeed enhanced nature, they were highly technical and provided with all up-to-date equipment. Nevertheless, in our time we categorize as organic primarily styles which also in the forms of the buildings reflect nature by their curves and curved shapes.

The Hungarian Imre Makovecz adopted an 'organic' approach in his entire oeuvre. He frequently employs wood structures, with shingle roofs, shingled domes and timber members, using them in their natural form without attempting to impart a regular shape. The buildings of Makovecz inspired a number of younger architects both in Hungary and further afield. Their design ideology is to draw from the real or imaginary forms of ancient Hungarian folk architecture, such as tents and yourts. Makovecz sometimes derives inspiration from the human body or face (an anthropomorphic approach), or from trees or plants (zoomorphic approach). Makovecz's internationally acclaimed Hungarian Pavilion at the Sevilla Expo, Spain, 1990–92, is representative of his style.

A number of basically modernist, or post-modernist architects chose to use the style, but unlike Makovecz, whose entire oeuvre is hallmarked by it, these architects were inspired by the organic style because of the function, location or surroundings of the actual building. Renzo Piano's Kanak Museum

Figure 1.12 Communal building, Szigetvar, Hungary, 1985, architect: Imre Makovecz. Organic architecture with revivalist traditional, nationalistic ornaments.

in New Caledonia could be mentioned as an example, where local ethnographic, technological and artistic features were utilized. Others, like Itsuko Hasegawa, availed themselves of contemporary materials and geometry in the organic manner to evoke mountains, trees and artificial landscapes. Regional modern architecture usually draws its inspiration from the local traditions and skills, in combination with modern or post-modern elements. Because of its links with the tradition, the style may assimilate the local historical forms and decoration. For these very reasons the style can also relate to organic (but eventually to other types of) architecture.

An individual type of organic architecture was developed by the Austrian Friedenreich Hundertwasser who rejected all linear and angular features in design. He declared that straight lines are an instrument of the Devil. His multi-storey buildings (as, for example, in Vienna at the corner of the Löwengasse and the Kegelgasse) resemble certain vernacular houses. In their construction much freedom was granted to builders and future users. Whilst these buildings are much-visited attractions (some of his buildings may be considered as belonging to deconstuctivism; see next section), they remained a solitary trend in new architecture.

1.2.5 Deconstructivist architecture

Deconstructivism can be considered as a group of independent stylistic developments within the post-modern period (Norris and Benjamin, 1988, Papadakis et al., 1989, Jencks and Kropf, 1997). Its origin can be traced back to the Russian avantgarde of the 1920s as manifested in the work of Malevich and Tchernikov and the Suprematism of El Lissitzky and Swetin. In Europe it had its roots in the Dada movement. In the USA one of its birthplaces was the East (primarily New York), the other being California. It discontinued the historical architectural language, the autocracy of horizontal and vertical elements and deconstructed the tectonic and orthogonal system (Bonta, 2001).

The partnership Coop Himmelblau designed the first actual deconstructivist realizations in Europe: the lawyers' practice in Vienna, Falkenstrasse

(1983–85) and the Funder factory building in St Veit Glan, Austria (1988–89) (Plate 31). Zaha Hadid's Vitra fire-fighting station in Weil am Rein (1993) went on to world fame.

In the USA Peter Eisenman, one of the group New York Five, designed buildings with crossing frames and distorted building grids. A special innovation was the use of folding applied by Eisenman at Colombus University (1989) but also by Daniel Libeskind at the Berlin Jewish Museum (1988–95).

The theoretical impact of deconstructivist architecture, however, only emerged after the Second World War when the French philosopher Jacques Derrida defined its principles in art and literature. During preparations for the design of the Paris La Villette complex, Bernard Tschumi contacted Jacques Derrida and invited him to participate in a discussion about deconstructivism in architecture (Wigley, 1993). As Tschumi reported: 'When I first met Jacques Derrida, in order to convince him to confront his own work with architecture, he asked me, "But how could an architect be interested in deconstruction? After all, deconstruction is anti-form, anti-hierarchy, anti-structure, the opposite of all that architecture stands for". "Precisely for this reason," I replied!' (Tschumi, 1994). Deconstructivist architects, after analysing the project brief and the site conditions, usually reach quite unconventional design solutions. The main initiator of the style in the USA was Frank O. Gehry in California who often applies the techniques of scenography, movie making and theatre, using inexpensive, stage-set materials. In Japan, Hiromi Fuji followed the style. His buildings have been described as having a grid-based light framework, shaken out of order by an earthquake.

The 1988 Exhibition at the New York Museum of Modern Art curated by Philip Johnson and Mark Wigley promoted the deconstructivist architecture of Frank O. Gehry, Peter Eisenman, Daniel Libeskind, Rem Koolhaas, Zaha Hadid, Bernard Tschumi and the group Coop Himmelblau (Johnson and Wigley, 1988). Mark Wigley wrote in the prospectus: 'In each project, the traditional structure of parallel planes – stacked up horizontally from the ground plane within a regular form – is twisted. The frame is warped. Even the ground plane is warped.'

Whilst deconstructivism never attained dominance amongst architectural styles, it continually attracts adherents. Undoubtedly, the most spectacular example of the style hitherto is Frank O. Gehry's titanium-clad Guggenheim Museum at Bilbao, Spain (Plate 6). Considering the high cost of titanium, only the use of thin sheets made the application possible. Consequently, the individual cladding sheets move and distort, due to thermal and mechanical stresses, thus displaying a range of colour variations and reflections according to lighting conditions (Jodidio, 1998, van Bruggen, 1997). Also titanium cladding was proposed in the winning competition project for the Beijing Opera by the Frenchman Andreu. It equally based its façade design on thin titanium sheet.

Philip Johnson hailed the Bilbao museum building as the century's greatest work and Gehry declared: 'Poor Frank. He will never top Bilbao, you only get to build one miracle in a lifetime!' However, Gehry's Los Angeles Disney Concert Hall (2275 seats), completed after a halt and several design revisions, is also a (deconstructivist) masterpiece (Figure 1.16).

Another deconstructivist building, Gehry's Nationale Nederlanden Building in Prague, Czech Republic (1992–96) (Plate 7) has a curved glass façade, in striking contrast to the historic ambience of its surroundings.

The use of titanium could result in the misleading conclusion that deconstructivist architects are fond of expensive materials. The truth is rather the contrary, they frequently use cheap materials, which earlier would not even qualify for being used as building materials. The source of this trend can be found in stage architecture, which by its very nature is accustomed to low-cost materials, even with a short lifespan, and this also explains why such choices of materials have appeared first in California, the home of movie making. It is typical that Philip Johnson referred to Eric Owen Moss, a Californian architect, as 'the master jeweller of junk'.

Amongst other notable deconstructivist buildings, Bernard Tschumi's Le Fresnoy National Studio for Contemporary Art, Tourcoing, France (1991–97) and the Lerner Student Centre, Columbia University, New York (1994–97), as well as the Arken Museum of Modern Art, Copenhagen, Denmark

(1988–96) by Soren Robert Lund, merit mention but the list of realized buildings has grown immensely and deconstructivist approaches remain, if not dominant, very much alive.

Some of the deconstructivist buildings may be considered as being eccentric but the best of these are 'serious' architecture. At the same time buildings do exist for which the central objective of the designer was to be eccentric. These can hardly be accepted as valid central components of architectural development (Galfetti, 1999). We do not require that function define form and would even accept some slight unease in function and certain useless details (this would also permit the frenzied cacophony of some deconstuctivist buildings) if architectural considerations dictate such a compromise, but a deliberate search for extravagant forms to the detriment of the function is usually unacceptable.

1.3 Post-War Regional Survey

A contemporary identification of global trends is no easy matter because in our time competing trends exist in parallel. This is also valid for regions: there is no dominant single trend in any country. In spite of this there do exist certain characteristic features in individual regions and countries. Let us quote a typical statement: 'The aesthetics of architectural design seem more and more often to be dictated not by predetermined stylistic conventions but by the factors that influence a given site or a given program' (Jodidio, 1998). The picture is further blurred by the work of architects in foreign countries. Nevertheless, a comprehensive summing up of regional trends is attempted below.

France

Between the two world wars, Le Corbusier was the leading practitioner and theoretician, and it was he who introduced modernism into France. More than that, he also exercised considerable influence worldwide.

After the Second World War, France excelled in the innovation of industrialized building technologies

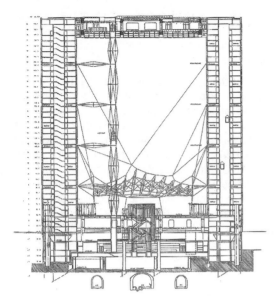

Figure 1.13 La Grande Arche (The Big Arch), La Défense, Paris, France, architect: Von Spreckelsen. One of the first major projects initiated by the then French President Mitterand, reflecting French ambitions for monumental architecture: a post-modern 'arc de triomphe'.

for housing, schools and offices, principally by such prefabricated large-panel systems as Camus, Coignet, Pascal, Costamagna, Balency-Schuhl, Fillod, etc. By now most of these have become outdated but contemporary French architecture continues to be on the highest level. Moreover, the centralized state administration contributed to architectural renewal by initiating and often financing many *grands ensembles*. The Institute of the Arab World (by Jean Nouvel), the Opera Bastille, the new National Library, La Grande Arche office building (by Von Spreckelsen, Figure 1.13) are just a few examples of this. Among others outside Paris, the Euralille complex designed by Rem Koolhaas and Jean Nouvel, Christian de Portzampac and Jean-Marie Duthilleul (1990–94), can be mentioned. Whilst some of these may not be of outstanding architectural quality, they all had an impact on architecture and planning beyond France, by demonstrating the possibilities of urban renewal through large cultural investments (Lesnikowski, 1990).

Among a number of notable realizations let us mention L'Avancée at Guyancourt, a Renault Research and Technical Centre, designed by Chaix and Morel (Philippe Chaix and Jean Paul Morel). This enormous centre, its construction inspired by similar centres of other automotive giants, covers 74 000 square metres. Other architects of a new generation are, among others, Marc Barani and Manuelle Gautrand.

Much has been also achieved in social housing (HLM – flats with controlled rent) and new residential complexes.

United States of America

In the USA, economic and technical progress and increased prosperity permitted major improvements in housing conditions. A new phenomenon was the appearance of tall buildings at first in Chicago, then in New York and later in most major American towns. The skyscraper rising above the city has become the widely recognized symbol of America (Stern, 1991). The modernist period culminated in the 'International Style'. As previously discussed, an early example of this was the Lever House and a later one, the much perfected Seagram Building, which provided a prototype for office buildings all over the world. Also belonging to this category were the tragically destroyed twin towers of the New York World Trade Center.

Since the 1960s, dissatisfaction with the often schematic appearance of office architecture and the plight of inner city areas spurred architects and their clients to search for a new style, which eventually acquired the collective label of post-modernism. Some leading proponents of the new style were Gehry, Meier, Stern, Venturi, Pei, Pelli, Portland, Graves, Moss, who had, and are still having, a strong impact on new architecture. During the 1970s the group of 'Whites' was formed, which included Peter Eisenman, Richard Meier, Michael Graves and Charles Gwathmey. They adhered to the pure idioms of modernist aesthetics. The 'Greys' (in the persons of Venturi, Moore, Stern), however, rejected the 'White' style and reintroduced some of the historical architectural elements. In time several of those listed above became world famous.

Figure 1.14
Climatron, St. Louis, Missouri, USA, designer Buckminster Fuller. Buckminster Fuller was the inventor of the geodesic dome, realized in great numbers all around the world. © Sebestyen: *Lightweight Building Construction*, Akadémiai Kiadó.

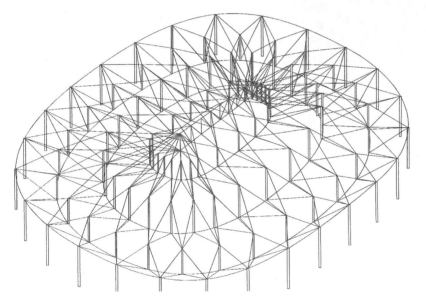

Figure 1.15
Georgia Dome, Atlanta, Georgia, USA, 1992, structural design: Mathys P. Levy, Weidlinger Associates. Wide-span roof, the longest span hypar-tensegrity structure made.

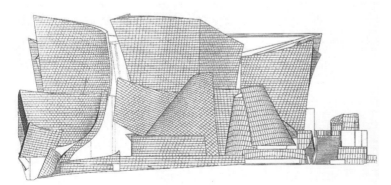

Figure 1.16 Walt Disney Concert Hall, Los Angeles, California, USA, architect Frank O. Gehry. Deconstructivist architecture, a typical F.O. Gehry design, thin titan sheet cladding (as also at the Bilbao museum, Spain), a technological innovation in construction and also with new aesthetic effect.

19

Figure 1.17 Gordon Wu dining hall, Princeton, USA, architects: Venturi, Rauch and Scott Brown. Façade designed with symmetry and simple geometric patterns and an anthropomorphic approach.

Following the end of the Second World War, experiments were launched to introduce industrialized methods to new housing. Steel- or aluminium-framed houses or systems based on structural plastics proved not to be as yet economical. On the other hand, timber-framed houses, including panellized and modular components and mobile home constructions, stood their ground well. From the architectural point of view, these usually did not introduce major aesthetic novelties.

In the 1980s architecture in the USA appeared to have become somewhat ossified. However, American architecture has always had the capacity to renew and reinvigorate itself. For this reason, the developments in American architecture and construction techniques had always exerted a strong impact worldwide and, therefore, in this book we shall frequently revert to discussing its innovations.

Let us mention here just some of the new successful architectural practices: Asymptote, Wendell Burnett, Simon Ungers, Thompson and Rose Architects.

Great Britain

After 1945, based on the earlier and successful examples of garden cities, the 'New Towns' movement was launched, with the aim of easing the country's housing shortage. The architectural style of the new towns, as in Hemel Hempstead and Welwyn Garden City, was often traditional, rooted in the Edwardian legacy of Lutyens and Voysey.

However, urban local authorities were more inclined to experiment with the modernist style, frequently involving prefabricated system building on newly cleared sites with, it must be said, varying degrees of success and durability. Notable results, even though some remain controversial, were for example Ernö Goldfinger's residential and office scheme at Elephant and Castle, London (1965), and almost a decade later the Byker Estate, Newcastle. During this period, there was also much large-scale speculative office and commercial development in the war-damaged City of London, Bristol and other provincial cities, often with questionable results. One of the most prolific architects of this genre was Richard Seifert, whose controversial London Centre Point development has stood the test of time reasonably well. Another architect of the period, recognized for his high-quality modernist buildings, was Denys Lasdun whose early buildings were labelled as 'New Brutalist'. He died in 2001. His National Theatre on the South Bank in London eventually gained universal acceptance but only after considerable public doubt and debate.

Most of the important new buildings were designed by British architects who had a leading share in post-modern architecture. The Canary Wharf high office building, completed in 1991, was designed by American architect Cesar Pelli, with a somewhat late-modernist concept. In spite of, or perhaps as the result of, a popular backlash against modernist architecture, which was led by the Prince of Wales, a generation of younger architects succeeded in establishing a characteristic and innovative type of post-modernist 'high-tech' architecture, which has achieved worldwide acclaim. Norman Foster, Richard Rogers (Rogers, 1985), James Stirling (Stirling, 1975), Nicholas Grimshaw and Michael Hopkins could be cited as the leading architects. In addition to the buildings designed by them, which were realized in Great Britain, they became the architects of spectacular buildings abroad, such as the Pompidou Centre (Rogers with Piano), the Hongkong and Shanghai Bank in Hong Kong (1979–86), and the Commerzbank Headquarters Building in Frankfurt, Germany (1994–97), the last two designed by Foster.

Germany

Following the Second World War, much effort was expended on the reconstruction of destroyed cities and housing in which the art and craft of historical building restoration achieved considerable results. In the Federal Republic of Germany (Western Germany before the reunification) modernist architecture quickly replaced the somewhat pompous neo-historic style of fascist Germany. A major step forward was taken with the construction of the Olympic Stadium in Munich, 1972 (design: Behrens and Partner with Gunther Grzimek). This reinforced the move in many countries towards new types of tensioned and membrane structures.

Gradually late-modernism became combined with high-tech trends with some examples following the 'inside-out' style of buildings such as the Pompidou Centre in Paris. A major example of this was the New Medical Faculty Building in Aachen, 1969–84 (architects: Weber, Brand and Partners) with its 'boiler-suit approach'.

The impressive development of the German economy also meant that clients were in the position to invite foreign architects to Germany. A controversial but finally well-accepted realization was the new building of the Staatsgalerie in Stuttgart, 1977-82 (architect: James Stirling) with a neo-classicist trend. As a direct result of its fascist architectural past, historical trends did not readily find favour in Germany.

Another realization by a British architect is the Commerzbank Building in Frankfurt am Main, 1994–97, designed by Norman Foster. At the time of its exe-

cution it was Europe's tallest skyscraper (299 metres). Its central atrium serves as a natural ventilation system. Four-storey gardens spiral round the curved triangular plan. Several of the foreign architects also designed new buildings in Berlin when it became once again the capital of Germany.

Initially, East German architecture, burdened by the ideology of socialist realism, followed the style prevailing in the (then) Soviet Union. Notable new public buildings in the GDR were the Friedrichspalast and the Ministry of Foreign Affairs in East Berlin and the Neue Gewandhaus in Leipzig, designed by R. Skoda, 1975–81.

Meanwhile in West Germany the tradition of early modernism enjoyed a revival in combination with American influence, mostly with the neo-modernist approach of post-modernism. An important new building is Hall 26 in Hanover, 1994–96 (architect: Thomas Herzog and Partner). This 220 by 115 metre building is covered by a light tensile steel suspension roof whose pleasing wave-like form is eminently suitable for natural lighting and ventilation.

Following the reunification of the two parts, Berlin again became the capital of Germany and very intensive construction programmes were launched. These also included important commissions to architects from abroad. In Germany, as well as in other countries, a new generation of architects is increasingly making important realizations, for instance, Schneider and Schumacher; Otto Steidle; and Gerd Jäger (Klotz and Krase, 1985).

The Netherlands

After the war the strong traditions of Dutch modernism continued. Possibly its most striking manifestation was the rebuilding of war-destroyed Rotterdam, where the Lijnbaan, designed by J.H. van den Broek and J.B. Bakema, became a model for modern inner city pedestrian shopping centres. As part of the Lijnbaan complex, Marcel Breuer's timeless Bijenkorf department store merits special attention.

N. Habraken, a Dutch professor of architecture, initiated the 'Open Architecture' approach in which the primary load-bearing structure is separated from the secondary structures (light partitions, equipment, etc.).

Architects of the next generation, typified by Rem Koolhaas, adopted the newest trends in American architecture, at first the International Style and then post-modernism and deconstructivism. Notable buildings by Koolhaas are the Euralille complex in Lille, France, the Kunsthal in Rotterdam and the Dance Theatre in The Hague. Other noted practitioners were or are Aldo van Eyck, Herman Hertzberger, Jo Coenen and Erick van Egeraat. Jo Coenen designed the Institute of Architecture in Rotterdam, and Hertzberger the Centraal Beheer office complex. The Netherlands has made a point of being open to offering architectural design contracts to foreign architects: Renzo Piano (Institute of Science and Technology, Amsterdam; KPN Telecom Building, Rotterdam), Richard Meier (Town Hall, The Hague) as well as to its own younger architects (Group Meccano, Jo Coenen, etc.).

Scandinavia and Finland

In these Nordic countries of Europe a limited number of buildings designed in one of the historical styles exist. In modern times, several eminent architects have worked in the region. Some of them emigrated, such as the Finnish Eliel Saarinen, to the USA. His son, Eero Saarinen (1910–61), established a practice in the USA. His New York Idlewild air terminal building (1956–61), and the Dulles Airport Building (1958–61), this latter designed in cooperation with engineers Amman and Whitney, with their imaginative undulating forms, became well known globally.

Hugo Alvar Aalto (1898–1976), also Finnish, must be counted as among the outstanding modernist architects. His Congress Building in Helsinki and others are rightly held to be no less than landmarks of modernist architecture.

Another Scandinavian master of the first half of the twentieth century was the Swedish architect Erik Gunnar Asplund (1885-1940).

Timber structures are extensively constructed in these countries, as in Norwegian, Swedish and Finnish housing, and wide-span structures are also accorded prominence. At the same time the use of concrete attained high technical and qualitative levels. The Swedish Skanska Cementgjuteriet, the Finnish Partek and the Danish Larsen-Nielsen companies developed various up-to-date concrete technologies, which found widespread use by architects in the design of various buildings.

Post-modern trends certainly did not lack enthusiastic practitioners. The Arken Museum of Modern Art, near Copenhagen in Denmark, 1988–96, architect: Soren Robert Lund, is conceived in the spirit of deconstructivism (Jodidio, 1998). Other emerging architects that can be singled out in this region are: in Denmark, Entasis Arkitekter; in Sweden, Claesson Koivistu Rune, Thomas Sandell; in Finland, Artto Palo and Rossi Tikka.

Southern Europe

Through their designs, architects and structural engineers in the countries of this region (Nervi, Torroja, Piano, etc.) contributed to the progress of architecture. The Pirelli Tower in Milan, Italy, completed in 1959 (design: Gio Ponti) can be counted as a notable European realization at the close of the modernist office construction period.

In contrast to traditional and historical architecture, rich with ornaments and decorative stylistic approaches, modern architecture in this region tends rather to be characterized by sober, geometric approaches, as is the case with the Italian architects Aldo Rossi (Rossi, 1987) and Giorgio Grassi and the Swiss architect Mario Botta. Their buildings frequently are designed with the use of bricks and stone on the external envelope. Among the newer names in architectural design the following readily spring to mind: from Spain, Bach and Mora Jesus Aparicio Guisado; RCR Aranda Pigem Vilalta; Estudio Cano Lasso; Sancho Madridejos Moneo; Miralles; Pinon and Viaplan; Garcès and Soria; Lepena and Torres; and from Italy, the Studio Archea.

The (former) Soviet Union and the countries of Eastern Europe

In Russia, the constructivist movement of the early post-1917 years was the first during the twentieth century to break with ideas of classical balanced harmony and hierarchical design and to introduce a measure of randomness (see e.g. Tchernikov's designs) (El Lissitzky, 1984). In the countries of the region various architectural trends prevailed, including modernist and neo-historic trends.

After the war, restoration of war damage preoccupied the building industry of the region. In new projects there was a brief revival of the modernist style, mainly following the tradition of the Bauhaus and under the influence of Le Corbusier.

However, after the Communist takeover of Poland, Hungary, Czechoslovakia and later East Germany, architects there were expected to conform to the socialist realist style, which, as already mentioned, was characterized by a form of monumental and often banal classicism. Despite considerable restraint on experimentation and artistic development, some innovative and noteworthy architecture did emerge. During the years 1964–69 the tall buildings of Kalinin Avenue, Moscow, designed by M.V. Posohin, were constructed following late-modernist trends. In the meantime a traditionalist trend got the upper hand. The skyscrapers that were put up in Moscow bore some similarity to the beginning of the twentieth-century New York skyscrapers (Kultermann, 1985).

The only skyscraper in Warsaw designed by a Russian architect, who followed the style of the Moscow skyscrapers, is the Palace of Culture and Science. A notable example of the monumental historicizing architecture is also the Palace of the Republic in Bucharest, Romania's capital, for which an entire downtown district was razed. Finally, modernist and post-modernist trends took over in Russia and other East European countries.

In Czechoslovakia modernism and cubism had strong traditions and architecture was on a high artistic level: examples are the Tugendhat House by Mies van der Rohe, at Brno, 1930 and the Müller House in Prague, designed by Adolf Loos, 1928–30. After 1945 some modern designs found their way to realization, such as the buildings by the architects' group SIAL, those by K. Hubacek and (later) by J. Pleskot; S. Fiala; M. Kotlik and V. Králicek. In the GDR the 365 metres-high East Berlin Television Tower designed by F. Dieter, G. Franke and W.

Ahrendt, 1966–69, was a remarkable result of structural engineering.

In Bulgaria and Romania there were many places where architects succeeded in designing and realizing excellent buildings and complexes for tourism at the Black Sea and the Adriatic Coast. One example is the Hotel International designed by the Bulgarian G. Stoilov. New hotels in Sophia are the Rila and the Vitosha, the first designed by Stoilov, the second by the Japanese Kurokawa.

For new housing, mass production of large panels was introduced. Factories each producing large-size reinforced concrete panels for 1000–10 000 flats annually were established. By means of such methods it was possible to construct many new dwellings but the resulting overall quality and architectural levels generally left a lot to be desired. Cultural and political liberalization during recent years enabled architects gradually to join the mainstream of Western architecture, or in some cases even to develop their own individual style. In Hungary a number of modern hotels (the first one in 1964) and commercial buildings (West End) were designed in late-modern style by Josef Finta. As mentioned earlier, Imre Makovecz, using his individual organic-romantic style, designed and realized a number of restaurants, chapels, cultural buildings (Heathcote, 1997). T. Jankovics, G. Farkas, S. Dévényi, Gy. Csete, F. Lörincz are some of the Hungarian followers of I. Makovecz.

In Bulgaria, during the first twenty post-war years, the socialist realist style still prevailed, for example, on the Headquarters Building of the Communist Party designed by I.P. Popov (1951–53); the building of the Institute of Technical Sciences, Sofia (1971–74), already reflects modernist influences.

Yugoslavia, to some extent, constituted a special case in the region because of its different relations with the Soviet Union. In this country also, a great number of Adriatic Coast hotels were built, some indeed showing remarkable architectural quality and imaginative adaptation to challenging sloping terrains: Hotel Rubin, Porec, designed by J. de Luca (1970–72), and Marina Lucica, Primoshten, designed by L. Perkovic (1971). The new countries of what was Yugoslavia (Slovenia, Croatia, etc.) can all lay claim to having some eminent architects and structural engineers. A garage building type designed by S. Sever was put up at 130 sites. In the countries of this region, after 1990 large-panel technologies were abandoned or greatly diminished in use, and new housing now adopts Western trends.

Asia and the Pacific Rim

The world's largest continent has always produced some fine architecture, for instance in China, Japan, India, the Middle East and elsewhere. As the twentieth century progressed traditional (regional) national architecture has been increasingly combined with Western architecture. During the colonial period Western architects were active but gradually domestic architects occupied a growing – and ultimately a dominant – share of design work. The region has today evolved into a showplace of fine designs, not least as exemplified by the work of Western architects: earlier Le Corbusier, Louis Kahn, Frank Lloyd Wright and in our time Norman Foster, Renzo Piano and others as well as national architects from these countries. This book does no more than to sketch a survey.

India (formerly including Pakistan and Bangladesh)
Balkrishna Vithaldas Doshi (born 1927) studied in India, worked with Le Corbusier and Louis Kahn and

later independently. Doshi developed outstanding architecture, an important realization of which is the Hussein-Doshi Gufa Art Gallery in Ahmadabad (1993) (Figure 1.18). Several of its interlined circular and elliptical spaces are concealed under an undulating earth surface. Charles M. Correa (born 1930) studied in the USA. Having founded his own firm, he designed many housing complexes (New Bombay, Delhi) and other buildings: museums, offices, etc. Uttam C. Jain (born 1934) studied in India and Argentina. Most of his buildings are for educational purposes (universities) and hotels. Usually he was constrained by the restricted financial resources of the clients and so made much use of cheap, local materials (sandstone, etc.).

Pakistan
Nayyar Ali Dada, chief of an architectural design firm, incorporated Islamic elements in his designs. Yasmeen Lari (born 1942) who studied in Europe at Oxford designed housing complexes in several places (Karachi, Lahore).

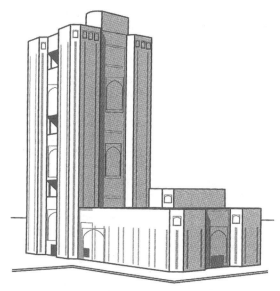

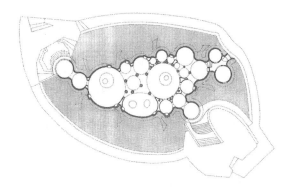

Figure 1.18 Gufa Art Gallery for the works of M.F. Hussein, Ahmadabad, India, 1993, designer: Balkrishna Doshi (Stein, Doshi and Bhalla). Overlapping circular and elliptical spaces formed under earth mounds, reminiscent of cave dwellings; a mixture of traditionalism and post-modernism (inspired by Portoghesi).

Figure 1.19 Sapico office building, Islamabad, Pakistan, 1990, architects: BEEAH and Naygar Ali Dada with partners: Abdul Rahman Hussaini and Ali Shuabi. Modern architecture combined with traditional (Mogul) ornaments; dark blue cladding tiles on the façade.

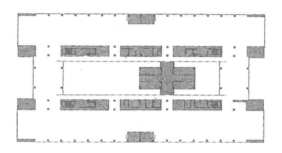

Figure 1.20 NTT Makuhari Building, Makuhari, Japan, 1993. Late modern building with large-scale components, central atria, filled-in middle floors, 100 per cent air-conditioning.

Japan

Kenzo Tange was the first Japanese architect of the modernist period to gain worldwide recognition. His major 'megastructure' designs had a modern as well as a uniquely Japanese flavour.

Following Tange, Arata Isozaki, Fumihiko Maki, Kazuo Shinohara and Kisho Kurokawa became the best known architects of the country. The Metabolist Movement, which was launched in the 1960s, was the first Japanese initiative to embark on an independent path. Members of the next generation, all born after 1940, have been Tadao Ando (Futagawa, 1987), Toyo Ito, Itsuko Hasegawa, Katsuhiro Ishii, Riken Yamamoto, and Shin Takamatsu, and they have been instrumental in raising Japanese architecture to international prominence.

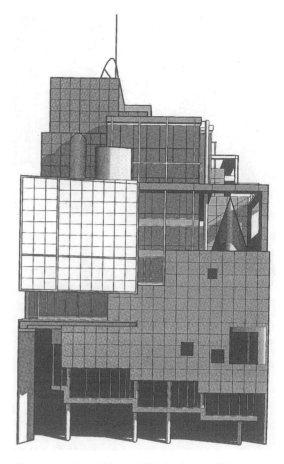

Figure 1.21 Spiral Wacoal Media Center, Minato, Aoyama, Tokyo, Japan, 1982–85, architect: Fumihiko Maki. Dominant geometric forms (square, cone, etc.) and articulation, characteristic of Japanese architecture.

Their approach is characterized by a combination of tradition, modern technology, sophistication and simplicity, which is sometimes referred to as 'constructed nothingness'. Japanese architects display a different approach to the site and the surrounding environment (the *genius loci*) from their Western colleagues.

On occasion the approach seems to ignore the existing milieu, or perhaps the design is not afraid to emphasize the contrast of the new. Another difference in approach is the avoidance or even rejection of the use of historical forms in preference to

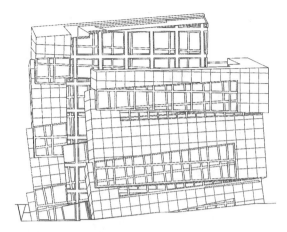

Figure 1.22 Nunotani Headquarters Building, Edogawa-ku, Tokyo, Japan, 1991–92, north elevation, architect: Peter Eisenman. Deconstructivist architecture.

pure geometry such as the circle or the square, geometrical patterns and modules.

However, at the same time, Japanese designs can incorporate very refined and articulate forms, often reflecting industrial age methods, or, according to Fumihiko Maki, 'industrial vocabulary'. Japan's rapid economic and technical development also had other consequences for its architecture, resulting in a vast number of new buildings, great diversity and, sometimes, chaotic complexes. Also, there does tend to be an element of the temporary in some of the new urban developments.

In spite of, or perhaps because of the difference in approach, Japanese architecture gained international recognition. Thus, self-confidence and the demand for Japanese architects abroad conversely opened the door to extend invitations to Western architects to work in Japan. The Italian Renzo Piano, the Dutch Rem Koolhaas, the British Norman Foster, the French Christian de Portzamparc and the Swiss Mario Botta are only some of those who have been engaged in the country.

China
(Mainland) China's architecture was based on principles similar to those in other 'socialist' countries. Hong Kong's architecture (before unification with China) followed Western trends. Tao Ho (born 1936) studied in the USA and modernism (the 'International Style') through Walter Gropius, and Buckminster Fuller influenced his early designs. His practice later expanded to mainland China.

Iraq
Several architects, including Mohamed Saleh Makiya (born 1917) and Rifat Chadirji (born 1926), studied in England and other Western countries but were engaged mostly in Iraq and also abroad (Kuwait, Bahrain).

Iran
Both Nadar Ardahan and Kamran Diba studied in the USA. In partnership with Anthony John Major they designed the Teheran Museum of Modern Arts.

Turkey
Sedad Eldem (1908–87) designed his buildings by applying local technologies (timber frame, high-pitched roof). This applies also to Turgut Cansever who attempts to combine modernism with vernacularism.

Jordan
Perhaps the best known end-of-twentieth-century architect is Rasem Badran, who studied in Germany and whose active practice extends beyond Jordan to other Arabic countries (Abu Dhabi, etc.).

Malaysia and Singapore
Most architects are of Chinese origin, for example, William S.W. Lim (born 1932). He studied in England and the USA and designed (in various partnerships such as with Chen Voon Fee, Lim Cheong Keat, Mok Wei Wei) large-size complex buildings and shopping centres in Singapore and Kuala Lumpur. Other successful architects in the region are Tay Kheng Soon, Ken Yeang and Tengku Hamzah (the two latter in partnership).

Thailand
Sumet Jamsai (born 1939) designed buildings in Bangkok and Pattaya that follow the principle of the inseparability of people and machines ('robot architecture') and, together with modernist trends, reflect an interest in local architectural traditions.

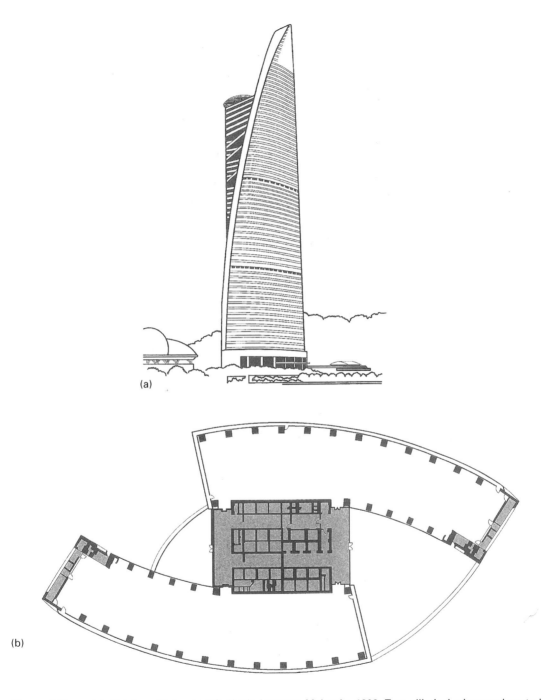

(a)

(b)

Figure 1.23a and b. Telekom Malaysia HQ, Kuala Lumpur, Malaysia, 1998. Two elliptical wings and central core, 77 floors full height (55 occupied). © Harrison et al.: *Intelligent Buildings in South East Asia*, E & FN Spon.

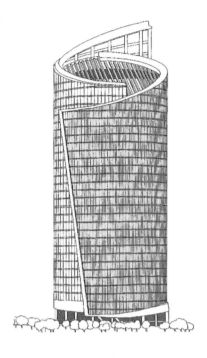

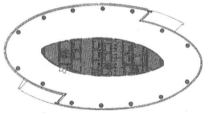

Figure 1.24 Wave Tower, Bangkok, Thailand, 1988, building with a central core, 27 floors. Late modern office building with post-modern curved façade, in a developing country. © Harrison et al.: *Intelligent Buildings in South East Asia*, E & FN Spon.

Korea (South)

Both Swoo Geun Kim (1931–86) and Kim-Chung-up (1922–88) worked at the outset of their careers for Le Corbusier and designed a number of buildings in Korea. Now a new generation (Kim Wou, Kim Sok-chol and Zo-Kunyong) have taken over their place.

The Philippines

Leandro V. Locsin (born 1928) achieved international fame through the forceful dynamic effects of his designs.

Indonesia

Among several eminent architects Tony Candraw-inata (born 1946) and the Atelier 6 Group of six architects can already lay claim to a number of notable realizations.

Latin Americas

Pre-Colombian cities were mostly destroyed, with the exception of some major complexes of monuments. During the twentieth century, Latin American architects attempted to introduce traditions into modern architecture.

Brazil

The oeuvre of Oscar Niemeyer (born 1907) has acquired global fame, including the planning and design of Brasilia, the new capital (urban planning in cooperation with Lucio Costa (born 1932)). Joaquim Guedes (born 1932) designed various modernist buildings. In Bahia the construction of the city of Caraiba was commenced during the late 1970s.

Mexico

Felix Candela (born 1910) contributed to the international development of shells by his reinforced concrete shells. Gonzales Gortazar (born 1942) designed several buildings in Guadalajara, which clearly reflect his double education as architect and sculptor.

Argentina

Argentina's most famous architect is M.J. Testa, born 1923 in Italy and who emigrated as a child to Argentina. His buildings (partly designed in partnership with others) have strong visual undertones.

Africa

Africa ranks as the world's most problematic continent. The wealthiest state is South Africa, which keeps abreast of the world's architecture. Here it is only the minority that enjoys high living standards. Major programmes are afoot to improve the housing conditions of the poor population. In some North African countries (Egypt, Tunisia, etc.) new architecture is progressing, for example in Morocco where Elie Azagury (born 1918), the partnership of Faraoui (born 1928) and Patrice de Maziere (born 1930) have designed some remarkable buildings. Here it can be stated that a new generation of architects is emerging.

Bibliography

Abel, Chris (Ed.) (1991) *Renault Centre, Swindon, 1982, Architect: Norman Foster*, AD, Architecture Design and Technology Press

Beedle, Lynn S. (Ed.-in-Chief), Armstrong, Paul, J. (Ed.) (1995) *Architecture of Tall Buildings*, Council on Tall Buildings and Urban Habitat, McGraw-Hill, Inc.

Blaser, Werner (Ed.) (1992) *Norman Foster Sketches*, Birkhäuser Verlag

Bonta, János (2001) Deconstructivism in Architecture, *Epités-Epitészettudomàny*, Vol. XXIX, No. 1–2, pp. 83–91

van Bruggen, Coosje (1997) *Frank O. Gehry: Guggenheim Museum Bilbao*, The Solomon Guggenheim Foundation New York

Crosbie, Michael J. (Ed.) (1997) *The Passive Solar Design and Construction Handbook*, John Wiley & Sons, Inc.

de Vallée, Sheila (Ed.) (1995) *L'architecture du futur*, Terrail

d'Huart, Annabelle (1989) *Ricardo Bofill*, Electa Moniteur

Frampton, Kenneth (1980) *Modern Architecture: A Critical History*, Oxford University Press.

Futagawa, Yukio (Ed.) (1987) *Architect Tadao Ando, GA Architect*, ADA. Edita

Galfetti, Gustau Gili (1999) *Maisons excentriques*, Seuil (1st edn), Gustavo Gili

Ghirardo, Diane (1997) *Les architectures postmodernes*, Thames & Hudson (original: *Architecture after Modernism*, Thames & Hudson, 1996)

Giedion, Siegfried (1973) *Space, Time and Architecture: Growth of a New Tradition*, 5th edn, Harvard University Press

Gössel, P. and Leuthauser, G (1991) *L'architecture du XXe siècle*, Benedikt Taschen

Graves, Michael (1982) *Buildings and Projects 1966–1981*, Ed. K.V. Wheeler et al., The Architectural Press

Gropius, Walter (1955) *Scope of Total Architecture*, Harper & Broth

Harrison, Andrew, Loe, Eris and Read, James (Eds) (1998) *Intelligent Buildings in South East Asia*, E & FN Spon

Haughton, Graham and Hunter, Colin (1994) *Sustainable Cities*, Jessica Kingsley Publishers

Heathcote, Edwin (1997) *Imre Makovecz:. The Wings of the Soul*, Academy Editions, AM No. 47

Himmelblau, Coop (1983) *Architecture is Now: 1969–1983*, Rizzoli

Hitchcock, Henry-Russell and Johnson, Philip (1966) *The International Style: Architecture Since 1922*, exposition catalogue, New York

HRH The Prince of Wales (1989) *A Vision of Britain: A Personal View of Architecture*, Doubleday

Hutchinson, Maxwell (1989) *The Prince of Wales: Right or Wrong?*, Faber and Faber

Ibelings, Hans (1995) *20th Century Architecture in the Netherlands*, NAI Publishers

Iselin, Donald G. and Lemer, Andrew C. (Eds) (1993) *The Fourth Dimension in Building: Strategies for Minimizing Obsolescence*, National Academy Press

Jacobs, Jane (1961) *The Death and Life of Great American Cities*, Random House, Inc.

Jencks, Charles (1978) *The Language of Post-Modern Architecture*, 2nd edn, Academy Editions

Jencks, Charles (1980) *Late-Modern Architecture and Other Essays*, Academy Editions

Jencks, Charles (1982) *Current Architecture*, Academy Editions

Jencks, Charles (1985) *Symbolic Architecture*, Academy Editions

Jencks, Charles (1986) *What is Post-Modernism?*, Academy Editions/St Martin's Press

Jencks, Charles (1987) *Post-Modernism: The New Classicism in Art and Architecture*, Academy Editions

Jencks, Charles (1988) *The Prince, the Architects and New Wave Monarchy*, Academy Editions

Jencks, Charles (1988, 1993) *Architecture Today*, Academy Editions

Jencks, Charles (1990) *The New Moderns from Late to Neo-Modernism*, Academy Editions

Jencks, Charles (1996) *What is Post-Modernism?*, Academy Editions

Jencks, Charles (1999) The Dynamic, Noisy, Beautiful (and Kitsch) Earth, *Architectural Design*, Vol. 69, No. 11–12, Profile 142

Jencks, Charles and Kropf, Karl (1997) *Theories and Manifestos of Contemporary Architecture*, Academy Editions

Jodidio, Philip (1995) *Contemporary European Architects*, Volume III, Taschen

Jodidio, Philip (1996) *Contemporary European Architects*, Volume IV, Taschen

Jodidio, Philip (1997) *Nieuwe Vormen in de Architektur, De Jaren '90*, Taschen/Librero

Jodidio, Philip (1997) *Contemporary European Architects*, Volume V, Taschen

Jodidio, Philip (1998) *Contemporary European Architects*, Volume VI, Taschen

Jodidio, Philip (1998) *Contemporary American Architects*, Volume IV, Taschen

Jodidio, Philip (1999) *Building a New Millennium*, Taschen

Johnson, Philip and Wigley, Mark (1988) *Deconstructivist Architecture*, The Museum of Modern Art

Kähler, Gert (Ed.) (1990) *Dekonstruktion? Dekonstruktivism?: Aufbruch ins Chaos Oder Neues Bild der Welt?*, Vieweg & Sohn

Khan, Hasan-Uddin (1995) *Contemporary Asian Architects*, Benedikt Taschen

Khan, Hasan-Uddin (1998) *Le Style International. Le modernisme dans l'architecture de 1925 à 1965*, Taschen

Klotz, Heinrich and Krase, Waltraud (1985) *New Museum Buildings in the Federal Republic of Germany*, Rizzoli

Koolhaas, Rem (1978) *Delirious New York: A Retroactive Manifesto for Manhattan*, Oxford University Press & Le Chene

Kultermann, Udo (1980) *Architekten der Dritten Welt, Bauen Zwischen: Tradition und Neubeginn*, Du Mont Buchverlag

Kultermann, Udo (1985) *Zeitgenössische Architektur in Osteuropa*, Du Mont Buchverlag

Kultermann, Udo (1993) *Contemporary Architecture in the Arab States: Renaissance of a Region*, McGraw-Hill

Kurokawa, Kisho (1977) *Metabolism in Architecture*, Studio Vista, London

Larson, M.S. *Behind the Postmodern Façade, Architectural Change in Late Twentieth Century America*

Lesnikowski, Wojciech (1990) *The New French Architecture*, Rizzoli

Lillyman, William J., Moriarty, Marilyn F. and Neuman, David J. (Eds.) *Critical Architecture and Contemporary Culture*, Oxford University Press

Lissitzky, El (1984) *Russia: An Architecture for World Revolution*, The MIT Press

Lüchinger, Arnulf (1981) *Strukturalismus in Architektur und Städtebau. Structuralism in Architecture and Urban Planning. Structuralisme en architecture et urbanisme*, Karl Krämer Verlag

Meehan, Patrick (1991) *Frank Lloyd Wright Remembered*, The Preservation Press

Melet, E (Ed.) (1999) *Sustainable Architecture: Towards a Diverse Built Environment*, NAI Publishers

Meyhöfer, Dirk (Ed.) (1993) *Contemporary Japanese Architects*, Taschen

Monnier, Gérard (1996) *L'architecture du XXe siècle*, Presses Universitaires de France

Mulder, Bertus (1997) *Rietveld Schröder House*, V + K Publishing

Norris, Christopher and Benjamin, Andrew (1988) *Was ist Dekonstruktion?*, Verlag für Architektur Artemis

Papadakis, Andreas and Watson, Harriet (Eds) (1990) *New Classicism*, Omnibus Volume, Academy Editions

Papadakis, Andreas (1997) *L'architecture moderne classique*, Terrail

Portoghesi, Paolo (1981) *Au delà de l'architecture moderne*, l'Equerre (original: 1980)

Robbin, Toby (1996) *Engineering a New Architecture*, Yale University

Richard Rogers and Architects (1985) *Architectural Monographs*, Academy Editions/St Martin's Press

Rossi, Aldo (1987) *Architecture 1959–1987*, Electa

Saxon, R. (1993) *The Atrium Comes of Age*, Longman

Schulz-Dornburg, Julia (2000) *Art and Architecture: New Affinities*, Gustavo Gili (Spanish: 1999)

Stern, A.M. Robert (1991) *Selected Works, Architectural Monographs*, Academy Editions/St Martin's Press

Stirling, James (1975) Thames and Hudson

Thompson, Jessica Cargill (2000) *40 Architects Under 40*, Taschen

Tschumi, Bernard (1994) *Architecture and Disjunction*, The MIT Press

Van der Ree, Pieter (2000) *Organische Architectuur*, Uitgeverij Vrij – Geestesleven

Whitney, David and Kipnis, Jeffrey (1996) *Philip Johnson Glass House*, Italian edn, Electa (French edn, Gallimard/Electa, 1997)

Wigley, Mark (1993) *The Architecture of Deconstruction: Derrida's Haunt*, The MIT Press

Wright, Frank Lloyd (1977) *An Autobiography*, Horizon Press

Zabalbeascoa, Anatxu and Marcos, Javier Rodriguez (2000) *Minimalisms*, Gustavo Gili

Zipper, Jean-Philippe and Bekas, Frédéric (1986) *Architectures vitalistes 1950–1980*, Editions Parenthèses

2

The impact of technological change on building materials

2.1 General Considerations

Construction earlier was based on practical experience. Gradually, more and more has come to be grounded on science: strength of materials, development of new and improved building materials, structural analysis and design, heat and moisture transfer, acoustics, natural and artificial illumination, energy conservation, fight against corrosion, fire, smoke, wind, floods, environmental protection, information and telecommunication technology, mathematical methods and application of computers, management and social sciences.

Several of these affect the architectural appearance of buildings, although not all changes in architecture can be explained by technical progress. In what follows an analysis will be made of technological progress and changes in architecture. This will not be restricted to perceptible changes; the hidden influences, which affect the design and characteristics of buildings without their visible modification will also be examined.

The central science of mechanics of building materials itself has undergone basic progress. The collective knowledge about elastic and plastic state, stress and strain, micro-cracking and fracturing, stability, buckling, ductility, probability influences, risk, ultimate states and others has resulted in the complex science of present-day mechanics of materials. Parallel to the progress in materials sciences, the technology of construction and manufacturing

of building materials have also evolved tremendously.

Architectural design at all times has had to reckon with the available technology: materials and processes. These, however, have never completely defined the work of designers. The ideas and objectives of society, of the clients and of the architects, have also always exercised a significant impact on the product of design. The different architectural styles developed as a sum of technical development and ideas of architects. The ambition of architects together with developing requirements of clients had a repercussion on technological development. As a consequence, architectural trends can be explained not merely by changes in technology but also by changes in architectural ideas and requirements of clients. This will be done in the following. Technological progress has always had its impact on architecture. However, so massive has been the progress of science over the recent past and so continuous the changes in architectural design that the question has now arisen as to whether we are not standing at the dawn of a completely new era. Is new science not evoking a completely new architecture?

Are the new computer-based design techniques and the new curved buildings not heralding the period of a new, non-linear architecture? The question has indeed been raised (Jencks, 1997) but could not be answered definitively, for no definitive answer can ever be provided concerning the future as affected by social and human factors. What, however, is certain is that technological progress has an increasing influence on architecture.

Engineers, as has been stated in previous contexts, are partners of architects; while some are themselves designing structures with architectural ambitions, others are active partners in providing a solid basis for architectural dreams and ambitions. Peter Rice, an English structural engineer, having cooperated with architects on several important objects (Pompidou Centre, Sydney Opera House, Paris La Villette, etc.) declared that whilst the architect's work is creative, the engineer's is essentially inventive (Rice, 1994). This may sound like an oversimplification but it does come somewhere near to the truth. Similar declarations were made by a number of other cooperating architects and engineers.

In the following we commence with a discussion of the impact on architecture of the changing building materials and, following this, examine the influence of other factors.

Building materials and their potential performance have right from the very outset formed the starting basis for shaping buildings. Thus, the available technologies in stone, timber and bricks in earlier historical periods; in iron/steel and concrete since the nineteenth century and, very recently, in glass and plastics, have all influenced the appearance of buildings.

Traditional materials (such as timber, stone and bricks) find their application in new architecture. As a matter of fact such materials are much favoured by individual architects and some groups of architects. The science of materials has, however, gone forward by leaps and bounds for traditional materials also. Traditional materials have been perfected; new types and composites of materials developed. Now, the new fabrication and jointing methods equally affect the design work of the architect.

Steel sections are hot- and cold-rolled, welded or bent. Aluminium sections are extruded, aluminium panels cast. Glass sheet is manufactured by different continuous automated methods with differing compositions of the glass. Plastics components are extruded, thermoformed. New sealants and fasteners have been invented. Concrete and rein-

forced concrete have opened up new vistas for manufacturing and construction, including the design based on up-to-date technologies. For concrete and other materials, prefabrication (off-site processes) provides novel opportunities (Gibb, 1999). There exist various components which may be prefabricated: wall panels (cast as a whole or unitized from elements), volumetric units (modules or boxes), floor, ceiling and roof panels, sanitary blocks (WCs, bathrooms, kitchen units), partitions and others. Fabrication methods have to be selected; those for example for reinforced concrete panels include casting in horizontal position, casting in vertical position individually, or in batteries (i.e. in group forms). The design of prefabricated components must solve new problems, such as transportation in the factory, on the road or by rail, on the building site.

Adequate structural design must not neglect problems of building physics: avoidance of thermal and sound bridges. Building materials have certain properties, which depend on their composition (type of alloy, etc.), and the conditions surrounding them (polluted urban or seashore air, or clean natural air). Weathering, corrosion, thermal expansion, durability may be of decisive importance. The performances of traditional and new building materials, their new fabrication and jointing methods are to a greater or lesser extent known by the architect. Formerly, new knowledge about modern manufacturing methods tended not to be included in the stock of architectural education or the architect had to rely on the experience of industrial technologists. In many cases the role of the architect is to be a partner to the industrial engineer and to participate in the development of fabrication methods and of materials with new or improved properties. A number of major industrial manufacturing companies (for instance, Hoesch and Thyssen in steel, Alusuisse and Alcoa in aluminium, Pilkington and Saint Gobain in glass, Höchst and Dow in plastics) have created their own research and development units, eventually with the participation of architects, engaged on product development adjusted to up-to-date manufacturing methods. This is a process that continues to flourish.

The choice of building materials for façades depends to a great extent on the functions of the building. Industrial and agricultural buildings are usually large premises without a need for windows to the outside. Therefore, façades may be designed as uninterrupted large surfaces and these may be assembled from identical components suspended on a frame. What results are claddings assembled from corrugated steel or aluminium sheet, eventually from reinforced concrete components. Façades of buildings requiring windows are designed from masonry or panels made from steel, aluminium, concrete or timber and recently from glass.

The properties of building materials (strength, thermal and sound characteristics, corrosion, behaviour in fire, durability, etc.), economic data concerning them, as well as their impact on structural and architectural design have long been extensively documented and detailed repetition is unnecessary. Concise references to such properties are provided in cases where their impact on design is of great importance. However, there is a new area that greatly affects architectural design: aspects of the environment, ecology and sustainability. These will be discussed in a subsequent chapter because they require a more general introduction and analysis. Prior to that later analysis, this chapter will concentrate on a comprehensive survey of the environmental effects of building materials. In this we are taking account of a survey published in The Netherlands (Anink et al., 1996). It is essential to bear in mind that it is not only the environmental aspects of the production of building materials that are important, but also the materials' impact in use and after use (demolition, recycling).

Natural resources for stone, brick and glass in general exist in abundance although their geographical distribution is uneven and the actual availability affects the selection. For most of the materials in this class, energy requirements for fabrication are reasonably limited, with the notable exceptions of glass and binding materials (cement, lime, and gypsum). Cement production not only requires considerable energy but also is the source of a substantial amount of CO_2 emission. The energy content of reinforced concrete structures is increased by the steel reinforcement. Pollution created by the use of materials in this class is limited. Durability is (with some exception) satisfactory, with recycling possible without being excessively expensive. Exceptionally, contamination may cause problems. Extraction or quarrying may have displeasing natural consequences, a situation that is being accorded increasing attention. Materials in this group are bulky and moving them to the building sites requires substantial transport activities (with much energy consumption) on roads, railways and waterways. Glass production also consumes much energy although it must be said that glass can be recycled with relative ease and at reasonable cost. Iron and some other metals (copper, lead, etc.) have been used in construction since ancient times but their wider application is a modern phenomenon. Ore mining precedes transformation into metals and their alloys. Mining ores may cause serious damage to nature. Much energy is necessary for metal fabrication (metallurgy, etc.) and processes cause extensive pollution, but the required countermeasures are now feasible.

The prevention or reduction of corrosion is a problem for several metals (steel, etc.). Reuse of metals is technically and economically feasible, which is of course of environmental benefit. Lead is available in limited quantity and it is the source of various health hazards. The basic raw material for synthetics is petroleum. Whilst only a small part (4 per cent) of petroleum consumption is attributable to the production of synthetics, the overall consequences of the use of petroleum have to be taken into account. The extraction and transport of petroleum repeatedly causes disasters and its consumption depletes a limited natural and non-renewable resource. Production, use and demolition (or recycling) of plastics (synthetics) may be technically complicated and expensive while also giving rise to pollution, contamination, harmful emissions and various health hazards.

Polyethylene (PE) and polypropylene (PP) are well suited for recycling. Polyvinyl chloride (PVC), one of the most common plastics, on the other hand entails a number of negative environmental effects: in production, use and recycling. Polyurethane (PUR) is also the source of different health hazards. The use of CFCs (contributors to the depletion of the ozone layer) in the production of foamed PUR and polystyrene (PS), in cooling and refrigeration is gradually being replaced by other agents.

Timber also has long been used in construction and remains to this day a basic material in some regions although mostly in an industrialized form. Timber is an important renewable raw material for construction but with the attendant condition to realize sustainable forestry. This is easier for softwoods, more difficult for hard ones, and extremely difficult for special tropical ones. Most of the paints and sealants contain additives harmful to human health and the environment and these could exercise an adverse influence during production (e.g. to painters) and during use. Environmental aspects have been mentioned somewhat cursorily above. At the present time detailed analytical studies on assessment methods and their results exist (Berge, 1992, in Norwegian, 2000, in English).

2.2 Timber

Timber and other natural organic materials were among the very earliest building materials and in its modern form timber continues to serve as a basic building material. Its properties greatly affect architectural design (Actualités, 1998/99). Timber has a high strength to weight ratio. Its strength and stiffness are dependent on the direction of load in relation to the grain. It is strong and relatively stiff parallel to the grain. However, it is prone to cleavage along the grain if tension stresses are perpendicular to it. It has low shear strength and shear modulus. Higher moisture content reduces both the strength and elasticity, and a part of the original strength will anyway be lost over time. Under load, timber creeps and deforms. Serviceability therefore often governs structural analysis.

Structural analysis, detail design and processes of technology take care of a number of the specific problems of timber structures, such as buckling, behaviour around notches, prevention of interstitial condensation, protection against moisture, insect and fungal attack, and fire (Sebestyen, 1998). Technical progress in the use of timber has some major repercussions on architecture. Apart from those in organic architecture as described in Chapter 1, these concern the:

- selection of the type of timber
- transformation of the basic timber material into one with new properties

- new timber products, for example, stressed skin panels and various types of boards (plywood, fibreboard, particleboard, oriented stranded board, waferboard, flakeboard), tapered, curved or pitched cambered beams, glued thin-webbed beams, sandwich panels, portal frames and arches
- new types of organic adhesives, including those able to withstand outdoor exposure
- improvement of properties and performances (e.g. improving behaviour in fire)
- enhancement of the structural performance of softwoods for use in glued structures (Gilfillan et al., 2001)
- use of new fasteners, hangers, connectors (Bianchina, 1997)
- new principles in structural analysis and design, including adequate consideration of the interaction between loads and material properties.

Gluing opened up new possibilities for timber. Glued laminated timber (Glulam) and adhesive-bonded timber components (boards and others) are the basic materials for a great variety of products. The first type of fasteners are those where the load is transferred along the shank, such as dowels, staples, nails, screws and bolts (Larsen and Jensen, 2000). A second category of fasteners are those where the load is transmitted over a large bearing area at the surface of members, such as split-rings, shear plates and punched metal plates. One of the new connectors is a sectioned steel tube embedded into the end grain of heavy-timber structural members using a vinyl-ester-based mortar (Schreyer et al., 2001). The new types of fasteners lead to more efficient structures. The performance of attachments has a particular importance in regions with high winds and/or seismic action. Low-rise timber-frame structures fail rapidly under high wind loads after the failure of the first fastener (Rosowsky and Schiff, 2000, Rosowsky, 2000, Dolan, 2000, Stathopoulos, 2000). Therefore, the tributary area of the single fastener should be small enough (e.g. less than 10 square feet). Deformed shank nails (such as ring shanks, or threaded nails) have a greater uplift capacity than smooth shank nails. Screws offer more uplift capacity than is usually assumed. Specially shaped connecting hardware is also used for mechanical timber jointing.

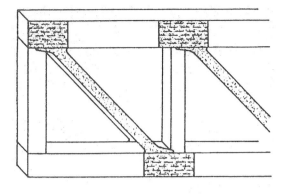

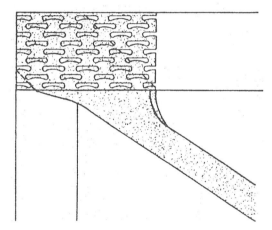

Figure 2.1 Gang-Nail steel plates for timber trusses (Sanford).

sheets forming the skins on one or both sides. They can be produced by gluing or with mechanical joints. The webs are usually of solid timber and the panels improve stability and resistance to strong wind and earthquake. The stressed skin principle, introduced in the previous century, enables the inclusion of the panels in the structural calculations. Naturally, family houses can be designed not only with a timber frame but also with a metallic (primarily steel) frame and stressed skin panels. With Glulam and mechanically connected timber components long-span structures covering large spaces may be constructed. One of the largest timber-structured buildings is the Olympic Stadium in Hamar, Norway, which was completed in 1992 (Architect: Niels Torp). It houses no fewer than 13 000 seats, and 2000 cubic metres of glued laminated timber were used for its construction. Its vaulted roof is supported by arched timber trusses. Another important timber building is the Dome in Izumo, Japan, which was also completed in 1992 (design: Kajima). The diameter of the building is 143 metres. In appearance its dome gives the impression of being shaped like an open umbrella but its structure is based on quite another principle. Thirty-six half-arches were assembled, each 90 metres long and these were then raised to their final position. As a general principle, it can be stated that the scope of applying timber in construction is widening, including to multi-storey buildings (Stungo, 1998). Over recent years fire research has also produced results (including such specific topics as the self-ignition of insulating fibreboard panels), which have increased the fire safety of timber structures (Buchanan, 2000, Mehaffey et al., 2000).

Fasteners designed in a specific form and appearing in some pattern (articulation) on the surface provide new sorts of decoration.

New types of timber applied in building are on the one hand hard (tropical and other) woods such as teak and sequoia and, on the other hand, soft-woods solidified and identified. The use of hardwoods is limited by environmental protection and, due to their high price, to up-market applications: de luxe residential housing and prestigious offices. Stressed skin panels consist of webs in the direction of the span connected with wood-based

2.3 Steel

Iron (cast and wrought) has long been utilized in building but steel was introduced only in the course of the second half of the nineteenth century (Blanc et al., 1993). Its introduction resulted in the construction of tall structures (skyscrapers and towers) and long-span structures in the form of bridges and spaces covered by domes, shells and space trusses (Seitz, 1995) but it has been used in all sorts of standard buildings as well as industrial halls, agricultural buildings, etc. Carbon steel is the base metal used for most steel products. An increase in the amount of carbon improves the hardness and tensile strength of steel. Carbon content, however, inversely affects the ductility of steel alloy and the weldability of the metal. Various elements – phosphorus, manganese, copper, nitrogen, sulphur and others – modify the properties of steel. Some of the most important product categories are hot-rolled, cold-rolled and cast steel products. Welding, mechanical jointing, painting, coating, enamelling are some of the technologies transforming basic steel products. New fabrication methods, new alloys, new structural schemes and new fastenings were invented, all of which exerted varying impact on architecture:

- high-strength steel
- stainless steel and weathering steel
- high-friction grip bolts, shot pins, welding
- hot rolling and automatic welding of sections
- cold forming (cold working): rolling, bending, pressing
- various sections: sheet and strip, open and tubular, corrugated and others
- protection against corrosion and fire
- tensile (tensioned) structures, suspended and stressed cable structures
- various systems of framing, diagonal bracing, dampeners
- surface treatment methods: coil coating, enamelling and others.

The American architect Frank O. Gehry declared that for him 'metal is the material of our time' and that 'metal is sculptural allowing for free-form structures inconceivable in any other material'.

The first metals to be used in building were iron (wrought and cast), copper, bronze (copper and tin alloy), brass (a copper alloy containing zinc), zinc and lead. In our time new metallic alloys based on steel, aluminium and titanium have been introduced. Steel alloys containing chromium in excess of 10 per cent are known as the stainless steels (Zahner, 1955). Stainless steel alloys may contain also manganese, chromium, nickel, molybdenum, silicon, carbon, and nitrogen. Stainless steel was developed in the nineteenth century, and brought to architectural applications in the first half of the

twentieth century. The same products as in normal steel can also be produced in stainless steel but the thickness of plate and sheet can be reduced and surface finishing can be different. The Chrysler Building in New York (designer: William Van Allen), built in the late 1920s, was one of the first major architectural projects constructed with a prime architectural surface. Notable early realizations in stainless steel were the roof of the Pittsburgh Plate Glass Company Plant in 1924 and the Gateway Arch in St Louis, 1966, designed by Eero Saarinen.

Since that time many other important buildings have been designed with a stainless steel envelope, such as the 36-metre diameter sphere of the Museum of Science and Technology in Paris (architect: Adrien Fainsilber). Metals may have different types of surface finishing: polishing, embossing, metal or paint coating.

Hot-rolled steel sections (eventually also in welded form) were the first to be used in construction on a large scale. Then, cold forming brought new forms, first of all with corrugated sheet and also with hollow profiles. Codes for various types of steel structures were introduced. There exist simple but accurate methods to be selected by the engineer depending on various circumstances. For example, there are proposals for the simplified design of steel trusses with different types of joints. These can be applied in less complex cases or as a first approximation to a later and more precise analysis (Krampen, 2001).

The simplest building form with a steel frame is the single-storey building and within this category the single-bay and the multiple-bay buildings (see also Chapter 3). They are commonly designed with a pitched or flat roof, columns, portal frame or a space frame and roof lights. In many countries there are firms (steel and aluminium manufacturers and enterprises constructing halls with a metallic frame) that specialize in offering and constructing industrial halls and storage buildings (Newman, 1997). Such standard halls are designed based on up-to-date codes and analysis methods, including finite element (FE) methods (Pasternak and Müller, 2001).

For multi-storey buildings appropriate frames and different types of floors were developed, eventually also making use of concrete. Suspended (hanging) ceilings and double deck floors were introduced. The lower surface of hanging ceilings and of roofs was frequently shaped in a highly articulated pattern. Structural design took care of bracing, here again in steel alone or in combination with concrete (shear walls and cores). The structure interacted with services, which themselves acquired increasing sophistication. The heights of multi-storey buildings have shot up from about 100 metres to about 500. The high-rise or tall buildings became known as skyscrapers and those with a height of over 500 metres as super-scrapers. Architectural consequences have been manifold.

Whilst the lightweight claddings dominated the market, heavyweight (traditional) external walls occasionally found application. A new development was the structural glass façade. The frame was positioned in its relation to the cladding or the glass either externally or internally, sometimes in a mixed way. The progress achieved in technology prepared the way for the super-scrapers as described above. The world's newest tallest buildings are the Petronas Towers in Kuala Lumpur, the (planned) 580 metre-high MTR Tower in Chicago and the 609 metre-high 7 South Dearborn Tower, also in Chicago (both the latter were designed by SOM). Cold rolling and coil coating resulted in corrugated sheeting, which is eminently applicable for industrial buildings, but which can be somewhat problematic for multi-storey office buildings. For the latter, individually pressed panels have been extensively used, in particular for skyscrapers. In recent years enamelled steel sheet panels have been used by architects in New York and elsewhere, the initiator and best-known proponent being the American architect Richard Meier. Coated metal (steel, stainless steel, aluminium, and copper) constitutes the basis of a multitude of thin sheet products. The basis of these in most cases is thin sheet in coil form, which is then roll-formed and coated, i.e. coil coated (Oliver et al., 1997). Prior to coating, steel sheet may be galvanized. A great number of coatings have been developed including, at first PVC plastisols, and later, in view of the deficiencies of plastisols, PVF2 resins, polyurethanes, plastic film laminates, thermoplastic polyamide incorporating polyurethane and polyester, powder coatings and others. Developments in design include the use of curved sheet, ribbed profiles, laminated and composite panels, secret-concealed-fix systems with standing seam and tapered curves (Oliver et al., 1997). The products are manufactured by major steel and aluminium companies and increasingly used for metal cladding and roofing purposes. There also exist a number of companies specialized in manufacturing and assembling such claddings and roofing. Some companies went on to develop specific products based on coated metal sheet (Hunter Douglas, Robertson, etc.). Design details are the fixings (fastening), roof lights, edge solutions and it must be noted that earlier these have been the source of many failures. The present situation is that correct solutions have been devised. Considering the increasing use of coated metal sheet cladding and roofing and also the wide variations in potential appearance, architects must become familiar with performance and aesthetic possibilities and design details or take steps to ensure close cooperation with experts in these technologies (Eggen and Sandaker, 1996). Further application of steel (and aluminium) will be discussed in Chapter 3.

2.4 Aluminium and Other Metals

Steel and aluminium (in the USA aluminum) are the most commonly used metals (not as chemically pure metals but in the form of alloys) as structural building materials. Copper, lead, zinc, titan (titanium) and their alloys are applied for specific purposes and various surface finishing, primarily metallic or paint or plastics coatings (Zahner, 1995). Aluminium was introduced in building later than steel but its use is increasing. The first spectacular architectural application of aluminium was the cast aluminium pinnacle of the Washington Monument in 1884. The architectural use of aluminium accelerated after the First World War. The range of application is broad: curtain walls, suspended ceilings, claddings, windows, louvres, space frames, domes and others.

The two basic classes of aluminium and its alloys are cast and wrought aluminium. The modulus of aluminium is about one third that of steel. The consequence is that the deflections of aluminium members under load are greater than those of steel. Aluminium's thermal conductivity and thermal expansion also exceed those of steel. On the other hand the corrosion behaviour of aluminium is superior to that of steel. These and some other properties have an impact on structural and architectural design. Aluminium products can be fabricated partly by similar methods as steel (casting, hot and cold rolling, machining), and partly by extrusion, the latter providing specific potentials for design. Specific fabrication methods are used for various shaping purposes and to achieve different surface patterns and properties. A wide range of joining methods are available for aluminium (and steel), such as mechanical fastening (bolting, pinning, riveting, welding, gluing and others (Lane, 1992). For surface finishing, anodizing, coating (including coil coating), enamelling and lacquering are the main possibilities. The three basic anodizing processes are integral curing, two-step colouring and impregnated colouring. The electrolytic process of anodizing thickens the thin protective surface of the aluminium oxide layer and simultaneously is used to provide a coloured surface. A variety of anodizing processes has been invented producing various colours and visual quality. Paint and lacquer coatings are also increasingly applied. Different metallic alloys have different properties, but at a price. Usually steel is corrosive but certain alloys, like stainless steel, are protected from corrosion. Metals may be coated to prevent corrosion and also in order to obtain a certain colour and surface, e.g. lead-coated copper. Aluminium basically does not corrode but a higher level of protection may be required and attained through the use of special alloys or by coating. Aluminium windows are often designed with a thermal break, for example, by containing a solid strip of insulating plastic such as polyamide. Aluminium curtain walls have undergone many innovations over the years as was described earlier for steel curtain walls. Corrugated steel and aluminium sheets are very common building components used for claddings, roofs, suspended ceilings and permanent shuttering. Most space frames are designed with steel members (MERO, etc.) but some are based on aluminium. One of the best-known aluminium space frames is

Triodetic, which features aluminium tubular members coupled together using specially shaped joints. Various forms such as flat structures, vaults and domes have been built with Triodetic with spans ranging from 50 to 100 metres. The Shah Alam mosque at Selangor, Malaysia, is one such dome.

Architectural and structural design must take care of certain specific failure modes of aluminium structures. Aluminium, for instance, is more prone to fatigue (the consequence of loads repeated many times) than steel. Various forms of buckling also play an important part in the failure of aluminium structures (Dwight, 1999). There exist adequate codes for the analysis of aluminium structures, such as the Eurocode 9. Aluminium joints in particular (bolted, riveted, welded, adhesively bonded) require careful consideration (Kosteas, 2001,

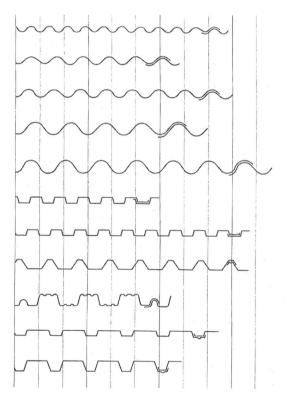

Figure 2.2 Sinusoidal, trapezoidal and other corrugated, cold-rolled aluminium sheets (Alusuisse). © Sebestyen: *Lightweight Building Construction*, Akadémiai Kiadó.

Meyer-Sternberg, 2001). The various fabrications and connecting techniques affect the design of steel and aluminium structures. The results are specific frameworks, trusses, vaults, curtain walls, space frames, domes, sometimes developed as subsystems available commercially for any new project. Several uses of aluminium in building are the equivalent of those in steel but certain fabrication processes are specific for aluminium, for example extrusion of sections and casting of alu-

minium panels. The architectural consequences follow from the specifics of fabrication. Practically all major producers of aluminium possess equipment and plant to produce corrugated sheet from coils by cold-forming sheet (Alucolux, etc.). The two major aluminium companies producing large-size cast aluminium panels are the Japanese Kubota and the Swiss Alusuisse.

In the wake of steel and aluminium, titanium may become an architectural metal. Cost and the priority of aerospace and military uses earlier constituted an obstacle to its extended architectural use. Titanium has an extremely low rate of thermal expansion and has excellent strength properties. Japan was the first country to use titanium in construction; the United States followed. A significant novelty has been the construction of the Guggenheim Museum in Bilbao, Spain, designed by Frank O. Gehry with an external titan (titanium) cladding. Titanium is resistant to corrosion and it has a low thermal expansion coefficient. Its yield strength is similar to that of stainless steel. Titanium sheet can be formed, joined and welded by conventional sheet-metal methods (Zahner, 1995). Seaming is a common form of joining. Earlier, the high price of titan meant that it was prohibitive for the construction of buildings. However, the gradual reduction in price and the use of much thinner sheets have placed it within the reach of designers.

Titanium is not supposed to tarnish, so that it was an unpleasant experience when its sheen partly faded at the Bilbao Museum. The probable cause has been the oxidization of chemicals used to fireproof the steel structure beneath the titanium shingles, which leaked into the cladding during construction. Various attempts had to be made (cleaning or partial replacement of sections of the cladding) to restore the sheen. The case furnishes further proof of just how much caution is recommended when introducing new materials into construction.

Titan increasingly finds application in the construction of façades. The prize-winning design by Paul Andreu, a French architect, for the new Beijing Opera House envisaged titan cladding. The spectacular new Glasgow Millennium Natural Science complex, on the River Clyde, consists of three more

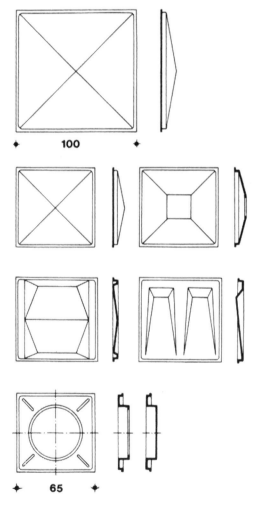

Figure 2.3 Aluminium cladding components (Reinhold and Mahla, Germany). © Sebestyen: *Lightweight Building Construction*, Akadémiai Kiadó.

or less independent buildings: a three-dimensional IMAX cinema, the Glasgow Tower, and the Natural Science and Technical Centre. The IMAX cinema and the Glasgow Science Centre are the first buildings in Great Britain to have a titanium cladding. The 7600 square metres roof area of the Centre (architect: Building Design Partnership, structural design: Buro Happold) has an isolated titanium sheet cladding. The 127 metre-high Tower is innovative in that the whole building can turn around its vertical axis and not only the top level as is the case for many other tall buildings and towers. The Science Centre and other buildings provide new potentials to combine education and entertainment and will greatly contribute to a renewal of Glasgow, a phenomenon that is a specific feature of new architecture and urban development: other examples (Lille, etc.) are mentioned elsewhere in the book.

2.5 Brick, Stone and Masonry

Brick and stone are among the oldest materials having been used in ancient Babylon and Egypt. They are still a material for masonry, or are used by prefabricating large panels with a thin exposed brick surface and backed by a thin reinforced concrete layer and, finally, gluing also provides a solution. The Wilbrink House, Amersfoort, The Netherlands, designed by the Dutch architect Ben van Berkel, 1992–94 (incidentally also the designer of the striking Rotterdam Erasmus Bridge), has a not entirely vertical wall consisting of bricks glued together. The Eurocode 6 is the new European standard for masonry structures.

Mario Botta, a Swiss architect, likes to design large-surface façades with exposed brick surfaces. Several other features characterizing new architecture's different trends can also be identified on Botta's buildings: large plane surfaces uninterrupted by windows or other openings thereby also camouflaging the number of floor levels behind the façade; a strong brick-red colour contrasting with black and white coloured surfaces on other parts of the façade; simple geometric contours: rectangles, circles, articulation of the façade by parallel or radial lines. All these features characterize, for example, the San Francisco Museum of Modern Art created

by Botta during the first years of the 1990s (see photograph in Philip Jodidio, *Contemporary European Architects*, Volume III, Taschen, 1995, page 56) and the Evry Cathedral, France, another design by Botta, 1992–95. These buildings may also be mentioned as containing certain new characteristics in Botta's designs. The large circular forms are in a slanted plane and occur not only as forms for structures but also for openings.

Masonry uses various types of bricks and concrete blocks. In recent times innovative new types of masonry products have been introduced, such as flashing block, moisture control block, dry stack masonry systems, thin brick systems, new mortar additives and new masonry ties (Beall, 2000). Masonry for low-rise buildings usually suffers much in earthquakes, although various ways to improve resistance to seismic actions are known (Casabonne, 2000).

In modern, post-modern and contemporary architecture stone has relinquished its position as a structural (load-bearing) material. However, it is much favoured in specific functions, such as cladding for curtain walls, floor paving and sculptural and decorative purposes. In curtain walls it is used as thin slabs suspended on a steel frame. In Saudi Arabia stone (marble veneer) has seen increasing application over the last 30 years (Idris, 2000).

2.6 Glass and Structural Glass

Glass performs a significant function in space divisions and heat and light control. It has been known since early times so it fully justifies being considered as a traditional material. Glass, however, was expensive and so enjoyed only restricted use up to the nineteenth century. Mass production of sheet glass, the development of steel frames, cable structures, fixing devices and systems as well as of elastic and elasto-plastic sealant changed this and resulted in a number of innovative solutions and systems. During the twentieth century the curtain wall emerged with new types of glazing. However, on the façades of the skyscrapers, linear glass fixing components were still present. The ambition was to develop all-glass façades with uninterrupted glass surfaces. Gradual progress in materials and systems achieved this objective (Wigginton, 1997).

The basic glazing material used for external envelopes is the glass pane, which may be clear white, body tinted, photosensitive, or photochromatic. For glass roofs with increased safety laminated glass may be used. The low tensile strength of glass can be improved by its thermal or chemical toughening. Thermally toughened glass (tempered glass) fractures into small pieces and thereby reduces risk in the case of glass breakage. Such glass is referred to as 'safety glass'. Glass coated by one or by several thin coating layers may be heat and light absorbent and/or reflective. These properties affect the appearance of buildings and even eventually their colour. The glass is usually transparent or translucent and these are properties that the designer may wish to make use of. Heat insulation may be increased by insulating glass, which is composed of two or more panes separated by a cavity (filled by dehydrated air or inert gas) and glued together and sealed along the edges. The solution most widely applied (with alternatives in the details) is the system that fixes the corners of the panes to a structure that itself is fixed to the main load-bearing structure, and ensures adequate tolerances and movements in space as a consequence of various actions, such as wind and other forms of deformation. The expression 'structural glass' is used for glazings that (when used in the external envelope) can withstand certain actions such as bending and buckling.

If the façade is shaped as an uninterrupted glass surface, we use the expression 'all-glass'. In the 1920s Le Corbusier and Mies van der Rohe attempted to develop all-glass systems but the technology evolved only gradually and at a later date. For such façades tempered or toughened glass is needed, which is produced by heating the glass panes in a furnace, having first cut them to their final shape, and then chilling them with cold air from a jet system. The result is that the outer surface is placed in compression and the inner part under tension. All-glass glazing systems evolved from earlier curtain wall systems in which the glass panes were fixed between linear frame components: glass beads, gaskets or pressure profiles.

Later, systems were developed where the glass panes were fixed at the corners only, either individually, or with two or four panes being fixed by a single fixing device. The glass façade is suspended by stressed cables to the structure. All-glass façades have a different aesthetic appearance from framed curtain walls, as a consequence of the absence of external metallic frame sections. One of the first buildings constructed with bolted corner-plate fixing points (so-called patch fittings) was the Faber and Dumas building in Ipswich, Great Britain, 1975 (architect: Norman Foster, glazing system developed in collaboration with Pilkington). A subsequent development was the countersunk 'Planar' fixing system where bolts flush with the glass pane were applied. It was first applied to the Renault Centre in Swindon, Great Britain, 1982 (also designed by Norman Foster, the glazing system in

Figure 2.4 City of Science, La Villette, Paris, 1986, designer: RFR Partners and Adrien Fainsilber. Structural glazing. © P. Rice and H. Dutton: *Structural Glass*, E & FN Spon.

collaboration with Pilkington). In 1986 the bolted fixing system with swivel joints (RFR system) was developed. This still forms the basis for several present-day structural glass systems. The RFR system was developed in 1986 by Adrien Fainsilber and the specialists Rice, Francis and Ritchie and first used at the La Villette complex in Paris (Figure 2.4). The main designer of the glazing system was the Briton Peter Rice (1935–92) who regrettably died at an early age.

An alternative solution for all-glass façades is to glue the panes at their corners to the load-bearing frame. However, this has not developed into a generally applied solution for the reason that movements of the components can cause problems. The solution most widely applied (with various alternatives in the details) is the one with fixing points in the glass façade as demonstrated in some early realizations, as in Ipswich, Swindon and Paris. Some notable additional realizations are:

- the Glass Pyramid at the Louvre, Paris, 1988, architect: I.M. Pei and Partners
- The Netherlands Architecture Institute, Rotterdam, The Netherlands, designer: Jo Coenen, 1988–93 (Plate19)
- Waterloo International Railway Station, London, 1994, architect: Nicolas Grimshaw and Partners
- Western Morning News, Plymouth, England, 1992, architect: Nicolas Grimshaw and Partners

and many other buildings in various countries.

Big halls, lobbies and entrance halls on the ground floor may have a glass wall assembled from suspended thick and large-size panes, as in the central building of the Radio in Paris. Originally buildings usually had one façade skin (single-skin façades) even if the single skin itself is comprised of several layers. A new concept is the construction of multiple-skin façades in which the space between the two layers can be utilized for ventilation and other purposes. Such a principle was used at the new building of the Dutch Ministry for Housing (VROM). In recent times glass envelopes (façades and roofs) have developed into high-tech components: 'polyvalent' or 'intelligent' (smart) envelopes. These have a role to play in the control of heating, ventilating, cooling, air conditioning and lighting.

The intelligent façade may also contribute to the improvement of environmental conditions by enabling the designer to plan green areas on various floors, as at the Commerzbank Headquarters, Frankfurt, Germany (architect: Norman Foster and Partners). Paul Andreu of the Paris Airports designed the 1200 tonne glass and steel dome of the Osaka Maritime Museum (engineering design by Ove Arup and Partners). The shell 'emerges' from the sea, access to it is through an underground tunnel. The 70-metre diameter hemisphere is one of the largest ever built and it acts as a casing for four floors of the museum. Its structure is a diagrid of tubular membranes connected by nodes and prestressed rods to resist earthquake action. The hemisphere was manufactured by Kawasaki Heavy Industries.

Almost all glass façades are assembled from plane glass sheets. A notable exception is the Hermes store building in Tokyo designed by Renzo Piano. Its skin is a continuous curtain of glass brick assembled from nine-piece panels. Each block is manually mirror-varnished along its edges and polished on its smooth side, the opposite side being corrugated. The bricks are encased in a tubular metal grille with fire-retardant rubber protected by a ceramic cord. The unit is then sealed on site with silicone. The 22 millimetre joints guarantee a tolerance of 4–5 millimetres for each block in the case of an earthquake.

Glass structures provide a most important field of cooperation between architects and engineers with consequences for the architectural design and the appearance of buildings.

2.7 Concrete and Reinforced Concrete

Research and innovation resulted in various new or improved types and properties of heavy and lightweight concrete, new production technologies such as prestressing, and new structural analysis and design methods for various loads and actions, prestressing, etc. Relatively recent is the intelligent and high-performance concrete (see below). The use of glass, polypropylene and steel fibres (including textiles and fabrics made from such fibres) in concrete (more generally, in cementitious materials) has come a long way over recent years (Sadegzadeh et al., 2001). Enhanced composite properties have been the result. Cladding panels have been developed, which utilize the new potentials.

Self-compacting concrete was first developed in 1988 in order to achieve durable concrete structures. To produce a self-compacting concrete, requirements are a high deformability of the paste or mortar and a resistance to segregation between

Figure 2.5 Apartment block, Expo '67, Montreal, Canada, 1966–67, architect: Moshe Safdie. Modular, three-dimensional reinforced concrete box architecture.

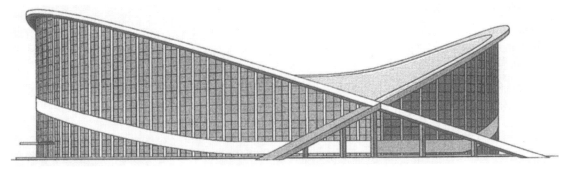

Figure 2.6 Exposition Hall, Raleigh, North Carolina, USA, 1952–53, designers: M. Nowicki, W.H. Deltrick and F. Severud. Structure suspended on two inclined intersecting reinforced concrete arches by cable nets. © Sebestyen: *Construction: Craft to Industry*, E & FN Spon.

43

coarse aggregate and mortar when the concrete flows through the confined zone of reinforcing bars.

To achieve these, a limited aggregate content, a low water/powder ratio and the use of a superplasticizer are recommended. By now, the process has been executed in several countries and self-compacting concrete is becoming a standard type of concrete (Okamura et al., 2000). Structural analysis and design have certain principles common to all types of concrete but some deviations are necessary for specific types of concrete (CEB and FIP Recommendations, 1998, 2000). The EN 206-1:2000 is the new European standard for concrete, reinforced concrete and prestressed concrete structures. High-strength concrete has a higher compressive strength and usually also has other attributes superior to normal concrete, such as durability. Such concrete is then considered high-performance concrete. High-performance concrete has a compressive strength exceeding 60 N/mm^2 and, with a special composition mix, over 100 N/mm^2: ten times stronger than ordinary concrete. High-performance concrete is prepared with special cement, mineral and chemical admixtures (fly ash, superplasticizers, polymers, silica fume, granulated blast furnace slag, high-reactivity metakaolin) and is reinforced with fibres instead of steel rods (Nawy, 1996, Shah and Ahmad, 1994). Structural design must follow the general methods applied to normal reinforced concrete but some specific characteristics require additional considerations (for example, slab-column and beam-column intersections), partly with some impact on the appearance of structures. Some of the realizations with high-performance concrete are high-rise buildings, such as:

- Lake Point Tower, Chicago, total height above ground 197 metres, 1966–67
- Water Tower Place, Chicago, 76-storey concrete building, 1976
- Texas Commerce Tower, Houston, 75-storey composite steel and concrete building, 1981
- South Wacker Drive, Chicago, 70-storey, 295 metres-high reinforced concrete building, 1989.

For buildings, high-rise is the principal field of application of high-performance concrete and this has made it possible to construct concrete tall buildings with increasing height. Another application is for bridges. The Americas cable-stayed bridge near Vancouver, Canada, completed in 1986, has a maximum span of 465 metres and has a high-performance concrete deck. High-strength lightweight aggregate concrete also finds some fields of application although on a much more limited scale than high-performance normal concrete.

New developments in concrete are concrete with resins and concrete with fibre-reinforced polymer (FRP) reinforcement. Both, eventually in a combined form, are used in repairing damaged or cracked concrete structures (rehabilitation and strengthening) as well as for some specific types of new constructions. As structural reinforcement, fibre-reinforced polymers are based on armada (AFRP), carbon (CFRP) or glass fibres (GFRP). The resin matrix is based in most cases on epoxy or vinyl-ester. A most recent innovation is the twin application of FRP reinforcement and fibre optical sensing, which produces 'smart structures' automatically monitoring structures. Among the new technologies, concrete with exposed surfaces has developed and these surfaces have an influence on architecture. Blemish-free surfaces of uniform colour can be produced with adequate mix, careful compacting and curing. Pre-cast components can be produced with sculptured surface. For such purpose, various materials (concrete, timber, steel, and plastics) can be used for the formwork. To obtain a coloured surface, either the top layer has to have a coloured mix, or the surface has to be painted (Sebestyen, 1998).

Prefabrication affects the morphology and geometry of the buildings but also has an impact on design principles and organization. The primary effect of prefabrication on forms is to favour shapes advantageous for shuttering forms and industrial production. Although this in itself is a rather vague requirement it does acquire importance in actual design. It should not be identified with the simplistic rule to design simple shapes. Ricardo Bofill designs all of his buildings with neo-classicist components (see Bofill-designed buildings in Montpellier and elsewhere). However, he realizes such historicizing forms from pre-cast concrete components.

If a façade wall panel is manufactured in a horizontal position, the decision must be made as to whether the external surface should be formed on the upper or the lower surface of the panel. The lower surface is better suited for producing a relief-like surface. On the upper surface this is possible by pressing, a technique that is seldom applied, however. Hammering the surface may produce different reliefs. Embedding special decorative aggregates (coloured glass, stone or porcelain) is possible into either the lower surface of the panel or the upper one. Washing out or brushing the cement from the surface within a certain time is also applied and for this purpose a retardant may be added to the cement mortar. Internal wall panels have a smooth plane surface on both sides and may be manufactured either horizontally or vertically. For casting panels in a vertical position, the manufacturing floor space in the production hall may be reduced by casting two or more panels in a vertical position in a single form: twin-forms for two panels or a battery of forms for casting several panels. This technology was introduced for large-size wall panels. Some prefabrication firms specialize in the casting of concrete components with quite intricately sculptured forms.

Exposed concrete surfaces were applied quite frequently during the modernist period, for example, by Le Corbusier. After 1945, for some years, exposed concrete was applied in many constructions. Buildings with large surfaces of exposed concrete even received the label of 'New Brutalism'. Several British (and other) architects adhered to such a trend for some time and indeed New Brutalism appeared in many countries but the trend did not last for too long. After some time the perception was that an excessive use of concrete surfaces might lack sufficient appeal.

Architects in recent times do not adhere to the earlier principle to let forms reflect their structural function. For instance, when designing columns linked to beams above them, architects and engineers favoured quadratic cross-sections for the columns and higher cross-sections for the beams. This design principle has lost its validity and beams may be designed with similar widths to columns; see some buildings designed by the Japanese architect Arata Isozaki (the Museum of Modern Art, Gamma Prefecture, Takasaki, Japan, 1974 and the Team Disney Building, Orlando, Florida, USA, 1991). Another example is the Museum of Contemporary Art, Chicago, Illinois, USA, designed by Josef Paul

Kleihaus, 1992–96; the number of similar realizations is virtually limitless.

To produce an exposed concrete surface, a careful composition of the mix, of the shuttering and of the whole technological process is required. In certain cases the joints between the shutters and end points of the distance-holding components of the shutters are left visible. This equally requires advance planning and strict adherence to the planned technological process. This can be seen, for example, on several buildings designed by the Japanese Tadao Ando (for example, the Koshino House, Ashiya, Hyago, Japan).

One of the most common trends of industrialization in building is the development of 'systems', i.e. 'system building'. Such systems were developed in housing (Camus, Coignet, Larsen-Nielsen, etc.), in educational constructions (CLASP, etc.) and in industrial and other buildings. Systems are characterized by some kind of load-bearing structure (in steel or concrete) and a façade system with either large panels manufactured from reinforced concrete or a lightweight system (with a timber or steel frame). Research on structural concrete focusses on certain topics, such as:

- designing for durability
- developing a uniform and balanced safety concept
- bridging the gap between material science and structural design
- designing with new materials
- quality of construction and production
- consistency between calculation methods
- minimum reinforcement and robustness
- external prestressing
- redesign of existing concrete structures
- aesthetics of concrete structures
- various individual topics, such as lightness of structures, corrosion of prestressing steel
- fire resistance of complex structures as a whole
- design by testing
- the growing role of information technology (IT) in design and education (Walraven, 2000).

2.8 Plastics, Fabrics and Foils

For structural and space-enclosing purposes, synthetic materials, mostly polymers and polymer composites, are also used to produce building components. Their properties are so different from those of traditional materials that design from them calls for specialized knowledge and care. Their fabrication processes usually favour curved surfaces, which in themselves result in new forms, unfamiliar in former construction. The main groups of polymers are: the thermoplastics (polyvinyl – PVC, polyethylene – PE, polypropylene – PP, polystyrene – PS, etc.), the thermosets (polyurethane – PU, epoxies, etc.) and the elastomers (synthetic rubbers). Plastics and the composites manufactured from them have low moduli of elasticity. The required rigidity of a structure must therefore be derived from the shape rather than from the material. Shapes with high rigidity are three-dimensional surface structures such as domes, shells, or folded plates. To achieve or increase rigidity, fibre-reinforced sheets in appropriate forms are used, e.g. by troughing, ribbing or supporting the sheet in a sandwich structure. Corrugated sheets are rigid in one direction but not in the other. In sandwich panels, the polymer foam (or another material with similar properties e.g. rock wool, softwood-based layer) constitutes the core; the two faces may be metal sheet or some form of hardboard. The use of a soft cover layer such as paper is also possible. The most productive technology for making sandwich panels is continuous manufacture. The two cover faces are produced from coated steel or aluminium sheet coils, which are corrugated with rollers. The foam is produced, equally continuously, between the two metal faces of the future sandwich panels. Following heat treatment and a hardening of the foam, the three-layer sandwich is cut to its definitive length. Such sandwich panels are used for both walls and roofs.

In designing structures from plastics, deformation and temperature (even if only slightly higher than normal) are of paramount importance. Several types of plastics do not weather well, i.e. they change under the influence of outdoor circumstances. Some are susceptible to crazing, which is a network of fine cracks on or under the surface of the material. Crazing may have different causes, one of which originates in stresses caused by excessive loading. Most plastics are combustible and special compositions are required to protect

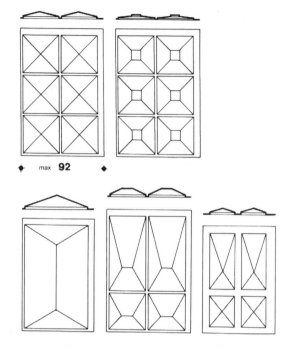

Figure 2.7 Vacuum-formed impact-resistant hard PVC cladding components (Hoechst, Germany). © Sebestyen: *Lightweight Building Construction*, Akadémiai Kiadó.

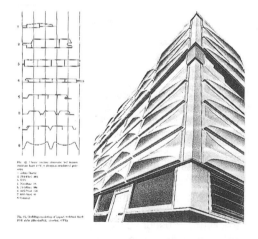

Figure 2.8 Plastic impact-resistant hard PVC and fibreglass reinforced polyester façade components. © Sebestyen: *Lightweight Building Construction*, Akadémiai Kiadó.

them from fire. Full account should also be taken of potential hazards to health. Jointing and sealing joints have been developed with special consideration to the properties of plastics (Montella, 1985). Due to the properties listed as well as others, the design of components from plastics must take a number of criteria into account, such as:

- structural requirements: types and distribution of actions and loads (static and dynamic, regular or random distribution, dead and live, wind, seismic, snow, stresses, strains, deflection, elastic and plastic properties)
- environmental conditions: service temperature range, thermal insulation and movement, moisture, fire hazards, behaviour to light (transparent, translucent, opaqueness, colour, discoloration, dust and other air impurities)
- fabrication methods and consequences: mechanical (cutting, piercing), casting, welding, extrusion, thermoforming (free blowing, vacuum forming, strip heat bending, drape forming, ridge forming), combinations with other materials
- detail design: size, shape, quantity, colour, edges, ribs, laminations
- tolerances: jointing, sealing, fastening, reinforcements.

Obviously, the above is not a complete list and it is not only in the design of plastics components that many of the parameters occur. In addition to having certain basic aspects in common, components from plastics, or from any other material, have their own specific requirements as well. Plastics are applied in construction for many purposes: glazing, skylights, roofs, heat, sound and water insulation, enclosures and claddings, windows and doors, lighting, etc.

Roofs are frequently covered by plastics. Suspended roofs (membranes) are made from coated fabrics or foils: PVC or Teflon-coated glass fibre, polyester fabrics, or ETFE foils. PVC-coated polyester fabrics were mostly used in Europe: some realized buildings that are covered by such materials are:

- Covered Tennis Court, Gorle, Italy, 1991
- Trade Fair Stand, Frankfurt, Germany, 1994
- Recreational Clinic, Maserberg, Germany, 1993–94
- Auditorium Roof, Tarragona, Spain, 1993.

In North America PTFE-coated glass fibre is more widely used. Elsewhere two applications are the Amenities Building of the Inland Revenue Centre in Nottingham, Great Britain, completed in 1995 (architect: Michael Hopkins and Partner) and the Climate-Controlled Parasols in Medina, Saudi Arabia, 1992 (architect: Kamal Izmail, structural consultant: Buro Happold). In some cases nets, shade fabrics or grid fabrics are applied, eventually without any water insulating layer, their objective being purely a visual separation of space (Schock, 1997). Various types of plastics serve as sealants in joints between building components. The rate of curing of sealant affects their performance under movement. Silicones and the two-part sealants are superior to polysulphide and polyurethane, for sealing joints that are subjected to high movement stresses immediately upon installation (Chew, 2000). Various experiments were undertaken into the production of whole buildings to be assembled from components made from plastics. In many cases these were successful for small buildings (kiosks, one-family houses) but not so for larger buildings. Larger buildings invariably require a frame or other load-bearing structure made of concrete, steel, or other non-plastic structural material. A great number of buildings with a combination of different materials, including plastics, have been assembled. A special class of lightweight long-span structures is the buildings covered by air-inflated (pneumatic) structures; see also Chapter 3. A globally known early realization was the one constructed for the Osaka, Japan EXPO. A more recent example is the Pneumatic Hall 'Airtecture', Esslingen-Berkheim, Germany, 1996 (architecture and structure: Festo KG).

Bibliography

General considerations

Anink, David, Boonstra, Chiel and Mak, John (1996) *Handbook of Sustainable Building: An Experimental Preference Method for Selection of Materials for Use in Construction and Refurbishment*, James & James (Science Publishers)

Berge, Bjorn (2000) *The Ecology of Building Materials*, Architectural Press (Norwegian: 1992)

Gibb, Alistair G.F. (1999) *Off-site Fabrication: Prefabrication, Pre-assembly and Modularisation*, Whittles Publishing

Illston, J.M. (1994) *Construction Materials*, E & FN Spon

Jencks, Charles (1997) Nonlinear Architecture: New Science = New Architecture? *Architectural Design*, Vol. 67, No. 9–10, September–October, pp. 7–9

Rice, Peter (1993) *An Engineer Imagines*, Ellipsis

Timber

Bianchina, Paul (1997) *Builder's Guide to New Materials and Techniques*, McGraw Hill

Buchanan, Andrew H. (2000) Fire Performance of Timber Construction, *Structural Engineering and Materials*, Vol. 2, No. 3, July-September, pp. 278–89

Cramer, S.M. (2000) Expectations Regarding Fire Performance and Building Design, *Focus, A Journal of Contemporary Wood Engineering*, Vol. 11, No. 2, summer, pp. 7–12

Dolan, J.D. (2000) Mismatched Expectations Pertaining to 'Designed to Code' for Seismic Design, *Focus, A Journal of Contemporary Wood Engineering*, Vol. 11, No. 2, summer, pp. 3–6

Gilfillan, J.R. et al. (2001) Enhancement of the Structural Performance of Glue Laminated Homegrown Sitka Spruce, Using Carbonfibre-Reinforced Polymer, *The Structural Engineer*, Vol. 79, No. 8, 17 April, pp. 23–28

Gutdeutsch, Götz (1996) *Building in Wood. Construction and Details*, Birkhäuser

Larsen, H.J. and Jensen, J.L. (2000) Influence of Semi-Rigidity of Joints on the Behaviour of Timber Structures, *Progress in Structural Engineering and Materials*, Vol. 2, No. 3, July–September, pp. 267–77

Mehaffey, J.R. et al. (2000) Self-Heating and Spontaneous Ignition of Fibreboard Insulating Panels, *Fire Technology*, Vol. 36, No. 4, November, pp. 226–35

Rosowsky, D. (2000) Mismatched Expectations, Objectives, and Performance Requirements for Wood Frame Construction in High-Wind Regions, *Focus, A Journal of Contemporary Wood Engineering*, Vol. 11, No. 2, summer, pp. 13–16

Rosowsky, D. and Schiff, S. (2000) Performance of Wood-Frame Structures Under High Wind Loads, *Focus, A Journal of Contemporary Wood Engineering*, Vol. 11, No. 1, spring, pp. 14–18

Schreyer, Alexander et al. (2001) Strength Capacities and Behaviour of New Composite Timber-Steel Connection, *Journal of Structural Engineering*, Vol. 127, No. 8, August, pp. 888–93

Sebestyen, Gyula (1998) *Construction: Craft to Industry*, E & FN Spon

Stathopoulos, Th. (2000) Wind Loads on Low Buildings: Research and Progress, *Focus, A Journal of Contemporary Wood Engineering*, Vol. 11, No.1, spring, pp. 18–24

Stungo, Naomi (1998) *The New Wood Architecture*, Calmann & King/Laurence King Publishing

Steel

Blanc, A., McEvoy, M. and Plank, R. (Eds) (1993) *Architecture and Construction in Steel*, E & FN Spon

Chan S.L. and Teng, J.G. (1999) *Advances in Steel Structures*, Elsevier

Eggen, Arne Petten and Sandaker, Bjorn Normann (1996) *Stahl in der Architektur: Konstruktive und Gestalterische Verwendung*, Deutsche Verlags-Anstalt

Krampen, Jürgen (2001) Bemessung von Fachwerken aus Hohlprofilen (MHS): Leicht Gemacht, *Stahlbau*, Vol. 70, No.3, March, pp. 153–64

Newman, Alexander (1997) *Metal Building Systems: Design and Specification*, McGraw-Hill

Oliver, M.S., Albon, J.M. and Garner, N.K. (1997) *Coated Metal Roofing and Cladding*, British Board of Agreement, Thomas Telford

Pasternak, H. and Müller, L. (2001) Zur FE: Modellierung Leichter Hallenrahmen, *Stahlbau*, Vol. 70, No. 1, January, pp. 53–8

Seitz, Frédéric (1995) *L'architecture métallique au XXe siècle*

Toma, T. et al. (Eds) (1992) *Cold Formed Steel in Tall Buildings*, McGraw-Hill, Inc.

Zahner, William L. (1995) *Architectural Metals: A Guide to Selection, Specification and Performance*, John Wiley & Sons, Inc.

Aluminium and other metals

Dwight, John (1999) *Aluminium Design and Construction*, E & FN Spon

Lane, J. (1992) *Aluminium in Building*, Ashgate

Kosteas, Dimitris (2001) Aluminiumverbindungen, Methoden und Normen, *Stahlbau*, Vol. 70, No.2, February, pp. 116–20

Meyer-Sternberg, Menno (2001) Aluminiumverbindungen: Berechnung nach Eurocode 9, *Stahlbau*, Vol. 70, No.2, February, pp. 121–5

Zahner, L. William (1995) *Architectural Metals: A Guide to Selection, Specification and Performance*, John Wiley & Sons, Inc

Brick, stone and masonry

Beall, Christine (2000) New Masonry Products and Materials, *Structural Engineering and Materials*, Vol. 2, No. 3, July–September, pp. 296–303

Casabonne, Carlos (2000) Masonry in the Seismic Areas of the Americas: Recent Investigation and Developments, *Structural Engineering and Materials*, Vol. 2, No. 3, July–September

Idris, Mahmoud, M. (2000) The Use of Marble Veneer in Building Façade in Riyadh: Materials, Adaptability and Construction, *Architectural Science Review*, 43.1, March, pp. 5–11

Glass and structural glass

Button, D. et al. (1993) *Glass in Building*, Butterworth Architecture

Compagno, Andrea (1995) *Intelligent Glass Façades*, Artemis

King, Carol Soucek (1996) *Designing with Glass: The Creative Touch*, PBC International, Inc.

Rice, Peter (1993) *An Engineer Imagines*, Ellipsis

Rice, P. and Dutton, H. (1995) *Structural Glass*, E & FN Spon

Wigginton, Michael (1997) *Glas in der Architektur*, Deutsche Verlags-Anstalt

Concrete and reinforced concrete

CEB-FIP (May 2000) Lightweight Aggregate Concrete. *Part 1: Recommended Extensions to Model Code 90. Guide*

Clarke, J.L. (Ed.) (1993) *Structural Lightweight Aggregate Concrete*, Blackie Academic & Professional

FIP (May 1998) *Recommendations. Design of Thin-Walled Units*

FIP/CEB-FIP (May 1998) *Recommendations for the Design of Post-Tensioned Slabs and Foundation Rafts*

High Performance Concrete (1995) *CEB Bulletin d'Information*, 228

Nawy, Edward G. (1996) *Fundamentals of High Strength High Performance Concrete*, Longman

Okamura, H., Ozawa, K. and Ouchi, M. (2000) Self-Compacting Concrete, *Structural Concrete*, Vol. 1, No. 1, March, pp. 3–17

Sadegzadeh, Massud, Kettle, Roger and Vassou, Vassoulla (2001) The Influence of Glass, Polypropylene and Steel Fibres on the Physical Properties of Concrete, *Concrete*, Vol. 35, No. 4, April, pp. 14–18

Shah, S.P. and Ahmad, S.H. (Eds) (1994) *High Performance Concretes and Applications*, Edward Arnold

Walraven, J. (1999) The Evolution of Concrete, *Structural Concrete*, Vol. 1, No. 1., March, pp. 3–11

Walraven, J. (2000) Message from the President, *Structural Concrete*, Vol. 1, No. 4, pp. 1–2

Plastics, fabrics, foils

Chew, M.Y.L. (2000) Evaluation of the Curing of High Performance Sealants, *Architectural Science Review*, 43.1, March, pp. 25–30

Hall, C. (1989) *Polymer Materials*, Macmillan Education

Margolis, James M. (1985) *Engineering Thermoplastics: Properties and Applications*, Marcel Dekker, Inc.

Montella, Ralph (1985) *Plastics in Architecture: A Guide to Acrylic and Polycarbonate*, Marcel Dekker, Inc.

Schock, Hans-Joachim (1997) *Soft Shells: Design and Technology of Tensile Architecture*, Birkhäuser

Sebestyen, Gyula (1998) *Construction: Craft to Industry*, E & FN Spon

3

The impact of technological change on buildings and structures

3.1 Some Specific Design Aspects

In the previous chapter we examined the impact of building materials on new architecture. Other technological factors affecting architecture are the function of buildings, the structures, components and equipment of buildings. Non-directly technological factors are computer-aided design, management, and the changing requirements of users, artistic aspirations, ambitions and fashion. In what follows, let us look at the role of the factors: buildings, structures and components. It will not be possible to deal in detail with various building types, structures and components but to the extent that they affect architectural design, they will be mentioned. Partitions, floors and foundations will not be discussed and façades, which are after all of extreme importance in designing the exterior of a building, were discussed partly in the sections on materials (on steel, aluminium, brick, glass and plastics) in Chapter 2.

For all types of building the positive satisfaction of users is important. This can be ensured in the design phase by involving future users. In buildings in which a great number of people work or which are used for other purposes, thorough studies are continuously being carried out to ascertain whether these do adequately respond to the users' requirements (Beedle, 1995).

3.1.1 Function and form

In the following some specific characteristics of new architecture design are identified. The architectural design and form of buildings is influenced by the type of the building and by its function. Buildings such as residential, commercial, industrial, transport, educational, health-care, leisure and agricultural buildings are designed with features characteristic for the individual building type. Structural systems also have an interrelation with the type and function of the buildings. As a consequence there exist school-building, residential-building and other systems. Technical progress (prefabrication, mechanization, etc.) resulted in the industrialization of building and, as a specific form of this, 'system building'. Early on, the various deficiencies inherent in system building (such as inadequate architectural quality and others) brought system building into discredit. Consequently it has ceased to be considered as the basic panacea for the problems of building. Nevertheless, the system concept may contribute to the combination of up-to-date technology and good architecture.

Basically we can differentiate two types of megasystem. The first of these is the technical system of buildings (Ahuja, 1997), which consists of:

- the structural system
- the architectural system
- the services and equipment (lighting, HVAC, power, security, elevators, telecommunications, functional equipment, etc.).

It was frequently claimed that ideally the form of a structure should correspond to the type of a structure and that the function of a building should harmonize with the structure form. Many realized examples seem to confirm this assumption; exceptions, however, already existed in historical architecture (e.g. hanging stucco ceilings in the form of vaults). In modern and post-modern architecture the use of steel and of reinforced concrete made it easy to design structures whose form did not really correspond to the type of the structure. The principle of the harmony of form and structure was in fact undermined by this development.

The second mega-system is composed of:

- the process of architectural, structural and engineering design and their documents
- economic analysis, data and results including quantity surveying, feasibility studies, risk analysis
- management of design, construction and use of buildings and structures (facility management) including cooperation of various organizations and persons involved in the construction process.

The architectural profession may rely on systems for buildings that are typical and occur with restricted variations in great numbers, but for any major commission individual approaches are favoured.

3.1.2 Bigness (mega-buildings)

The concept of megastructures had already been introduced during the modern period. Kenzo Tange's justification for megastructures was grounded on the idea that functions may change over the lifetime of a building and therefore megastructures might provide convenient bases to accommodate the altered internal functions. Another Japanese architect, Fumihiko Maki defined the megastructure as a large frame in which all functions of a city or part of a city may be housed.

In recent times new functions have appeared on the scene such as computer rooms, clean rooms, telecommunications premises and many others. A new type of building is that with flexible uses and

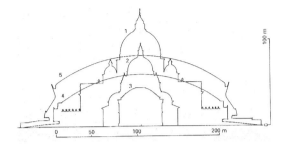

Figure 3.1 Dome spans: 1 = St. Peter's, Rome; 2 = St. Paul's, London; 3 = Pantheon, Rome; 4 = Astrodome, Houston, USA; 5 = Superdome, Louisiana, USA. Following the Pantheon dome in Rome, in the early second century AD, it was not until 1700 years later that domes of similar size were built and it was only in the twentieth century that the span of the Pantheon was surpassed.

with a combination of functions. Such buildings may be extremely large and beyond a certain scale their architecture acquires the properties of bigness (Koolhaas and Mau, 1995). Rem Koolhaas defined a latent theory of bigness based on five theorems (Jencks and Kropf, 1997):

1. Beyond a certain critical mass, a building becomes a Big Building with parts that remain committed to the whole.
2. The elevator and its family of related inventions 'render null and void the classical repertoire of architecture'.
3. 'In Bigness, the distance between core and envelope increases to the point where the façade can no longer reveal what happens inside.'
4. Through size alone, big buildings enter a new domain, beyond good or bad.
5. One of the consequences of Bigness is that such buildings are no longer part of the urban tissue. Bigness transforms architecture and generates a new kind of city.

A 1998 survey on outstanding European architectural realizations (Jodidio, 1998) demonstrated bigness by pointing to some recent buildings, such as:

- the Commerzbank Headquarters, Frankfurt am Main, architect: Norman Foster, 1994–97

51

Figure 3.2 Suspended stressed roof from PVC-coated textile.

- Hall 26, Deutsche Messe, Hanover, Germany, architect: Thomas Herzog and Partner, 1994–96
- Velodrome and Olympic Swimming Pool, Berlin, Germany, architect: Dominique Perrault, 1993–98.

The Commerzbank Building was at the time of its design and construction the tallest office building in Europe (298.7 metres with its aerial). Norman Foster described it as the 'world's first ecological high rise tower – energy efficient and user friendly'. The central atrium, together with the four-storey gar-dens, serves as a natural ventilation chimney. The offices are column free.

The Hall 26 of the Hanover Messe has a 220 by 115 metres structure and rises 25 metres above ground. It is composed as a complex of three steel suspension roofs with timber composite panels, which provide heat insulation covering the roof. A carefully thought-out ventilation system reduces mechanical ventilation needs. The wave-like shape of the building makes it attractive to users and visitors.

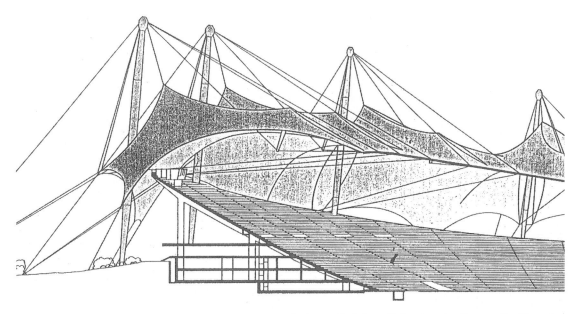

Figure 3.3 Olympic Stadium, Munich, Germany, 1972, designer: Frei Otto. Following the German Pavilion at the Montreal Expo, 1967, the next major cable and membrane structure was the Munich Olympic Stadium.

The Velodrome and Olympic Swimming Pool has as its visible feature the Velodrome's 115 metres clear-span 3500 tonnes spoked roof structure. The complex extends 17 metres below ground level, which renders the building extremely energy efficient.

A special category of large buildings are extensive covered spaces (Wilkinson, 1991). These serve greatly differing purposes: market halls, sports stadiums, auditorium halls, exhibition halls and others. We will discuss these not as buildings but as wide-span structures.

Following the construction of many large buildings, it can confidently be predicted that many more will be built in the future. Due to their 'bigness' and the vast number of users and visitors, they generate development around them, the implications of which have to be part of the architectural design.

For certain civil engineering works, for instance bridges, silos, telecommunications towers, the structural solution lies in determining the overall appearance. In other cases (for most buildings) the structural solution is only one factor that affects

appearance and other factors exercise an important influence.

3.1.3 Tall buildings

Structural design development has resulted in new types of structure. The new potentials in structural design were, on the one hand, results in science and engineering knowledge and, on the other hand, new demands of clients. This was the case, for example, with building higher buildings and with longer spans. The overall pattern of architectural design has been the interrelation of techniques, construction technology, artistic ambition and functions. Tall buildings required new façade systems. Underground premises and atria equally called for new architectural and engineering solutions.

Hal Iyengar wrote that 'The ability to form and shape a high-rise building is strongly influenced by the structural system. This influence becomes progressively significant as the height of the building increases' (Blanc et al., 1993: 227–8).

Figure 3.4 Façade with one- or two-part box-type bracings, eliminating thermal (cold) bridges, single, or thermal (double) insulating glazing, zipped-in plastic gasket sections (Pittco T-wall, USA). © Sebestyen: *Lightweight Building Construction*, Akadémiai Kiadó.

To build higher and higher has been an ambition of mankind ever since time immemorial. With traditional materials (stone, brick, timber) and technology, heights of 150 to 200 metres were achieved. It was in the twentieth century only that structures with heights exceeding 200 metres could be realized.

Tall buildings were first built in Chicago and the Chicago architects strove for modern design. In New York neo-classicist features characterized the first period of tall buildings. All through the history of skyscrapers, architects and structural engineers struggled to find more and more appropriate architectural and structural expression for the buildings and also to devise solutions regarding their adaptation to the surrounding urban environment. During the 1930s buildings climbed to 300 metres and above and, following the Second World War, the 400 metre mark was passed.

A novel phenomenon is that at the present time the tallest building is not in the USA or another industrialized country but in a developing country:

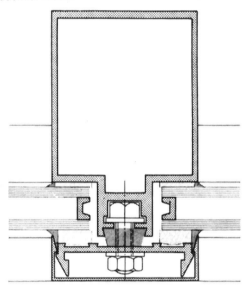

Figure 3.5 Façade system (two variants) with aluminium frame sections, fixed insulating glazing and plastic spacers (Mesconal, Germany). © Sebestyen: *Lightweight Building Construction*, Akadémiai Kiadó.

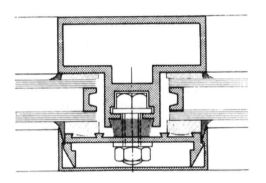

this is the twin towers in Kuala Lumpur, Malaysia. From the ten tallest buildings in the world four only are in New York and Chicago with the others being located in cities in developing countries (Kuala Lumpur, Shanghai, Guangzhou, Shenzhen, Hong Kong). On 11 September 2001 the twin towers of the World Trade Center in New York fell victim to a terrorist attack by hijacked aeroplanes. In the meantime the Tshinmao Building in Shanghai was completed (in 1998) with its tower 420.5 metres high. The construction of the Global Financial Center was commenced in Shanghai; it is planned to scale the height of 466 metres. In China's capital, Beijing, several new tall buildings are also envis-

aged. In 2001, the majority of buildings exceeding 90 metres were still in New York, followed by Hong Kong and Chicago, but it can be predicted that the share of the developing countries will grow.

It has become the prerogative of the twenty-first century to build higher than 500 metres. In the race for the world's highest building Hong Kong, Shanghai and Chicago are participants and others will certainly enter the competition. Buildings will soon climb to 600–800 metres in height (Campi, 2000).

To build that high, a number of technical problems had and have to be solved (Vambersky, 2001). In the forefront of these stands structural safety. This includes not only sufficient compressive strength of the superstructure and foundation but also safety against earthquake, strong wind, impact action (aircraft crash, explosion, etc.), human discomfort from vibration and horizontal movement. Some of the solutions involve a strong influence on the design of buildings. A conspicuous new component is the diagonal bracing appearing on the façade, such as the stiffened tube of the John Hancock Center in Chicago and many others since then. Another mostly hidden device is the passive and active damping system applied to reduce vibration of the structure.

The evolution of the vertical (lateral) system resulted in the following systems:

- shear (or 'Vierendel') frame with rigidly jointed columns and beams
- shear truss with diagonalized bracing between columns
- shear truss and frame with both shear frame and shear trusses and added knee braces
- shear-truss-frame outrigger and belt trusses: two-dimensional planar framework with the floor slab providing the lateral tie between them
- framed tube: closer spacing of columns and a continuous frame over corners
- truss tube with a form as framed tube but with wider spacing of columns and tied across by a system of diagonals
- bundled or modular tubes (diagonalized tube): grouped together framed or trussed tubes
- super-frame or mega-frame: a shear frame where horizontal and vertical members are large, several storeys deep and several bays wide
- composite systems: mixed reinforced concrete and steel systems with concrete shear walls or concrete framed tubes combined with steel framing.

For tall buildings many components had to be adapted to the specific conditions of such buildings, including frame connections, floors, ceilings, partitions and foundations. These also affected the aesthetic solution of the tall buildings.

Elevators and the supply systems are a source of a series of problems. Water pressure restrictions require zoning in height: many tall buildings demonstrate the zones on the façade; how this was to be solved became a design problem to be reckoned with. Water supply in case of fire, prevention against smoke propagation, safety of lifts, HVAC, lighting, communications in case of calamities call for planning in advance for all eventualities.

A survey on the history of skyscrapers defines the following periods (Bennett, 1995):

- the functional period, 1880–1900
- the eclectic period, 1900–20
- the 'Art Deco' period, 1920–40
- the 'International Style', 1950–70
- the period of giant towers, 1965–75
- the period of social skyscrapers, 1970–80
- the post-modern period, 1980 to date.

It is not the aim of this book to delve into any details about the history of architecture and we are also keeping the story of skyscrapers brief. The Empire State Building, New York, completed in 1931, originally 381 metres, remained the world's tallest for 40 years. Following the Second World War the Lever House, New York, completed in 1952 (architect: Gordon Bunshaft from Skidmore, Owings and Merrill) and the Seagram Building, New York, completed in 1958 (architect: Mies van der Rohe with Philip Johnson), served as models for all subsequent International Style skyscrapers. Within the long list of subsequent skyscrapers we would mention the John Hancock Center, Chicago, completed in 1969, design by Fazlur Khan. It has external diagonal bracing since imitated with various alternatives. For some time the Sears Tower, Chicago, completed in 1974, ranked as the tallest building in the world. It is 443 metres high and is composed of nine rectangular prisms. This has finally, or rather temporarily, been topped by the twin Petronas Towers, Kuala Lumpur, Malaysia, completed in 1998, architect Cesar Pelli with associates. These and all others realized or to be realized have been designed with a strong interrelationship with technological developments.

New skyscrapers were designed with new concepts. One such concept is the design of 'flat' buildings, which spread out the loads in the subsoil and can more efficiently withstand horizontal forces; one such project is the planned Swiss Re building in London. However, the terrorist attack against the twin towers of the New York World Trade Center may well prompt a searching reassessment of many planned future skyscrapers.

For the sake of completeness we must note within this section tall engineering structures: towers, silos, bunkers. These also constitute a new class of architectural design problems, see for example the structures by Calatrava, bridge pylons for suspension and for cable-stayed bridges and water towers.

3.1.4 Atria and elevators

Atria are defined as spaces within buildings surrounded by premises of the building and indeed have been built since ancient times. However, until the nineteenth century there was no solid roof over them.

The introduction of mass production of sheet glass enabled constructors during the nineteenth century to build large city atria ('galleries') with a glazed cover (Paris, London, Milan, etc.). During the twentieth century a wave of atria were built mainly in tall buildings. Whilst atria are today usually also in the interior of buildings, sometimes they are linked to the entry from the exterior and the lobby but in all cases they have a glazed roof and extend several storeys high. Nowadays atria are most commonly (but not exclusively) used in multi-storey hotels. They pose new challenges for the designer: structural safety, climate, fire, smoke, security and sound control, new types of internal contacts (corridors open to the atrium, eventually room windows overlooking the atrium), placing plants in the atrium space, positioning elevators in new ways (panoramic glass elevators). Assistance in the design of the structures, of the services and the building physics conditions is being rendered by various, sometimes quite complicated models, which may be analysed and solved by computers (see the AIRGLAZE model in Voeltzel et al., 2001). For fires, there exist different models, the best of which is based on computational fluid dynamics (CFD) (Yin and Chow, 2001). Where atria possess great height and dimensions new possibilities present themselves (lush garden restaurants, fountains, changing internal decorations and arrange-

ments) and there are spectacular new views within the building. Atria, just as entries and lobbies, have to provide good orientation for visitors or persons wishing to meet.

Atria offer a panoramic view, quite different from the usual perception of hotels. This also applies to entries and lobbies of large buildings whatever their destination. Elevators are one of the buildings' services. This book concentrates on the impacts of services on architectural design and not on engineering aspects. It is elevators that cause certain problems in the design of tall buildings. Even with increased speeds, travel to higher levels takes considerable time. The sudden change in speed can cause a sense of uneasiness. In large buildings with a number of elevators, complex control of the lifts is being introduced (So and Yu, 2001).

In tall buildings elevators may become a focal point for tension due to fear of crime or fire, or a feeling of claustrophobia. Rapid air pressure change causes discomfort or even pain. In the Chicago Sears Tower elevators had to be slowed down considerably.

In tall buildings used by very many, a great number of elevators is needed. Often the principle of zoning is applied. In such a case some of the elevators serve the lower storeys only, others the mid-range and others, at high speed, exclusively the upper floors. Ground, intermediate and sky lobbies are built for the convenience of those waiting for elevators.

3.1.5 Windows and curtain walls

Buildings in earlier periods usually had some basic structures: foundation, wall, roof, door and window. Windows were part of the wall and their form, size and framing had an impact on architectural design. In modern times windows underwent major technological changes. Their material could be wood, but also metal, concrete or plastic. At the same time performance requirements became more sophisticated. Finally, designers integrated windows into window walls: curtain walls, window structural glass façades or wall claddings. The various types of window wall, curtain wall and cladding have been discussed together with their basic material in Chapter 2.

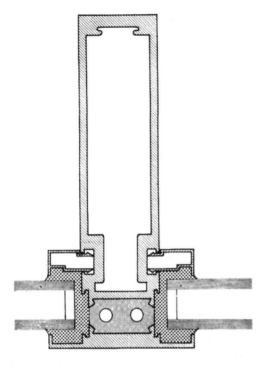

Figure 3.6 Curtain wall frame, insulating double glazing (Alusuisse, Switzerland). © Sebestyen: *Lightweight Building Construction*, Akadémiai Kiadó.

Windows fulfil a number of functions, such as:

- provide daylight to premises
- provide solar energy
- produce a therapeutically positive effect
- insulate sound
- provide heat insulation and ventilation (Muneer et al., 2000).

The basic parts of a window are the frame, glass, shading and sun directing construction, and ventilation device. Each has its function and also its impact on architectural design. The properties of glass and their performance have been discussed earlier in Chapter 2. Heat and sound and reaction to sunshine depend on the number of glass layers, their sealing, the property of the glass panes, coating on the glass and the type of filling in the air space between panes.

Daylight has an impact on the design of windows and buildings. This includes study of glare, which is

the excessive brightness contrast within the field of view. The frame also has an influence on these properties. In new architecture designers try to keep the frame sections as narrow as possible. An extreme result in this respect is structural glazing without any external visible frame sections.

Windows being part of the external envelope, a number of computer-based window and window wall design programs have been worked out and are in use.

Window frames may be produced from two different materials, for example, wood and plastics, steel or aluminium. In recent time plastics have gained considerable headway and developed into the most common material for window frames.

Today windows also impact on the aesthetic appearance of buildings through their form, structure and colour. A colour may be imparted to steel windows by coating or painting them. Aluminium window sections may be treated by various methods of coloration thereby obtaining brown, red, gold, or other colours. The most frequently applied plastic for manufacturing windows is the impact-resistant PVC and the colour most in use is white or grey although now other colours also can be applied.

The window walls were designed with a stick system, with a spandrel system or with individual panels made from steel or aluminium (coated or cast). The window wall itself progressed to the curtain wall and various cladding systems. Claddings were assembled either from lightweight metal panels or multi-layer panels or from pre-cast reinforced concrete panels.

During the period of the International Style the 'curtain walls' were developed. The earliest curtain walls in tall buildings had a 'stick' system, vertical mullions, and transoms, frames and insulated panels. From 1950 onwards, panel systems with pressure equalization were applied and later, steel or aluminium panels were pressed like a car body. The Japanese Kubota and the Swiss Alusuisse companies developed the manufacture of cast aluminium panels. The post-modern period saw the appearance of structural glass façades, which were discussed previously in Chapter 2.

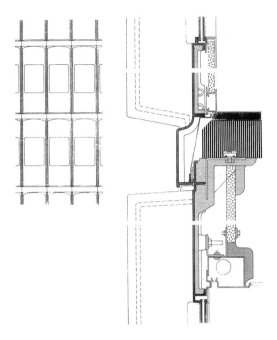

Figure 3.7 Façade with cast aluminium panels, Kubota, Japan. © Sebestyen: *Lightweight Building Construction*, Akadémiai Kiadó.

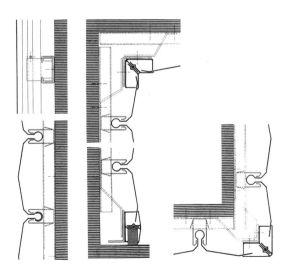

Figure 3.8 Façade from vacuum-formed hard PVC cladding panels, Hoechst, Germany. © Sebestyen: *Lightweight Building Construction*, Akadémiai Kiadó.

3.1.6 Roofing

Traditionally the selection of roofing material and detailing of roofs was a consequence of the availability of natural materials and local tradition. Roofing materials were shingle, reed, clay and concrete tile, stone slab (these were used for rain-shedding systems), copper, lead, and zinc sheet. In modern times metal (primarily aluminium) has been used in long strips joined with ingenious clips and mechanically assembled. Under the top layer frequently an additional weatherproofing layer was applied. These old materials are actually still in use but new materials have been added: stainless steel and aluminium sheet, asphalt, bituminous felt, plastics,

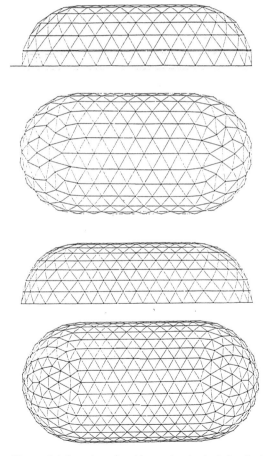

Figure 3.9 Barrel vault with semi-spherical domical ends.

59

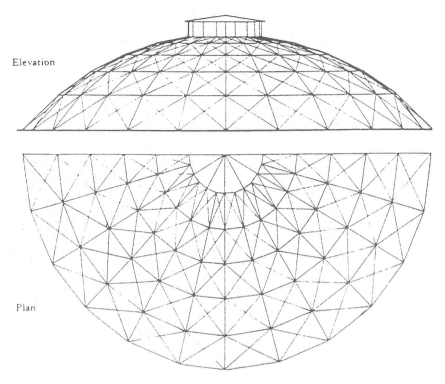

Figure 3.10 A type of a Schwedler dome.

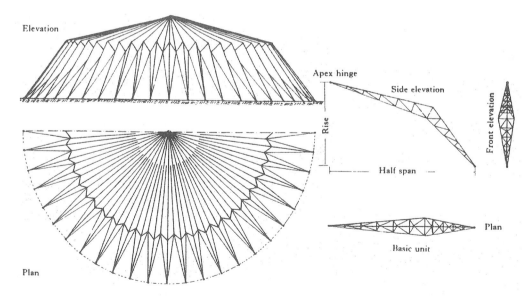

Figure 3.11 Prefabricated three-pinned arch-ribbed dome.

composites, and built-up structures. High-pitched roofs with hard roofing are still to be found but low-pitched and flat roofs are increasingly coming to be used.

The range of plastic (elasto/plastic systems) has been considerably expanded; they may now be 'single-ply' or elasto-plastic systems, modified bituminous systems, or 'multi-ply' but 'single-layer' systems. Tent roofs are making an appearance with new forms and are treated as part of membranes and tensegrity structures.

Among the technical solutions a new principle has been introduced with the inverted roofs in which the heat insulation is laid on top of the load-bearing structure and is protected against wind uplift and sunshine effect by gravel or concrete paving.

The selection of the type of roofing has become primarily a consequence of architectural and structural form: technical roofing solutions have been devised for all kinds of roof forms. This means that modern technology no longer restricts the architectural design of the building and specifically the design of roofs.

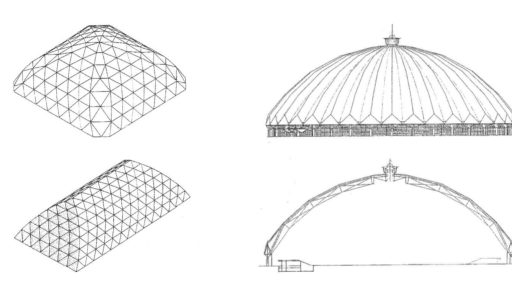

Figure 3.12 Basic forms of braced timber dome and vault.

Figure 3.14 Timber structure dome, Izuma, Japan, designers: Kajima; Masao Saitoh.

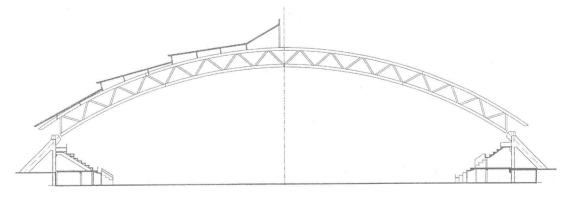

Figure 3.13 Stadium with timber roof structure, Hamar, Norway.

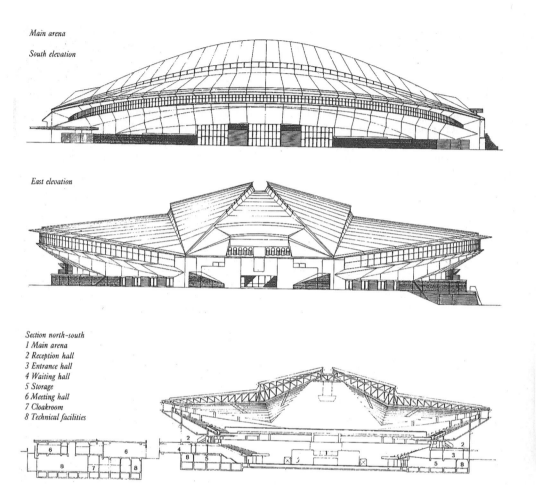

Main arena

South elevation

East elevation

Section north-south
1 *Main arena*
2 *Reception hall*
3 *Entrance hall*
4 *Waiting hall*
5 *Storage*
6 *Meeting hall*
7 *Cloakroom*
8 *Technical facilities*

Figure 3.15 Tokyo Metropolitan Gymnasium, Tokyo, Shibuya, 1990, designer: Fumihiko Maki. The diameter of the main sport area 120 m, steel truss roof: seam-welded stainless steel, 0.4 mm, on cement board backing, 2.5 mm + 2.5 mm urethane/fibreglass insulation sheet.

3.2 Selected Types of Building

3.2.1 Housing

The requirement for housing is truly an ancient one and the earliest known man-made residential structures are more than 5000 years old. It is noteworthy that within building, residential constructions are the most numerous when compared to other buildings, such as commercial, cultural, educational, etc. Among this great mass only a certain part is designed with such a degree of architectural care as to justify their being accorded a mention in architectural literature.

Whilst most residential buildings are anonymous products, on the other hand there do exist carefully designed and constructed social or prestigious units that warrant careful study and record (Price and Tsouros, 1996, Gottdiener and Pickvance, 1991).

Houses and flats are the most expensive consumer items in the lives of most families. They serve not only as shelter but also as investment. The manner

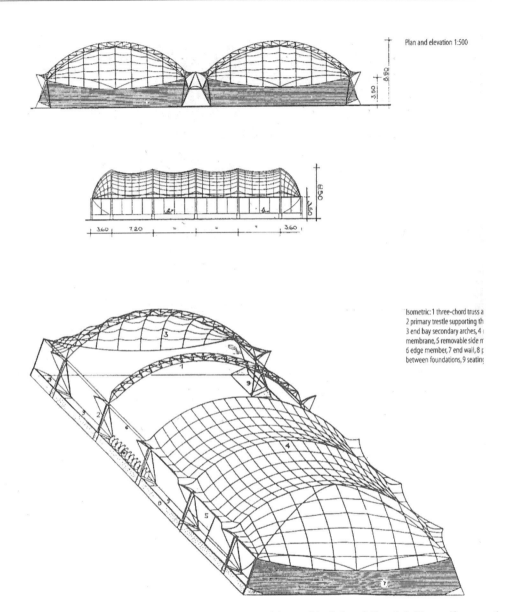

Plan and elevation 1:500

Isometric: 1 three-chord truss a
2 primary trestle supporting th
3 end bay secondary arches, 4 i
membrane, 5 removable side m
6 edge member, 7 end wall, 8 p
between foundations, 9 seating

Figure 3.16 Covered Tennis Court, Gorle, Italy, 1991, architects: Merlini and Natalini. Five self-supporting arches, roof membrane: PVC-coated polyester fabric; translucency: 15 per cent (sufficient for daylight illumination).

in which the expenditure on housing is met is of signal importance. Tenure is the expression used to cover various forms of housing, the most important categories of which are private ownership, rental housing and cooperative housing.

These are supplemented by intermediate forms of ownership including ownership of the residential unit but only rental of the land. The architectural characteristics comprise factors of tradition, local habits, lifestyle, ethnic and religious customs, family composition, special requirements of children, adults, aged and handicapped persons. In short there are a great many components and the consequence is that houses and flats themselves display a varied diversity.

A common problem but one that is met by alternative solutions is the need for privacy without foregoing social contacts. Both of these have to be assisted by architectural solutions. All over the world the size of households and families is decreasing. Smaller families require other types of dwelling than do larger ones. Growing children set up their own dwelling at an earlier age. Old people tend to live increasingly on their own and not as members of the family, as was general practice in former periods. These trends affect architectural design and standards for housing.

Housing has a number of characteristics in common with other types of building. Its architecture, materials and construction technologies are influenced by the style and technology of its era and geographical conditions. The users of housing, i.e. the human population itself, cannot afford expensive solutions. Consequently, it is primarily local materials and technologies established locally that are used. Design is often not the work of professional architects and the execution is frequently carried out by informal means: by the future user's family, perhaps with the assistance of neighbours or individual craftsmen. If we make a distinction between informal and formal construction methods, then housing is the largest construction subsector of informal building. This is still true today for less-developed countries and informal building goes on even in industrialized countries (Lawrence, 1987).

In addition to technology, the lifestyle of the occupants as manifested in the functions of a dwelling, has an impact on architecture in housing. Some of the characteristics are general over time and location. Others change with time and place and many are quite individual. Therefore, there exist studies and commentaries about housing functions in general, over functions concerning certain groups of the population: large or small families and households, young or aged persons, requirements for children, women, singles, couples, ethnic minori-

ties, religious communities, and individually, concerning one specific client or user. Studies of this kind are referred to as housing or sociological studies. An overall survey on housing shows that basically there are two types of residential unit: the majority consisting of units for individual households, including families, and the minority with living premises for groups of people, not forming complete households or families. The individual residential units may be:

- one-family houses and
- multi-storey blocks of flats.

There are certain intermediate types:

- two-family houses (twin houses)
- terraces (row houses, i.e. low-rise buildings containing from 5–15 houses united in a single row)
- other types of densely grouped low-rise dwelling units
- various types of low-rise building (town houses) with staircases providing access to several flats and buildings with direct access to flats.

Multi-storey blocks may be:

- low rise (with 2–5 levels)
- high rise (with 6–16 levels)
- tall buildings (16–100 or more levels).

Flats may have an entrance from:

- a staircase
- an external side corridor
- an internal corridor.

Flats are usually planned on a single level but sometimes may be on two or three levels. A special arrangement is the one of 'scissors' where the flats are combined in space, either with an access to the flat on each level or on each second level. The number of ground-floor arrangements, the contacts between rooms and their sizes, and the type of equipment are infinite but certain typical solutions within a given area and period have become rather general. In multi-storey buildings with large floor space access from a staircase is more justifiable; if the flats are small, access through a corridor is used frequently.

If walls bear the vertical loads, transversal walls are called for if the flats are small, longitudinal walls are applied if the flats are large. Load-bearing walls may be designed as masonry or from reinforced concrete, steel frames or timber. The decisions concerning the listed parameters are dependent on tradition, climate, habits and cost restrictions and have to be selected by the architect in consultation with the client and future users. The decisions made affect the overall architectural design and are a source of research and experimentation.

Experiments in housing usually attempt to consider not only technological aspects but also sociological ones and experiments are devised and executed in most cases not on one single building or house, but on a smaller or larger group of dwellings or housing. Experimental housing, realized for a long time in many countries, occurred on a large scale, during the 1930s (e.g. in Stuttgart, Frankfurt/Main, Vienna, etc.) and later, after the Second World War the practice also spread to developing countries and countries with central planning (Experiment Wohnen, 2001). One orientation of such experiments was the so-called 'Satellite Town' in Sweden and the 'New Town' initiated in Great Britain and carried forward in other countries: France, Sweden, USA, etc. The idea of New Towns was to stimulate the creation of new housing not by expanding existing major cities but rather by means of creating new towns with a limited size, for example, a population of 40 000 per new town. The rationale was that this strategy would relieve the pressure on existing cities and promote better housing conditions. The idea did prove to be to some extent successful but it achieved rather less than originally envisaged. The New Towns grew beyond the originally planned population and provided only a very limited solution to the large housing shortage. Other experiments, as for example, Operation Breakthrough in the USA during the 1970s, and one in what was West Berlin, called IBA (Internationale Bau Ausstellung), all yielded limited results. Internationally renowned architects (Aldo Rossi, Herman Hertzberger, Zaha Hadid, Peter Eisenman) participated in IBA. Many other experiments focussed on technical innovations and social aspects, for example, some on 'intelligent dwellings', others on 'growing residences'.

A very important specific area of studies is urban planning, which concerns communities in an urban or rural environment and optimum strateg develop healthy and attractive communities.

This also resulted in greatly differing solutions (as an example let us cite complexes by Ricardo Bofill, Lucien Kroll and others).

In most periods of history, new housing was created in single-storey or low-rise buildings. Multi-storey was rather the exception (in ancient Rome and Yemen). Its importance has grown only during the last centuries. High rise is more frequent for low-cost social housing but is also used for high-income households. In any case, large families not surprisingly favour medium- or low-rise blocks of flats. The characteristic two structural orientations seen throughout history – heavy (constructions with stone, clay or burnt brick walls) and light-weight (with various types of timber structure, bamboo, reed, palm leaves) – are encountered in new housing also.

The low income of the masses resulted in residential stocks providing inadequate and crowded living conditions. Various, partly utopian, projects attempted to improve housing conditions, until recently with only a modicum of success (plans and buildings by Le Corbusier and Ernst May). The housing units and estates planned by architects or developers in most cases proved to be too expensive, and usually failed to become self-sustaining and perished. Income levels have risen in several (but not all) countries during the twentieth century. This enabled interested developers and institutions to introduce technologies corresponding to contemporary standards of industrial manufacturing. Most of these were based on ideas of industrialization, prefabrication and system building.

The technologies applied in low-rise and in high-rise construction have been markedly different. In the low-rise category, lightweight systems primarily or partially based on timber structures evolved, as for instance in the Scandinavian countries, in Germany, North America and Japan. Some of the systems have a lightweight steel frame and some are designed with a combination of an antiseismic stressed-skin panel structure. Whilst the light-weight systems found an adequate market in many countries, the systems attempting to apply fully automated manufacturing methods, based, for example, on experience in ship or car manufacturing, in almost all cases failed. Success in this branch of construction, i.e. automatized manufacturing of new houses, lies still in the future. However, factory-constructed housing accounts for about 25 per cent of single family homes constructed annually in the USA (Albern, 1997). The same source claims that in the USA in 1995 there were no fewer than 18 million people living in 8 million (at least originally) mobile homes. In the USA within the category of factory-constructed housing – all factory-built or those with some semblance of assembly line – some special categories are distinguished, such as modular houses constructed from room modules (three-dimensional boxes), and panelized houses using factory-built panels. In Japan some large factories producing factory-constructed homes are operating, each of whose output can run into thousands of homes per annum (Sekisui, etc.).

Industrialization for multi-storey residential constructions has taken another direction. One of the new technologies has been the cast-in-situ concrete, called by the French: *béton banché*. This has been applied successfully but only to a limited extent. It still finds application not as an overall but as a partially applied technology combined, for example, with concrete prefabrication and/or lightweight components. Efforts in some countries were concentrated on the development of systems with large prefabricated, and in many cases room-sized, reinforced concrete panels. Such systems were developed in Scandinavia (Jespersen, Larsen-Nielsen), France (Camus, Coignet, Costamagna, Pascal), in the former Soviet Union and several East European countries between 1960 and 1990. These systems produced a great number of new residential units and provided decent housing conditions for millions of families. In the beginning such (large-panel) buildings contained a number of defects: driving rain penetration through the façade panel joints, surface and interstitial condensation, insufficient heat insulation and for that reason excessive humidity in the internal air and mould in corners and behind furniture, spalling of façade slabs, and others. These faults were eliminated over a period.

Driving rain penetration was caused earlier by (unsuccessfully) attempting to stop the rain immediately on the façade surface by watertight joints. However, dimension change and movements of the panels caused cracks, which allowed the rain to penetrate. This was stopped by the so-called *vide de décompression* (decompression chamber). The principle of this is to create behind the façade surface in the joints of the panels an increased air hollow in which the pressure of the driving rain is reduced and the intruding raindrops can be led to the outside at the bottom of each joint. Interstitial vapour condensation is prevented by a correct order of layers, i.e. by putting the vapour insulation on the internal side of the heat insulation. Surface condensation is eliminated by more effective heat insulation and ventilation. As a consequence the technical inadequacies were removed. Nevertheless what often remained was an unattractive appearance and the situation whereby the excessively fast tempo of construction, together with a too heterogeneous composition of the users, resulted in neglect of the buildings and vandalism.

A final adverse result of the various system building approaches in housing was the much lower (if indeed there was any at all) economic advantage as against more traditional forms of construction (Russell, 1981). Finally, many (or even most) of the large-panel system manufacturing plants closed down, or switched to more profitable mixed and more flexible (i.e. more 'open') technologies.

During the concluding decades of the twentieth century we have witnessed new trends in experimentation, for example by the French Jean Nouvel and by Japanese and other architects including some in developing countries. These experiments readily accept affordability as a constraint but at the same time strive to plan dwellings with better equipment and human comfort than was the case earlier. The homes with top-level technical equipment and automation have been called 'smart homes'.

This section of the book cannot ignore some spectacular (and expensive) houses usually designed for wealthy clients by internationally renowned architects. Let us cite selected examples:

- Frank Lloyd Wright designed a number of 'organic modern' houses, perhaps the best known of these being the Waterfall House.

- Richard Meier designed the Raschofsky House, Dallas, Texas, 1991–96, applying his white, pure geometric style to a 1000 square metre structure.
- Thom Mayne together with Morphosis designed the Blades Residence, Santa Barbara, California, 1992–96, a 750 square metre house.
- Michael Rotondi with his partner Clark Stevens (RoTo) designed the Teiger House, New Jersey, 1990–95, a 600 square metre house.
- Robert Stern designed a number of new or reconstructed apartments and houses, all with a much larger than average surface.

Each of the architect-designed large residential units and houses applies the architect's style and aesthetic orientation to this specific area.

The examples quoted represent the applications of modern and post-modern architecture to the houses of the wealthy. A small number of individual, architect-designed housing projects have been focussed on helping people in need: Sambo Mockbee and the Rural Studio (architectural students at the time of design) were authors of:

- Bryant House, Mason's Blend, Alabama, 1995–97, an 80 square metre house built at low cost using among other materials hay and corrugated acrylic.

Yancey Chapel, although not a residential object, is mentioned here because its authors are the same persons who were responsible for the previous two buildings; it was built from scavenged materials: tyres, rusted I-beams, pine from a 100-year-old house, sheets of tin from an old barn and river slate.

As has been seen, housing, despite its peculiarities, is also a field of construction in which the rule is valid that technology has a strong impact on architecture. Housing, however, must always reckon with the input of disciplines that differ from those in architecture and technology: human health research, sociology, physical planning, demographic and lifestyle changes.

Economics is an important aspect of housing. It deals first of all with the cost of building a unit and the cost of structures and equipment of a unit. Many studies discuss the factors of total cost and

others provide simple functions for quick cost estimates. Financial relations include the comparison of the cost of rental with owned housing. Constructing new residential buildings is assisted by subsidies, loans and mortgages. The final result of various schemes depends also on the level of interest rates and on the conditions for credit and mortgage.

These differ on any given date but are also subject to changes in time and, hence, involve a risk about future interest rates.

Whilst an architect does not need to be a financial expert when it comes to financial conditions and efficiency calculations, he may have to be a partner in such investigations, whose outcome may affect the design.

3.2.2 Public (cultural, leisure and other) buildings

In our era, a prime cause of change in architecture stems from alterations in the functions of and within buildings. We shall restrict ourselves to identifying some basic changes in certain categories of buildings only (Myerson, 1996).

Over the last hundred years the construction of buildings in the category of public buildings has increased tremendously (Konya, 1986). This has been the consequence of increasing wealth, higher education standards and more free time for leisure. This trend was further strengthened after the Second World War, and the construction of new or renovated churches, museums, schools, libraries, theatres, cinemas, sports facilities and others has become the focal point in many urban developments. Among the new buildings, churches (cathedrals, mosques, etc.) in certain cases have also acquired a special place in the evolution of architecture, as with the Ronchamps Chapel, the Evreux Cathedral and some others.

The new functions of certain buildings enabled architects to seek out new forms, volumes, colours and aesthetic qualities. Function has a varying impact on architectural design. Office, school and library buildings must satisfy well-defined requirements of users.

Libraries originally were repositories of written and printed publications. The growth of the population and of reading brought a commensurate increase in the demand for libraries. More publications meant calls for more space requirements. In modern times electronic services have appeared on the scene. So libraries had to cater for the needs of electronic services and for the future growth in information to be stored in different forms (Bazillion and Braun, 1995, Brawner and Beck, 1996 Multi-media libraries, 2001). The architect who is designing a library has to receive as clear a brief as possible not only concerning current stocks and services but also detailing probable future growth, the type of users and services. The provision of this data then enables the architect to design the spaces for stocking information, for information search and retrieval and for optimal working in the library. Among the *grands projets* of the late President Mitterand, the Bibliothèque Nationale de France in Paris, 1992–95 (architect: Dominique Perrault), is the one that comes closest to modernism or late-modernism. It is composed as a complex of four vast open books. Regrettably, this is not ideal for a library and what is worse, some high-tech ideas (e.g. the use of ultraviolet-resistant glass) have also been dropped.

Theatres are among the most ancient places of assembly and entertainment. Many of the ancient theatres were open-air establishments, often in the form of an amphitheatre. Much later, in fact during the last four centuries, new characteristics of theatres were developed. This applies as much to the stage as to the space for spectators. The technical equipment has developed into complex and automated machinery. The function of a theatre diversified, some remained all-purpose, others specialized according to size, audience, profile (prose theatres, opera houses, concert halls, and others). Acoustics has become a sophisticated field of science as much for the spoken word as for music.

Increased space above the stage and wings has increased the total volume of theatres and influences the form relations of building volumes. The purely theatrical function is often combined with others: premises for actors and external persons, so that theatres have assumed various functions of downtown area entertainment and meeting.

Versatility for the rapid transformation of a theatre into different arrangements has to be ensured by the design (Breton, 1989). During the last twenty years a considerable number of new theatres have been built (for example the Dance Theatre in The Hague, Netherlands, 1987, architect: Rem Koolhaas, the new Bastille Opera in Paris, 1985–89,

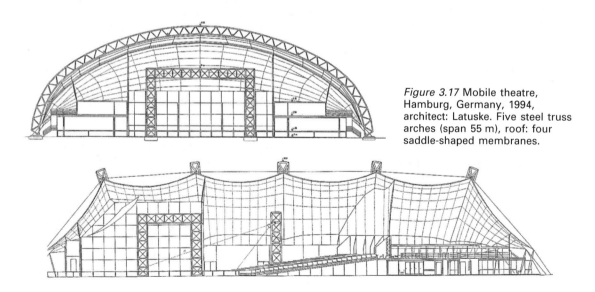

Figure 3.17 Mobile theatre, Hamburg, Germany, 1994, architect: Latuske. Five steel truss arches (span 55 m), roof: four saddle-shaped membranes.

architect: C. Ott and associates), all proving the notable impact of technological progress on architecture and, simultaneously, the changes in architectural and urban development principles (Monnier, 2000).

Auditoria, along with theatres, can be counted among the technically progressive establishments of culture and entertainment (Boulet et al,. 1990). They have increased in size and sophistication in acoustic and other respects. From among the many new concert halls, the one in Luzern, Switzerland, 1999 (design by Jean Nouvel) ranks as one of the most remarkable.

The construction of hotels was already proceeding apace during the nineteenth century. Following the First World War, a real hotel boom commenced (Rutes and Penner, 1985, Fitoussi, 1992). Hotels diversified and specialized, thereby satisfying different needs. Some of the hotel types are the downtown hotel, the residential hotel, the health hotel, the sport and holiday hotel and within each category there is further specialization. The locations, natural environment and local building materials and habits influenced design and construction technology. Different design patterns emerged, for example, on the guest room floor (of multi-storey hotels) single-loaded and double-loaded arrangements, some kind of standardization of guest room sizes, lobbies whose size depended on the function of the hotel (downtown, convention, airport or other), atria with corridors to the atrium and double-loaded arrangements with part of the rooms oriented towards the atrium, glass-walled lifts, meeting rooms and convention halls, partly utilitarian and partly elegant, and many other design characteristics.

Typical functional requirements, size of the various rooms and premises, general and specific design arrangements (for example for restaurants, bars, shopping, fitness facilities, swimming pool, etc.) were worked out and serve in the design and control of hotel plans. Many details in hotel construction developed into applicable inputs (subsystems, standardized components and equipment): this also occurred for office buildings and other types of building.

Offices can be subdivided into a number of sub-classes: headquarter and branch offices, low rise and high rise, one level and multi-storey office blocks, downtown and non-urban offices. In the case of high-prestige offices (such as headquarters of multinational corporations and major banks) direct economic efficiency may not be of prime importance. For most office buildings, however, economic considerations do have relevance. This includes an analysis of the relation of the property size to the total office surface, the cost per work place and the payback period of the investment. There is in existence a vast literature on economic feasibility investigations (e.g. Hensler, 1986 and many others).

Office buildings (headquarters and branch offices of large companies and smaller office buildings) are among the buildings typical of our time. The introduction of large workspaces without internal floor-to-floor partitions and more recently, interlinked workspace groups and, naturally, a high technical level of equipment with double-layer floors and suspended ceilings to house electrical wiring and cabling, telephone connection, lighting, ventilation, fire control and others, are among new trends in this category of buildings. Traditionally, offices (in particular, large ones) were built primarily in downtown areas, or linked to places of manufacturing, transport or commerce. In recent times, increasingly, offices are built outside the city centre, often as a cluster of offices (office parks), or in the form of a campus. This entails advantages from cheaper land prices, improved access and parking facilities for cars.

Cultural, educational and leisure buildings (theatres, auditoria, museums, sports halls) have to cater for various events and for that purpose require the facility to alter the seating configuration, partitions and other parts of the building.

Museums sometimes provide a rather free opportunity to exercise imagination in architecture. The last decades of the twentieth century were witness to a particularly vivid wave of new museums.

Some of these went on to acquire international fame, for instance, the Guggenheim Museum in Bilbao, Spain, designed by Frank O. Gehry, the Miho Museum, Shigaraki, Shiga Prefecture, Japan, by I.M. Pei, the new Groningen Museum in The Netherlands, the National Museum of Australia (architects

Ashton, Raggatt, McDonald) and others. In museums strictly defined levels of lighting, and air humidity must be ensured. On the other hand the architect enjoys considerable freedom to invent the appearance of the building and its internal spaces. When Renzo Piano designed the building for the Menil collection in Houston, Texas, he required a special diffuse lighting in the museum spaces. Steel-mesh-reinforced baffles moulded in special shapes, hanging from ductile iron trusses provide the light and also help to control the internal temperature.

In the design of a new museum, there are two basic situations as concerns the future objects to be displayed. The first is when these objects, or at least the most important ones and those with a special arrangement requirement, are known in advance. This, for instance, was the case when the Quai d'Orsay rail terminal building had to be transformed into a museum. The architect in such a case can shape optimal premises for housing the objects. However, when during the design and construction of a museum the objects are not as yet known, a certain flexibility of the future premises is needed. This was the situation during the creation of the Jewish Museum in Berlin (architect: Daniel Libeskind). Museums sometimes become focal points of fundamental city renewal.

Cinemas are clustered (with perhaps six to fifteen films running in parallel) thus enabling management to automate projection. Such multiplex cinemas require new design arrangements concerning the distance between the rows of seats, inclination of the floor, access to individual cinemas, ticket-selling lobby and projection spaces as well as fire safety. Such cinemas are sometimes linked to shopping centres (shopping malls, hypermarkets, shopping arcades), themselves new types of building, which may have, in addition to shops (for clothing, food, household articles, books, electrical and electronic equipment and furniture), various facilities for catering and leisure (Internet cafés, skating rinks, swimming pools, gambling premises, etc.) (Northen, 1984, Maitland, 1985, Mauger, 1991, MacKeith, 1986). Such shopping centres require careful preparatory actions: market analysis, site selection, car and pedestrian connections, dialogue with local authorities and, naturally, specific architectural considerations.

In the construction of buildings for sport and leisure, open and covered sport stadiums and recreational facilities (swimming pools, rock-climbing structures, artificial ski slopes, etc.) have an important function (Konya, 1986, Lemoine, 1998). They provide space not only for various outdoor and indoor sports (soccer, basketball, boxing, gymnastics, hockey, wrestling, tennis, swimming, fencing and others) but also for activities outside the realm of sport: concerts and meetings with a large attendance. Designers have reacted to this demand with structural innovations, for example with domes and membranes with wide-span and retractable roofs. The different sports also require specific arrangements concerning the material of the floor, the space necessary and its compartmentalization equipment, accessories, lighting, temperature and other parameters. Design must provide versatility in switching from one type of activity to another.

The great numbers of new types of building generate a renewal of city centres and urban structure.

3.2.3 Hospitals

The growth in population, the enhanced human life expectancy, the more efficient and more sophisticated healing technologies, all resulted in considerably broadening the demand for health care facilities, such as hospitals and others (James and Tatton-Brown, 1986, Jolly, 1988, Marberry, 1995, Wagenaar, 1999, Krankenhäuser, 2000, Wörner, 2001). Throughout the first half of the twentieth century very many hospitals were designed and constructed, many of them in the form of clustered pavilions for different branches of healing. Then in the second half of the century large multi-storey hospital complexes began to appear. Whilst these belonged to the most expensive and most voluminous investments in public life, they usually retained a degree of self-containment and did not associate themselves with the ongoing renewal of the central downtown areas. Hospitals retain some independence, which is a distinctly specific feature, in contradistinction to the development of museums, libraries, hotels, town halls and office buildings.

During the 1960s and the 1970s requirements for hospital investments grew significantly, not only in absolute terms but also when expressed as a ratio per bed. Even increased wealth was unable to satisfy the increasing demands. This conflict became the starting point for rationalizing demands.

This included a revision of the number of nights spent on average by a patient in the hospital which in turn also reduced the total number of beds needed and, as a consequence, lowered health care costs. The three basic zones of a hospital – the nursing, the clinical and the support zones – all underwent changes, creating a pressure to increase the areas in each of the three zones and, together with this, the investment and running costs. The rapid changes in medical technology and in the relative occurrence of various maladies pushed those responsible for preparing the briefs for hospital designs to ask for more flexibility to enable hospital managers to rearrange the hospitals according to changing requirements. Various actions attempted with varying measures of success to put a brake on this pressure for higher investments. The demand for more large and expensive hospitals was slightly alleviated by constructing smaller, less expensive district hospitals and by establishing alternative means for convalescent patients outside the expensive central hospitals. The struggle for more in all sectors of health care facilities was marginally reduced by various measures aimed at economies. In any case a marked development has been to reduce the average number of night stays in hospitals by patients, which to some extent has been achieved by replacing full hospital stays by day-care periods. The result of the above and other changes was a noticeably more flexible network of health care facilities and a restriction on rising health care expenditures. Let us quantify the above changes by quoting some tentative data:

- Prior to the First World War hospitals had a gross area of approximately 20 square metres per bed; this grew during the interwar period to 40 and, by the end of the twentieth century had reached 75–80 square metres, but in most countries was kept to 20–45 square metres.
- Earlier the average duration of a hospital stay was 15–20 days; by now this has been cut back to 8–10 days.

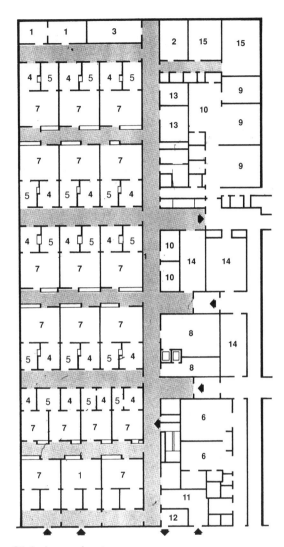

Clinical zone: key to drawings
1 Plaster suite
2 Plaster suite
3 Equipment
4 Anaesthetic room
5 Exit bay/recovery
6 Transfer, reception, bed park
7 Operating room/bay
8 Sterilising
9 Post-operation recovery
10 Staff base
11 Clean utility/supplies
12 Dirty utility/sluice
13 Stores
14 Trolleys/wheelchairs
15 Staff changing/toilets /rest

Figure 3.18 Sundsvall Hospital, Sweden. A total of 19 operating suites, arranged in six banks served by a single corridor system.

- The total floor area of operating theatres grew during the twentieth century from 60 to about 300 square metres and they contained more expensive equipment. In large hospitals complex units of operating theatres are established with at least three theatres per unit. Operating sections are set up in an interdisciplinary way so as to enable management to switch over from one medical field to another, including the combination of septic and aseptic processes. Individual operating units may share common auxiliary premises.
- Large open wards have been broken up into smaller rooms though each is better equipped.
- Wards with two beds have become the most common, although there are some deviations from this solution. Twelve square metres per bed in two-bed wards and 8 square metres per bed in multi-bed rooms have become widely applied.
- The equipment of patient rooms comprises shower, toilet, telephone and television connection.

These guidelines are intended to highlight trends but in actual practice there are substantial deviations in different countries.

Despite applying certain cost reductions, hospitals became more up-to-date, but obsolescence set in more quickly, which again called for greater flexibility in design and management. Precautions to prevent infections in hospitals have, in the meantime, become a matter of urgency, both in the nursing zone and even more in the clinical zone. In operating theatres a supply of ultra-clean air, for example clean air blown down from the ceiling over the operating area, has provided only a partial solution.

For architects designing hospitals, the increased size, sophistication and cost of hospitals brought with it the need to become intricately acquainted with modern medical technologies, hospital equipment, materials and structures best adapted to hospitals and different health requirements.

3.2.4 Schools

Following the Second World War a great demand for schools (primary and secondary schools, univer-

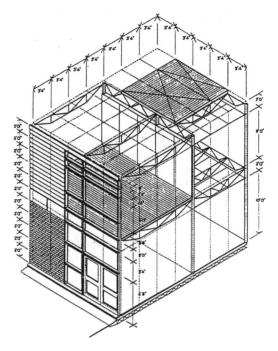

Figure 3.19 School 'system building', CLASP, UK. Industrialized school system buildings were developed after 1945, a period of high demand for new schools.

sities) arose. This meant a large number of very similar buildings and resulted in the development of school 'system buildings'. These had in common the modern education requirements stipulating buildings with premises easily adaptable in size, movable (eventually separate chairs and desks) furniture and equipment arrangement (Müller, 2001.) Today, consideration has to be given to facilities for the use of computers by students.

From the point of view of construction technology, 'industrialized' approaches were applied with standardized prefabricated components. In the United Kingdom the first such systems were the SCOLA, SEAC and CLASP (Figure 3.19) systems. They usually enabled the architect adopting one of these systems to design buildings with two to five storeys. Basic components for these buildings were the columns, girders, floor panels, cladding and partition wall panels. A similar French system

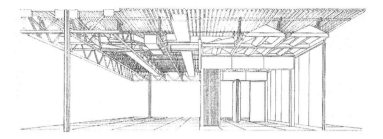

Figure 3.20 SCSD (Schools Construction System Development) System for the California Schools, Los Angeles, California, USA, leading designer: Ezra Ehrenkrantz. A system composed from four subsystems: a structural ceiling, air conditioning, lighting and partitions, an early USA industrialized school building system.

was the Fillod system. In the USA, in California and other regions single-level school building systems were developed. While conceding that the various systems did not give rise to extraordinary architectural levels it is fair to say that they did ensure an acceptable quality level.

Higher (university) education saw even more rapidly increasing enrolment figures than primary and secondary education. The number of different learning orientations (faculties, etc.) witnessed significant growth. However, together with greater specialization, a new requirement emerged: the wish to facilitate changes in and combinations of the fields of study. This itself has an impact on the design of university complexes. Other factors are the bringing together of education and research and education and practice. Traditional universities have been expanded and updated, e.g. polytechnics transformed into universities, while new university campus complexes, laboratories and other facilities have been designed and realized.

3.2.5 Buildings for manufacturing

The profile of industrial production has undergone significant change over the last 50 years. The manufacture of heavy machinery, for which halls with a strong framework and heavy overhead cranes are necessary, has been shrinking as a sector within total manufacturing. The industries that have gained ground are those that require light structures and spaces with a high degree of transformability (flexibility). Some industrial branches (electronics, biogenetics, etc.) require spaces with a high degree of super-clean air (clean rooms). The technological changes,

automation and robotization in manufacturing, transport and storage affect the design of industrial buildings (Lorenz, 1991).

Buildings for industry must satisfy the requirements of manufacturing (Ferrier, 1987) and be designed and constructed in an economic way. Various companies have specialized in industrial construction: designers, contractors, steel, aluminium, timber and concrete manufacturing firms. Such specialists have developed systems for industrial architecture enabling the system owner to apply their system for various commissions for industrial constructions.

The architecture of industrial buildings may have for some companies a marketing value. Some companies developed a specific image for the company, as did IBM. In such cases the company requires that its buildings be designed with that special feature, which for IBM means horizontally striped façade claddings; see the IBM complex in Basiano, 1983, designed by the Italian Gino Valle and the IBM Corbeil complex, Corbeil-Essonnes, France, 1982, designed by Vaudou and Luthi. Where external daylighting is not needed, industrial buildings may be designed as closed boxes with some kind of external cladding. Modular coordination is universally present. Flexibility and variability of internal space enables management to carry out changes in manufacturing processes. Overhead travelling cranes and rail connections (as mentioned above) are rarely required in contemporary industrial plants.

Industrial architecture embraced modernism and during the post-modern period retained this preference, a phenomenon that naturally is in harmony with industry's somewhat conservative character.

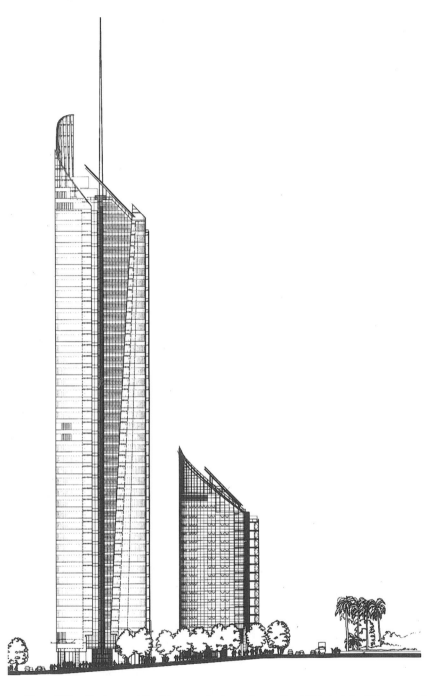

Figure 3.21 Aurora Place Office Tower and Residences, Sydney, Australia, 1996, height 200 m, architect: Renzo Piano, in cooperation with Lend Lease Design Group and Group GSA Pty, structural design: Ove Arup and Partners. The fins and sail form an extension of the curved cylindrical façade beyond the enclosure of the building and serve as protective screens to the winter gardens.

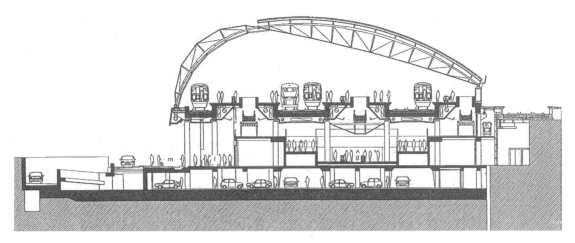

Figure 3.22 Waterloo International Railway Station, London, UK, architects: Nicholas Grimshaw and Partners. Integrating rail, car, bus and taxi services.

A great number of excellent late-modernist and neo-modernist industrial building complexes have been designed by British architects: Richard Rogers, Michael Hopkins, Nicholas Grimshaw and others in industrialized countries are among those who come to mind. These apply new construction features: masted buildings, suspended roof structures, etc.,as is the case with the Inmos complex, Newport, Great Britain, 1982, designed by Richard Rogers.

A particularly novel appearance of certain buildings was the consequence of suspension structures put outside the roof or even outside the main volume of the building. An example of this is the Renault Distribution Centre, Swindon, UK, designed by Norman Foster (Plate 10). The masts and cables are positioned outside the building. This, further accentuated by the conspicuous yellow colour of the structure, created a model for many other buildings. A similar principle has been applied at the Imnos factory, Newport, Gwent, Wales, designed by Richard Rogers (mentioned above), although its structure seems to be slightly clumsier than the one at the Renault building. Another building, the Schlumberger Research Centre, Cambridge, Great Britain, designed by Michael Hopkins, is equally characterized by its external suspension system but here its roof is covered by textile. Since these realizations a great number of designers have followed the above solutions.

3.2.6. Railway stations. Air terminals

The nineteenth century's rail construction boom produced grand terminals in large cities. This stimulated economic well-being. Then, during the first half of the twentieth century, rail transport ceded some ground to road transport. However, in the second half of the twentieth century, rail transport regained a new significance marked by intercity trains, high-speed trains (the TGVs, after the French expression), urban railways, underground railways (metros) and city tramways (Edwards, 1997, Ross, 2000). Different (public, private, combined) partnerships evolved for railways, rolling stock and stations. Over the past 50 years many new railway stations have been built. These were designed to comply with new functions: a procedure to allow large numbers of passengers to board and alight from trains without delay, automation of various functions, integration of rail and road (car, taxi, bus) transport. Functional development went hand in hand with new structural schemes and new architectural shapes. In our time, high-speed train lines are gradually being expanded with their stations seen as important economic catalysts. When the high-speed train connection was planned between Paris and London a fight broke out between Amiens and Lille for the hub station linking the line on to Brussels, Amsterdam and Cologne. Lille emerged as the winner thanks in

Figure 3.23 Dean Street Station, CrossRail, London, UK, architects: Troughton McAslan. A simple outlay to facilitate movement of masses.

part to the energetic intervention of its mayor. Since then the actual development has proved that such a decision serves as a major incentive for a city's development. In Lille, Eurolille and Cong-expo, designed by the Dutch architect Rem Kool-haas, were built.

A further development in railways has been the combination of major air terminals with the railway network, for example in Zurich and Amsterdam. Various types of railway station appeared: bridge station, square station, island station, rural and underground station (Edwards, 1997). In the down-town centres of large metropolises underground stations with multi-storeyed underground malls (Tokyo, Osaka, etc.) were constructed. Noteworthy among underground metro stations are those in Moscow. Whilst stylistically questionable, without

doubt these are impressive structures with lavish sculptural and other decorations, and top-quality building and cladding materials. Rail stations do present certain special problems requiring solution: platforms, tunnels or bridges to provide a trouble-free change from one line to the other. Stations are not only buildings but increasingly complex struc-tures, in part designed with picturesque canopies and other structures. These are well illustrated by Calatrava's structures, e.g. the Lyon–Satelas sta-tion (Figure 3.24)

The development of domestic, international and intercontinental air traffic has resulted in major investments in air terminals (Blow, 1991). The ini-tial system of linear terminals with direct arrivals was changed into terminals with finger access cor-ridors, satellites with piers and various combina-

Figure 3.24 Lyon-Satelas TGV railway station, France, designer: Santiago Calatrava. 120 m long, 100 m wide, 40 m high structure.

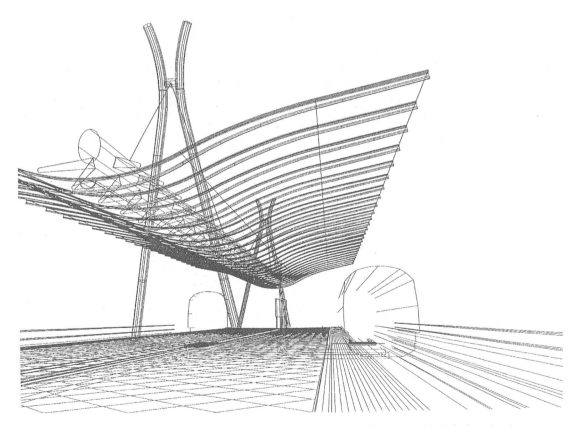

Figure 3.25 Platform canopy, architects: Ahrends Burton and Koralek. They should satisfy functional requirements and provide potential for imaginative architectural and structural forms.

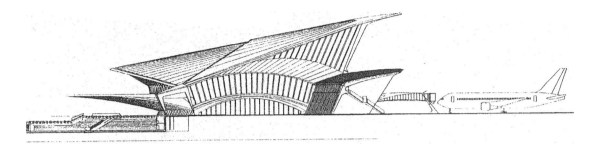

Figure 3.26 Sondica Airport, Bilbao, Spain, designer: Santiago Calatrava

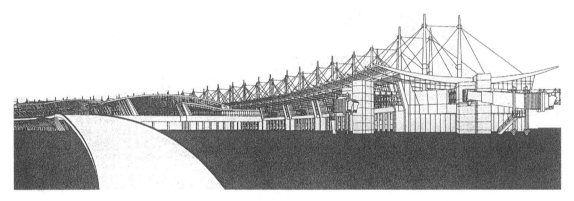

Figure 3.27 Inchon International Airport, Seoul, Korea, designers: C.W. Fentress, J.H. Bradburn and Associates, with BHJW (project).

tions of arrangements (Edwards, 1999). The new airports not only catered for the needs of passenger traffic and moving cargo but also became focal points for new clusters of buildings and infrastructure for services, commerce, hotels and restaurants. Recent realizations include such impressive complexes as the ones serving Tokyo, Osaka, London, Hong Kong, Paris, Denver, Chicago, New York, Singapore, Jakarta, Kuala Lumpur (Figure 3.28 and Plate 22), Shanghai and others (Binney, 1999, Zukovsky, 1996). Obviously, this is a trend that will continue in the future. Already in our time some architects and architectural firms have acquired specific experience in designing air and rail terminals and outstanding architects accept contracts for rail station and air terminal projects by themselves acquiring additional specialized knowledge or liaising with specialists. This situation incidentally is one that is taking place in various branches of design.

The design of airports reflects the technological progress both in air travel (movements of passengers and cargo), and in construction. The basic alternatives for major airports serving a great volume of air traffic (several tens of millions of passengers per annum) are those with one central terminal and those with several terminals, separated for domestic and international connections and, eventually, for different companies. Some metropolises have several airports serving sectors of the air traffic (New York, London, Paris). In most major airports there are separate levels for departures and arrivals, the departure level usually being situated above the arrival level. In some airports, however, both are on the same level. Some recent air

Figure 3.28 Kuala Lumpur International Airport, Malaysia, architect: Kisho Kurokawa.

terminals have double air bridges for departure and arrival served from the same level (Paris Charles de Gaulle, Terminal 2F and Chek Lap Kok in Hong Kong). In order to reach the aircraft with the minimum of walking distances, satellites, finger-corridors, or 'bastion'-piers are constructed.

The large number of persons arriving at, staying in, or leaving airports, requires spacious lounges that also have facilities for shopping and catering. Such lounges provide the architect with ample opportunities for imaginative designs. The wide-span hangars for aircraft are principally a design task that faces structural designers. The main passenger terminal buildings usually have a large surface glass wall oriented towards the area of aircraft arrivals and departures and a wide-span roof. The roof has become a major feature of these buildings, several with metaphoric or allegoric meaning, reflecting in some way the flight of birds or aeroplanes. The wide-span roof of air terminal buildings is sup-

ported by various structures, for example tree-like supports. The various functions in and around airports (baggage handling, check-in, access from the outside and departure by car, bus, high-speed train, provision of facilities for telecommunications, etc.) turn the airports into sophisticated complexes that require careful functional and technological design and facility management. These comments on buildings for air travel do serve to drive home their economic, managerial, technological, artistic and functional diversity.

3.3 Structures and Components

As for building types, it is not the purpose here to provide a full survey of structures and components. We are restricting ourselves to a selection of those that exercise a determinant impact on architectural design, the more so because certain structural details have been discussed in Chapter 2 (such as frames, curtain walls, structural glass and claddings).

3.3.1 Wide-span structures

Spaces with a large surface with or without internal columns (supports) and bridges with long spans have been constructed since ancient times. Domes, up to the nineteenth century, had a maximum span of 50 metres and it is only relatively recently that the progress in technology has allowed this restriction to be exceeded to the extent that in the twentieth century space coverings with spans of 300 metres and suspension bridges with a span of 2000–3000 metres were being constructed.

Wide-span hall roofs have some kind of supporting structure, which may bring the loads down into the soil, or be supported by separate supports such as masts, columns, frames. They also have a weather shield, which may be a membrane, panels laid on top of the supporting structure or a unified load-bearing and weather-shielding structure. As a consequence wide-span structures may be classified according to one of the three types of structure. This leads to overlapping classification systems since each of the three types of structure may be combined with various classes of the other two types of structure. A dome, for example, has one single structure with a load-bearing and weather-shielding function and may be supported in various ways. A membrane may be self-supporting or suspended from masts.

The last 150 years have not only brought with them a gradual increase in span (and height) but also a considerable number of new structural schemes and architectural forms for covering spaces: shells, vaults, domes, trusses, space grids and membranes (Chilton, 2000). A great variety of domes have been developed: Schwedler (see Figure 3.10), Kievitt, network, geodesic, and lamella folded plate domes.

Steel trusses were developed beginning in the nineteenth century. In the first half of the twentieth century reinforced concrete came on the scene as a competitor to steel for long-span structures, for

instance in the form of braced or ribbed reinforced concrete domes and roof structures (designs by Pier Luigi Nervi, Eduardo Torroja and Felix Candela). During the 1920s and 1930s thin reinforced concrete shells were constructed. Shells may be not only domes but also cylindrical and prestressed tensile membrane structures. Then up to the present time, a great variety of new structures were added to the list of wide-span structures: steel, aluminium, timber, membranes, space trusses (with one, two or three layers, polyhedra lattices) and tensile (tensioned) structures (Karni, 2000). Another aspect of categorization is the way in which vertical loads are transmitted to the ground: directly by the structure, as is the case with some domes, or by special supports: pylons, masts or columns. In this second category are the 'masted structures' (Harris and Pui-K Li, 1996). A masted building may have one, two or more (four, eight, etc.) masts and these can be placed interior or exterior to the building. A special category is formed by rotational structures, which may have one mast, or several within the building envelope or, alternatively multiple masts may be arranged around the perimeter of the building. Some of such rotational structures may be designed for grandstands. It is obvious that the masts not least due to their conspicuous appearance influence greatly the overall architectural design and its details.

Some of the load-bearing roof structures require an external layer on top for water and heat insulation purposes. Competitors to traditional roofing materials (wood shingle, reed, clay tile, stone slab, lead, copper) made their presence felt: corrugated coil-coated steel or aluminium sheet, plastics, foil or textile, factory-built-up composite panel (Selves, 1999). Some of these are also applied as wall cladding or suspended ceilings.

As mentioned earlier, stadiums are increasingly being constructed with a retractable roof, which makes sports events feasible in any kind of weather: typical are the stadiums designed by the Japanese Fumihiko Maki and others. The year 2002 saw the USA's first retractable football stadium completed in Houston. Here the travelling mechanism of the roof rides on rails along the tops of exposed structural steel super-trusses and during retraction the two trussed panels part in oppo-

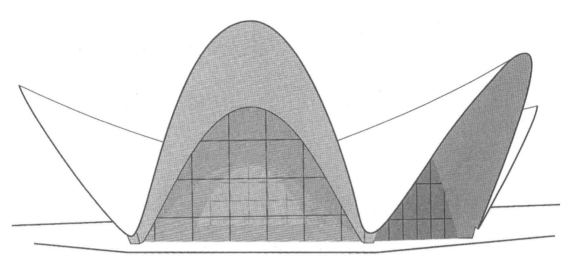

Figure 3.29a Restaurant, Cochimilco, Mexico, structural designer: Felix Candela. Eight thin hyperbolic paraboloid reinforced concrete shells.

site directions. The wheels of the mechanism ride on a single rail. Each of the two 287 metre-long super-trusses is borne on two reinforced concrete super-columns, which are nearly 210 metres apart, thereby eliminating the need for columns in the seating stands (*Engineering News-Record*, 2000). Plans have been put forward to rebuild the London Wembley Stadium with a retractable roof and with a capacity of 90 000 seats. Other recent designs of retractable roofs demonstrate a number of innovative solution possibilities (Ramaswamy et al., 1994, Levy, 1994).

3.3.2 Membranes. Tensioned structures

Membranes and other similar products (suspended structures, hanging roofs, membrane roofs, tensile structures, etc.) were initiated by some eminent structural designers, architects and builders: Frei Otto, Horst Berger, Ted Happold and others (Otto, 1954, Drew, 1979, Schock, 1997, Robbin, 1996). Following some smaller and experimental suspended roofs, the Olympic Stadium in Munich in 1972 was the first major realization of a long-span hanging roof. This had a roof assembled from acrylic panels, which, however, was an inappropriate material in view of the required lifespan of roofs.

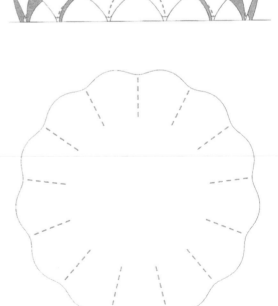

Figure 3.29b Market Hall, Royan, France.

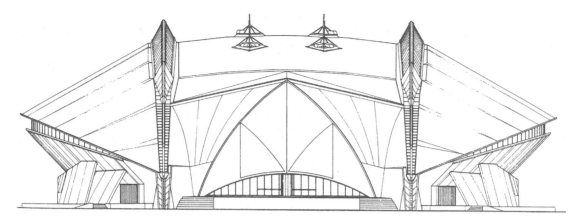

Figure 3.30 Fujisawa Municipal Gymnasium, Japan, 1984, designer: Fumihiko Maki. 0.4 mm thin stainless steel sheet roof; colour affected by weather conditions.

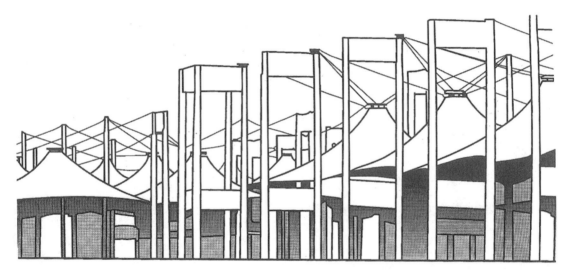

Figure 3.31 Haj Terminal, Jeddah, Saudi Arabia, 1981, structural designer: Fazlur Khan. Tent roof system, 460 000 square metres in area.

The next step was the introduction by the American Horst Berger of Teflon-coated fibreglass. This opened the way to a broad application of membrane roofs. The first such structural membrane roof was built in 1973 at the University of La Verne, California, USA. The most important membrane roof hitherto has been the Haj Terminal at the King Abdullah International Airport, Saudi Arabia, 1981 (Figure 3.31). Its Teflon-coated fibreglass membranes were designed by Horst Berger in cooperation with David Geiger and Fazlur Khan of Skidmore, Owings and Merrill. This roof covers 460 000 square metres and is up to now the largest roof structure in the world. It comprises 210 tents, each of them with a surface of over 2000 square metres. As could be expected, it required the elaboration and realization of complex structural design, fabrication and assembly plans.

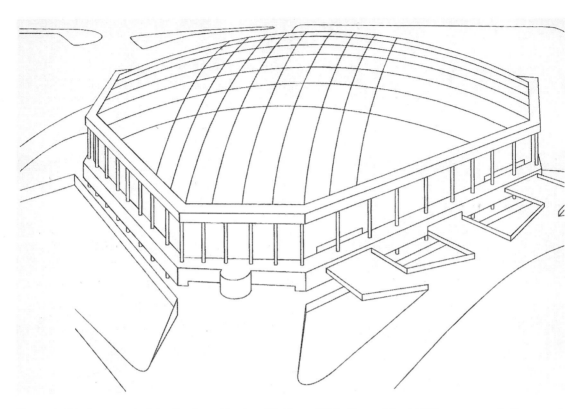

Figure 3.32 Balloon roof of the Stadium, Pontiac, Michigan, USA. Planned for 84 000 spectators, balloon roof consisting of large plastic membranes, stiffened by steel cables, curved by low air pressure.

Besides tents, tensioned roofs often follow in some way the form of umbrellas (Rasch, 1995). An equally important building covered by Teflon-coated fibreglass membranes was constructed at the Denver International Airport. The major designers were Horst Berger, Severud Associates and James Bradburn (Robbin, 1996). The roof is extremely light at 2 pounds per square foot. This is vividly illustrated by noting that if it were built from steel, its weight would be 50 times more and if from steel and concrete, yet more. In spite of its lightness, it bears the large snow loads of the region and it permits the passage of daylight sufficient for the requirements of the space below the roof. The roof consists of a series of tent-like modules supported by two rows of masts with a total length of 305 metres (Berger and Depaola, 1994). Along with the American firm Birdair, the Japanese Taiyo Kogyo Corporation may lay claim to being one of the world's leading fabricators and installers of architectural membranes.

In the major components of tensile or tensioned structures, tension stress only is present. The important components are the masts (pylons, etc.), the suspending cables or other supports (arches, trusses), suspended roofing: metal sheet, foil, or fabrics and specially designed and constructed edges (clamped edges, corner plates, rings and others). Two basic surface forms are mostly used, individually or in combination: the synclastic and the anticlastic shapes. Spheres and domes are examples of synclastic surfaces. Saddles (hyperbolic paraboloids, i.e. hypars) are common for anticlastic shapes.

A special class are the tensegrity (tensional integrity) domes (Buckminster Fuller, 1983, Kawaguchi et al., 1999). Tensegrity structures have

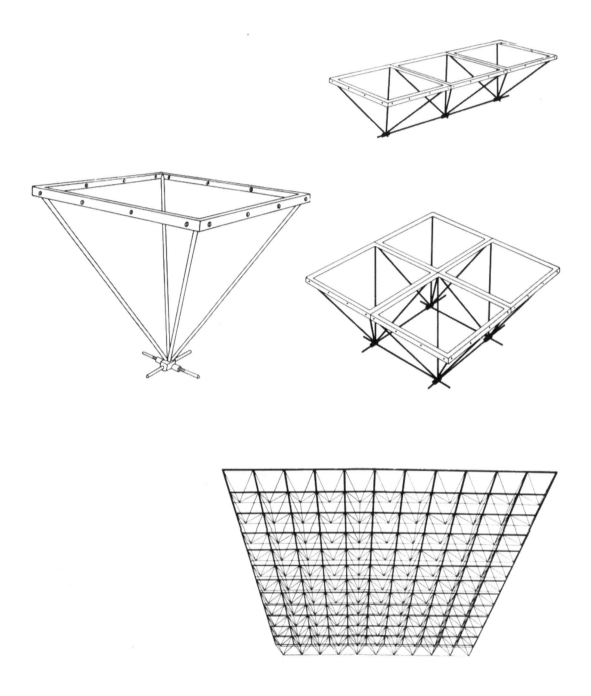

Figure 3.33 Double-layer space frame from prefabricated elements, readily transported (Space Deck, USA)
© Sebestyen: *Lightweight Building Construction*, Akadémiai Kiadó.

a geometry in which there are relatively few compression members and a net of pure tension members. The compression members do not touch, making a 'tensegrity'. Richard Buckminster Fuller (1895–1983), an American inventor, was the first to develop the tensegrity structures. His invention (and patent) was also the geodesic dome in which the bars on the surface of a sphere are geodesics, i.e. great circles of the sphere. Fuller based his domes on the geometry of one of the regular polyhedra (tetrahedron, cube, octahedron, dodecahedron, icosahedron). Other designs were using semi-regular poyhedra that comprise more than one type of regular polygon and other forms. One of the first geodesic domes was built at the Ford plant in Detroit in 1953 with a 28-metre diameter in which bars were connected to form triangles and octahedrons were built up from these. Following this, a great number of such domes were built all around the world, among them the 'Climatron' Botanical Garden, St Louis, Missouri (1960), and the one assembled in Montreal, Canada, 1967, with a height of 50 metres. Many variants of the geodesic dome have been developed during the years since its inception.

3.3.3 Space structures

The development of space trusses led to the creation and application of truss systems with specific types of node: MERO, Unistrut, Triodetic, Moduspan, Harley Mai Sky, Catrus, Pyramitec, Nodus and others. The MERO system in fact was one of the first space grid systems and it was introduced in the 1940s in Germany by Dr Max Mengeringhausen. To this day it remains one of the most popular in use. It consists of prefabricated steel tubes, which are screwed into forged steel connectors, the so-called MERO ball. Up to 18 members can be joined with this system without any eccentricity.

The two basic types of these systems are the flat skeletal grid and the curvilinear forms of barrel vaults and braced domes. In the flat skeletal double-layer grids two parallel lane grids are interconnected by inclined web members. The grids may be laid directly over one another (direct grid) or be offset from one another (offset grid). These basic relations lead to different geometries of the

system. Lamella domes and vaults consist of interconnecting steel or aluminium units. An important innovative step was the invention by Buckminster Fuller of the geodesic domes, to which reference has been made earlier.

The space grid systems mostly use circular or tubular members and their nodes may be characterized as solid or hollow spherical nodes, cylindrical, prismatic, plates, or nodeless. Most of these systems are double layered in that a top and a bottom layer composed from linear bars are interconnected by vertical or inclined, equally linear, members. The bars of single-layer space grids are usually positioned on a curved surface. A recently proposed new type of space grid is the 'nexorade', which is assembled from 'nexors'. Nexors have four bars (eventually scaffolding tubes) and these are connected at four connection points, two at the ends and two at intermediate points by swivel couplers (Baverel et al., 2000). The various space grids provide abundant inspiration for creating different structures including domes, vaults and irregular structures and, thereby, have an important role in architectural design.Domes and vaults assembled from space trusses have taken on a great variety. One of the world's largest is the hypar-tensegrity Georgia Dome (structural designer: Mathys Levy in cooperation with his co-workers at Weidlinger Associates, 1992). It has a sophisticated structural scheme (see Figure 1.15). Its ridge cables make rhombs and its cables lie in two planes.

Deployable structures make temporary scaffolding unnecessary. Mamoru Kawaguchi designed the Pantadome system employing a series of hinges so that the completed dome can be raised all at once (Robbin, 1996). Kawaguchi's first Pantadome was built in Kobe in 1985. He also designed the Barcelona Pantadome (Figure 3.34) in cooperation with architect Arata Isozaki, which was at first pre-assembled and then raised with jacks and temporary support towers. Tensile structures may be two dimensional (suspension bridges, cable-stayed beams or trusses, cable trusses), three dimensional (cable domes, truss systems), or membranes (pneumatically stressed surfaces, prestressed surfaces).

Structural design must deal with specific risks related to thin, tensile structures: non-linearity,

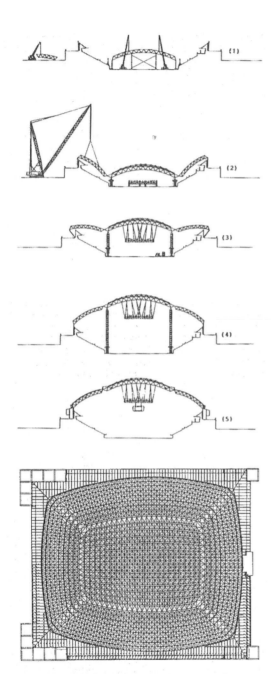

Figure 3.34 Palau Sant Jordi, Pantadome, Barcelona, Spain, design: Mamoru Kawaguchi and Arata Isozaki. The space frame was built in the arena floor bowl, then raised with jacks and temporary support towers; in total 12 000 parts, specified with only 40 Formex expressions.

wind uplift, buckling, stiffness, horizontal instability, temperature conditions, boundary conditions, erection methods.

3.3.4 Air-supported and air-inflated structures

Air-inflated structures (already mentioned earlier) have a fabric membrane, serving simultaneously as roof structure and as weather shield. The membrane is stabilized against flutter by the permanent air pressure being about 20 per cent higher than the atmospheric pressure outside. These find limited application due only to their energy requirements. Another category of air-inflated structures are those where the enclosure of the building is fully or partly assembled from air-inflated closed structures (structural ribs, sausages). The pressure differential in this case is considerably higher than 20 per cent (Vandenberg, 1998). Air-supported structures are mainly applied to buildings with one single main hall, such as covered tennis halls, swimming pools, or exhibition halls.

One of the realized buildings in the first category was also mentioned above. This is the 'Airtecture' Hall in Esslingen-Berkheim, Germany, completed in 1996. This consists of approximately 330 individual air-inflated elements in six categories (wall components, windows, etc.) The elements have different volumes and internal pressures (Schock, 1997).

3.3.5 Morphology

Morphology has extremely wide fields of application in architectural and structural design. First of all, it is the general study of forms in nature and human life including arts and architecture. A new discovery in this respect is the theory of fractals and chaos (Mandelbrot, 1977, Gleick, 1987). In spite of novelties in morphology and their broad potentials for applications, the direct relevance for architectural design remains to be investigated in the future. Then, morphology comprises a description and characterization of forms in various architectural styles and architectural realizations. This in fact has been practised for a long time and is a key part of the contents of this book. It also could be considered as the discipline for the study of the

Plate 2 Waterfall House (Fallingwater), Pennsylvania, USA, architect: F.L. Wright. Organic architecture but with modernist trends. Voted in 2000 by the American Institute of Architects the greatest building of the twentieth century. Photographer Terence Maikels. © Photographs of Fallingwater courtesy of Western Pennsylvania Conservancy.

Plate 1 The Sagrada Familia, Barcelona, Spain, 1883–1926 and continued in the present, architect: Antoni Gaudí. Organic-romantic, neo-gothic architecture with national-traditional decorations (coloured ceramics) but modern (reinforced concrete) structure.

Plate 3 Lever House, New York, USA, 1952, architect: Gordon Bunshaft from SOM (Skidmore, Owings and Merrill). One of the first models for the 'International Style'. The tower has the first sealed glass curtain wall.

Plate 4 Les Espaces d'Abraxas, Marne-la-Vallée, France, 1979–83, architect: Ricardo Bofill. Neo-historic architecture designed with pre-cast concrete components.

Plate 6 Guggenheim Museum Bilbao, Spain, 1993–98, architect: F.O. Gehry. Following other realizations, this is a masterpiece of deconstructivist architecture. © Van Bruggen: *Frank O. Gehry: Guggenheim Museum Bilbao*, Guggenheim Foundation, New York.

Plate 5 Georges Pompidou National Centre for Art and Culture, Paris, France, 1971–77, architects: Richard Rogers and Renzo Piano. A first realization of the idea of a 'high-tech', 'cultural machine' building; the external pipes painted in vivid colours, a staircase with a cylindrical plexiglas envelope, the overall boiler-house impression, open up a new approach in post-modernist architecture.

Plate 7 Nationale Nederlanden Head Office, Prague, Czech Republic, 1996, architect: F.O. Gehry. Deconstructivist design ignoring usual functional requirements (nicknamed 'Fred and Ginger' because its two towers seem to be dancing). © Van Bruggen: *Frank O. Gehry: Guggenheim Museum Bilbao*, Guggenheim Foundation New York.

Plate 9 The High Museum of Arts, Atlanta, Georgia, USA, 1980–83, architect: Richard Meier. Late-modern building with white porcelain enamel steel panels.

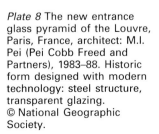

Plate 8 The new entrance glass pyramid of the Louvre, Paris, France, architect: M.I. Pei (Pei Cobb Freed and Partners), 1983–88. Historic form designed with modern technology: steel structure, transparent glazing. © National Geographic Society.

Plate 10 Renault UK Distribution Centre, storage depot, Westlea Down, Swindon, Wiltshire, UK, 1982–83, architect: Foster Associates, structural engineer: Ove Arup and Partners. Masted building, suspended roof, coloured appearance.

Plate 11 Law Faculty, Cambridge, UK, 1995, architect: Sir Norman Foster and Partners. Fully glazed north elevation.

Plate 12 New Railway Station at Frankfurt/Main Airport, glazed structure. Space frames are used in various structural systems. The German MERO is one of the first such systems. © MERO-VISION 2000 leaflet, No. 35, 1999/2000.

Plate 13 Jean-Marie Tjibaou Cultural Center, Nouméa, New Caledonia, 1991–98, architect: Renzo Piano Building Workshop. A combination of regional modern (high-tech) and organic-traditional approach. © Tim Griffith/ESTO, *The Pritzker Architecture Prize*, Harry N. Abrams Inc. Publishers.

Plate 14 Asian Games Village, New Delhi, India, 1982, Raj Rewal. Cluster housing in a Third World country, combining up-to-date and traditional technology and design.

Plate 15 Institutional Hill apartment building, Singapore, 1988, architect: Tang Guan Bee. Lively, articulated architecture, practically without any domestic, traditional influence.

Plate 17 Museum of Contemporary Art, Niteroi, State of Rio de Janeiro, Brazil, 1991–96, architect: Oscar Niemeyer. A beautiful combination of natural and built environment. The structure is likened to a chalice or a saucer. © Oscar Neimeyer, *The Pritzker Architecture Prize*, Harry N. Abrams Inc. Publishers.

Plate 16 Menara Mesianaga, Kuala Lumpur, Malaysia, 1992. Fourteen-storey building, post-modern in a developing country; side core building, metallic external skin, 'sky-courts'. © Harrison et al.: *Intelligent Buildings in South East Asia*, E & FN Spon.

Plate 18 National Museum of Roman Art, Merida, Spain, 1980–85, architect: José Rafael Moneo. Modern architecture with the use of traditional materials: (Roman style) brick masonry bearing walls, filled with concrete. © *The Pritzker Architecture Prize*.

Plate 19 Netherlands Architecture Institute, Rotterdam, The Netherlands, 1988–93, architect: Jo Coenen. Structural glass facade.

Plate 21 Hongkong and Shanghai Banking Corporation, Hong Kong, architect: Norman Foster. Post-modernist/late-modern, high-tech tall building.

Plate 20 Niigata Performing Arts Center, Japan, architect: Itsuko Hasegawa. A transparent glass façade. © Courtesy of Itsuko Hasegawa.

Plate 22 Kuala Lumpur International Airport, Malaysia, architect: Kisho Kurokawa.

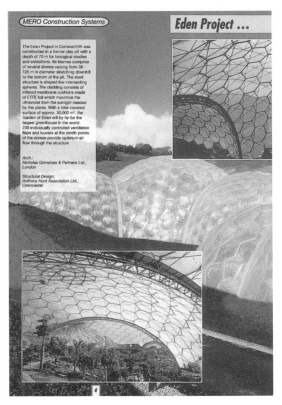

Eden Project ...

The Eden Project in Cornwall/UK was constructed in a former clay pit with a depth of 70 m for biological studies and exhibitions. Its biomes comprise of several domes varying from 38 - 125 m in diameter stretching downhill to the bottom of the pit. The steel structure is shaped like intersecting spheres. The cladding consists of inflated membrane cushions made of ETFE foil which maximize the ultraviolet from the sunlight needed by the plants. With a total covered surface of approx. 30,000 m², the Garden of Eden will by far be the largest greenhouse in the world. 230 individually controlled ventilation flaps and louvers at the zenith points of the domes provide optimum air flow through the structure.

Arch.:
Nicholas Grimshaw & Partners Ltd.,
London

Structural Design:
Anthony Hunt Association Ltd.,
Cirencester

Plate 24 Eden Project, Cornwall, UK, MERO construction system, architects: Nicholas Grimshaw and Partners, structural design: Anthony Hunt Association Ltd. Several spherical domes varying from 38 to 125 m in diameter, double-layer structure of hollow profiles, hexagonal geometry, bolted connections. © MERO.

Plate 23 Health Clinic, Bad Neustadt, Germany. 'MERO-Plus single layer system'. © MERO.

Plate 25 Carré d'Art, Nîmes, France, 1985–93, architect: Norman Foster. A cohabitation of ancient historical and modern architecture; new information centres ('médiatheques') contribute to the renewal of cities.

Plate 26 Planet Hollywood in Walt Disney World Orlando, USA, 1994, architect and interior designer: Rockwell Group). A building with entertainment restaurants, it is a translucent blue globe over 30 m high, at night covered with shimmering coloured lights. © {ai; Warchol.

Plate 27 The Trocadero Segaworld, London, UK, 1996, architects: RTKL UK Ltd, Tibbatts Associates. A multi-storey game centre, with futuristic neon-lit escalators. © John Edward Linden.

Plate 28 Low white Fish Lamp, 1984, designer: F.O. Gehry, material: Colorcore Formica. An enigmatic sign.

Plate 29 Standing glass fish, 1986, designer: F.O. Gehry, materials: wire, wood, glass, steel, silicon, plexiglas, rubber. A design which became an objet d'art, Walker Art Center, Minneapolis, USA.

Plate 30 Signal Box, Basel, Switzerland, architects: Herzog and de Meuron, 1992–95. In new architecture the external envelope frequently conceals internal functions of the building. © Taschen.

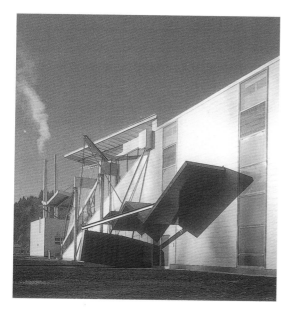

Plate 31 Funder Factory Works 3, in St Veit/Glan, Austria, architects: Coop Himmelblau, Wolf D. Prix and Helmut Swiczinsky. Deconstructivist architecture, with 'red comb', a power station with 'dancing chimney stocks'. © Taschen.

Plate 33 Cathedral, Rio de Janeiro, Brazil. Finely articulated architecture, different from historical, richly ornamented South American cathedrals.

Plate 32 'The Atlantis' Apartment Block in Miami Biscayne Bay, Florida, USA, 1979–82. Eighteen-storey building; pierced-through building volumes occur in new architecture.

aesthetics of forms. Next, morphology is the collection of methods for devising optimal forms for design. This is practised in particular for finding forms of thin curved surfaces, such as domes, shells, vaults, membranes, but also for space grids. In this section we concentrate on form finding.

Structural morphology is the discipline for studying the requirements for a structure in order to decide upon the characteristics and the form of the structural system. It is partly architectural and engineering design, which, however may be preceded by and founded upon a special branch of mathematics, geometry and topology (Motro and Wester, 1992). Morphology finds applications in chemistry, biology, astrophysics and other disciplines quite remote from construction but analogies between morphological properties in such different branches have proved to be useful in catalysing further progress.

In structural morphology the material, system, form and other characteristics of masts and other main load-bearing and load-transmitting components (cables, rods, tubes, trusses) have to be decided upon. For form finding, physical modelling, geometric (morphology) calculation and equilibrum calculation may assist the designer (Nooshin et al., 1993). The Formex algebra processes configuration with particular emphasis on the generation of patterns, surfaces and curved shapes, configurations modelled on polyhedra and various geodesic forms, and Formian is the structural morphology method comprising structural analysis requirements and applying Formex (Nooshin, 1984). In China a more sophisticated application of Formex (called SFCAD) was worked out and applied in the design of space frames (Robbin, 1996). Many other methodologies have been developed for general or specific form-finding purposes (Kneen, 1992).

Another program for generating polyhedra by rotation of polygons and other action is CORELLI, worked out in the Netherlands (Huybers and van der Ende, 1994). In this and other methods 'the goal is to enrich architecture and engineering with modern geometries' (Robbin, 1996).

Whilst most of the early form-shaping programs are based on some kind of regular geometric properties, some new methods can cope with arbitrar-

ily chosen forms. This was the case for the Guggenheim Museum in Bilbao designed by F.O. Gehry. The computer program for the design of the museum's façades was adapted from space

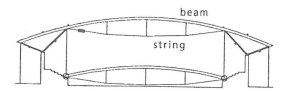

Figure 3.35 Sakata gym, Japan. The beam-and-string systems were prestressed at ground level and then hoisted into place.

Figure 3.36 King Abdul Aziz University, Sports Hall, Jeddah, Saudi Arabia, design: Buro Happold. Cable net roof; new types of structures enhance the range of architectural design. © Courtesy of Buro Happold.

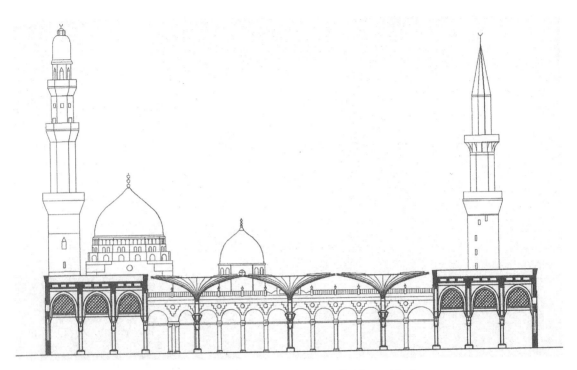

Figure 3.37 Mosque, Saudi Arabia. Super-light structures are applied increasingly.

technology. Its titanium cladding envelope was modelled by using the CATIA program developed by the French Dassault firm for the design of fighter planes (Jodidio, 1998).

The progress in morphology, fabrication methods and new ambitions by architects induce many researchers to seek for new types of form and, specifically, new types of curve. Such complicated curves have been defined as hyperstructures, and design with them, as hypersurface architecture (Perrella, 1998 and 1999).

Meta-architecture is the name given by architect-morphologist Haresh Lalvani to a technique to modulate sheet metal into a wide range of new configurations that can be easily manufactured using a patent fabrication process developed by Lalvani with Milgo-Bufkin (Lalvani, 1999).

The large long-spanned space enclosures (coverings) are characteristic new structures of architec-

ture. Due to the diverse structural schemes they offer many new design possibilities for architects and structural designers.

Bibliography

Ahuja, Anil (1997) *Integrated M/E Design: Building Systems Engineering*, Chapman & Hall

Albern, William, F. (1997) *Factory-Constructed Housing Developments: Planning, Design and Construction*, CRC Press

Bailey, Stephen (1990) *Offices, Briefing and Design Guides*, Butterworth Architecture

Baverel, O. et al. (2000) Nexorades, *International Journal of Space Structures*, Vol. 15, No. 2, pp. 81–94, 155–9

Bazillion, J. Richard and Braun, Connie (1995) *Academic Libraries as High-Tech Gateways: A Guide to Design and Space Decisions*, American Library Association

Beedle, Lynn S. (Ed.-in-Chief) and Armstrong, Paul J. (Ed.) (1995) *Architecture of Tall Buildings*, McGraw-Hill, Inc.

Bennett, David (1995) *Skyscrapers: Form and Function*, Marshall Editions Developments

Berger, H. and Depaola, E.M. (1994) Tensile Structures Highlight New Denver Airport, *Bulletin of the IASS*, Vol. 35, No. 115, pp. 110–16

Binney, Marcus (1999) *Airport Builders*, Academy Editions/John Wiley & Sons

Blanc, A., McEvoy, M. and Plank, R. (Eds) (1993) *Architecture and Construction in Steel*, E & FN Spon

Blow, Christopher J. (1991) *Airport Terminals*, Butterworth Architecture

Boulet, Marie Laure, Moissinac, Christine and Soulignac, Françoise (1990) *Auditoriums*, Editeurs du Moniteur

Brawner, Lee B. and Beck, Jun. Donald K. (1996) *Determining Your Public Library's Size: A Needs Assessment and Planning Model*, American Library Trustee Association

Breton, Gaelle (1989) *Theatres*, Editeurs du Moniteur

Buckminster Fuller, R. (1983) *Inventions: The Patented Works of R. Buckminster Fuller*, St Martin's Press

Campi, Mario (2000) *Skyscrapers: An Architectural Type of Modern Urbanism*, Birkhäuser-Publishers for Architecture

Chilton, John (2000) *Space Grid Structures*, Architectural Press, Butterworth

Douglas, G.H. (1996) *Skyscrapers*, McFarland

Drew, Philip (1979) *Tensile Architecture*, Westview Press

Edwards, B. (1998) *The Modern Terminal*, E & FN Spon

Edwards, Brian (1997) *The Modern Station: New Approaches to Railway Architecture*, E & FN Spon

Engineering News-Record (2000) 3/10 January, p. 14

Experiment Wohnen (2001), *Deutsche Bauzeitung (db)*, special issue, Vol. 135, 7 November

Ferrier, Jacques (1987) *Usines*, Electa France

Fitoussi, Brigitte (1992) *Hotels*, Editions du Moniteur

Gleick, James (1987) *Chaos*, The Viking Press

Gottdiener, M. and Pickvance, Chris, G. (Eds) (1991) *Urban Life in Transition*, Sage Publications

Gottschalk, Ottomar (1994) *Verwaltungsbauten: Flexibel, Kommunikativ, Nutzorientiert*, 4th edn, Bauverlag GmbH

Harather, Karin (1995) *Haus-Kleider: Zum Phänomen der Bekleidung in der Architektur*, Böhlau Verlag

Harris, James, B. and Pui-K Li, Kevin (1996) *Masted Structures in Architecture*, Butterworth Architecture

Hensler, Friedrich (1986) *Investitionsanalyse bei Hochbauten, Wirtschaftlichkeits- und Risikoanalyse von Investitionen in Büro- und Geschäftsgebäude*, Bauverlag GmbH

Huybers, P. and van der Ende, C. (1994) *Computing in Construction: Pioneers and the Future*, Butterworth-Heinemann

James, Paul and Tatton-Brown,William (1986) *Hospitals: Design and Development*, The Architectural Press

Jencks, Charles and Kropf, Karl (1997) *Theories and Manifestos of Contemporary Architecture*, Academy Editions

Jodidio, Philip (1998) *Contemporary American Architects*, Volume IV, Taschen

Jolly, Dominique (1988) *L'hopital au XXIe siècle*, Economica

Karni, Eyel (2000) Structural-Geometrical Performance of Wide-Span Space Structures, *Architectural Science Review*, 43.2, June

Kawaguchi, Mamoru, Abe, Masaru and Tatemichi, Ikuo (1999) Design, Tests and Realization of 'Suspen-Dome' System, *Journal of the IASS*, Vol. 40, No. 3, pp. 179–92

Kneen, P. (1992) Computer Aided Form Finding for Lightweight Surface Structures, In: Motro, R. and Wester, T. (Eds) *Structural Morphology*, IASS Working Group 15, University of Montpellier, II, p.82

Konya, Allan (Ed.) (1986) *Sports Buildings: A Briefing and Design Guide*, The Architectural Press

Koolhaas, Rem and Mau, Bruce (1995) *S, M, L, XL*, Monacelli Press, Inc.

Krankenhäuser- Hospitals, Architektur + Wettbewerbe, December 2000, No. 184

Lalvani, Haresh (1999) Meta Architecture, *Architectural Design*, Vol. 69, No. 9–10, Profile 141, pp. 32–8

Lawrence, Roderick J. (1987) *Housing, Dwellings and Homes: Design Theory, Research and Practice*, John Wiley & Sons

Lemoine, Bertrand (1998) *Les stades en gloire*, Gallimard

Levy, M. (1994) The Innovation of Lightness, *Bulletin of the International Association for Shell and Spatial Structures*, Vol. 35, No. 115, pp. 77–84

Lorenz, Peter (1991) *Gewerbebau. Industriebau*, Verlagsanstalt Alexander Koch

MacKeith, Margaret (1986) *The History and Conservation of Shopping Arcades*, Mansell Publishing

Maitland, Barry (1985) *Shopping Malls: Planning and Design*, Construction Press

Mandelbrot, Benoit (1977) *The Fractal Geometry of Nature*, Freeman

Marberry, Sara O. (Ed.) (1995) *Innovations in Healthcare Design*, Van Nostrand Reinhold

Mauger, Patrick (1991) *Centres commerciaux*, Moniteur

Mierop, C. (1995) *Skyscrapers Higher and Higher*, Norma Editions

Monnier, Gerard (2000) *L'architecture moderne en France, tome 3: De la croissance à la compétition*, Picard

Motro, René and Wester, Ture (Eds) (1992) *Structural Morphology*, IASS Working Group 15, University of Montpellier, II

Müller, Thomas (2001) Schuk-Zukunf, *Architektur, Innenarchitektur, Technisher Ansbau*, No. 7/8, pp. 69–77

Multi-media libraries, *Techniques and Architecture*, June–July

Muneer, T. et al. (2000) *Windows in Buildings: Thermal, Acoustic, Visual and Solar Performance*, Architectural Press

Myerson, Jeremy (1996) *New Public Architecture*, Laurence King

Nooshin, H. (1984) *Formex Configuration Processing in Structural Engineering*, Elsevier Applied Science Publishers

Nooshin, H., Disney, P. and Yamamoto, C. (1993) *Formian, Brentwood, Eng.*, Multi-Science Publishing Co.

Northen, Ian (1984) *Shopping Centre Development*, Property Development Library

Otto, F. (1954) *Das Hängende Dach*, Bauweltverlag

Perrella, Stephen (1998) Hypersurface Theory: Architecture >< Culture, *Architectural Design*, Vol. 68, No. 5–6, Profile 133, pp.7–15

Perrella, Stephen (1999) Commercial Value and Hypersurface: Theory, Art and Commerce Considered, *Architectural Design*, Vol. 69, No. 9–10, Profile 141, p.90

Price, Charles and Tsouros, Agis (Eds) (1996) *Our Cities: Our Future: Policies and Action Plans for Health and Sustainable Development*, WHO

Ramaswamy, G.S. (1994) A Design for a Football Stadium Roof Enabling Growth of a Natural Grass Playing Surface: Sydney Football Stadium, *Bulletin of the IASS*, Vol.35, no. 115, pp. 65–94

Rasch, Bodo (1995) Architectural Umbrellas, *Architectural Design*, Vol. 65, No. 9–10, Profile 117, pp. 23–5

Robbin, Tony (1996) *Engineering a New Architecture*, Yale University Press

Ross, Julian (Ed.) (2000) *Railway Stations: Planning, Design and Management*, Architectural Press

Russell, B. (1981) *Building Systems: Industrialisation and Architecture*, John Wiley & Sons, Inc.

Rutes, Walter A. and Penner, Richard H. (1985) *Hotel Planning and Design*, The Architectural Press

Schock, Hans-Joachim (1997) *Soft Shells: Design and Technology of Tensile Architecture*, Birkhäuser

Selves, N.W. (Ed.) (1999) *Profiled Sheet Roofing and Cladding*, 3rd edn, E & FN Spon/Routledge

So, A.T.P. and Yu, J.K.L. (2001) Intelligent Supervisory Control for Lifts: Dynamical Zoning, *Building Services Engineering Research and Technology*, Vol. 22, No. 1, pp. 15–33

Stafford Smith, B. and Coull, A. (1991) *Tall Building Structures: Analysis and Design*, John Wiley & Sons

Vambersky, J.N.J.A. (2001) Hoogbouwen: een kwestie van beton en staal, *Cement*, No.2, pp. 30–4

Vandenberg, Maritz (1998) *Cable Nets: Detail in Building*, Academy Editions

Voeltzel, A., Carrrié, F. and Guarracino, G. (2001) Thermal and Ventilation Modelling of Large Highly Glazed Spaces, *Energy and Buildings*, Vol. 33, No. 2, pp. 121–32

Wagenaar, Cor (Ed.) (1999) *De Architektuur van het Ziekenhuis*, NAI Uitgevers

Wilkinson, Chris (1991) *Supersheds: The Architecture of Long-Span, Large-Volume Buildings*, Butterworth Architecture

Wörner, Heinrich O. (2001) Innovativer Krankenhausbau, *Deutsche Bauzeitschrift (DBZ)*, special issue: Gesundheitswesen, No. 2, pp. 38–41

Yin, R. and Chow, W.K. (2001) Prediction of Pressure Distribution in Atrium Fires with CFD Models, *Architectural Science Review*, Vol. 44, No. 1, March, pp. 45–51

Zukovsky, John (Ed.) (1996) *Building for Air Travel: Architecture and Design for Commercial Aviation*, Prestel/The Art Institute of Chicago

4

The impact of technological change on services

The impact of technological change on new architecture is discussed in this book in three chapters: Chapter 2 on building materials, Chapter 3 on buildings and structures and this one, Chapter 4, on services. Chapter 5 discusses the impact of 'invisible technologies', e.g. research, use of computers. The contents of what follows on in Chapter 6 will deal with factors that are not primarily technological: urban planning, the economy, the environment, and sustainability. However, in the present chapter we include matters relating to climate and energy: whilst these are in the category of 'global values', or 'global commons' (meaning in our case resources, which are threatened by human activity and on which we all depend in various ways), they do have a direct impact on technology and, as a consequence, on architecture.

4.1 Ambience and Services

The ambience around and in buildings is the result of natural and of man-made causes: the climate, HVAC, lighting, etc. Whatever the nature of the cause, the responsibility falls squarely on the architect to reckon with it (Flynn et al., 1992). The extent and contents of the requirements concerning the ambience in buildings has grown ever more complex in recent times and embraces, for example, heat, moisture, mould, corrosion, water supply, energy control, fire, smoke, pure air and odour, natural and artificial illumination, sound, protection against lightning, vibration, security, electromagnetic radiation and various telecommunication services. Technical services cater for performance to satisfy the various requirements: HVAC equipment, water supply, telephone and telecommunications services, elevators, security and anti-fire equipment, etc. Each service may be and often is designed as a system and such systems increasingly are complex embracing two or more systems together with their interaction (Aspinall, 2001). For example, lighting may be combined with ventilation or may be incorporated in furniture. As a consequence, comprehensive environmental systems may be applied and the building as a whole may be considered as a comprehensive environmental system. When the architect designs a building, he/she must decide whether a new system or systems will be applied or whether existing systems will be incorporated in the design. Specialized firms develop their own (lighting, heating, etc.) system and system developers may develop complex systems to be applied by various designers (Flynn et al., 1992). Architects do not themselves design energy systems and services but have to be active partners with those who do design them since the dialogue must end up with comprehensive architectural-engineering solutions and the interrelation of services and structures results in specific aesthetic consequences.

4.2 Climate and Energy Conservation

An architect is not and in fact does not need to be an expert in climatology, which in itself is a sophis-

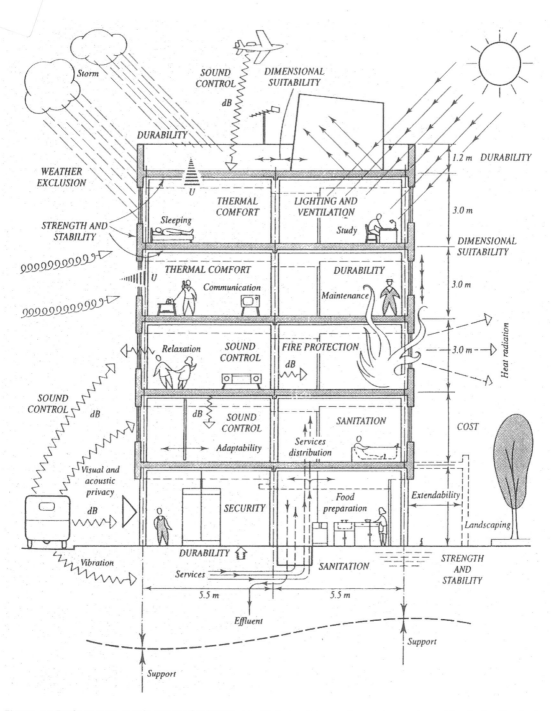

Figure 4.1 Performance requirements for buildings. Performance requirements serve as a basis for the design of buildings, compliance with codes and standards thus ensuring quality.

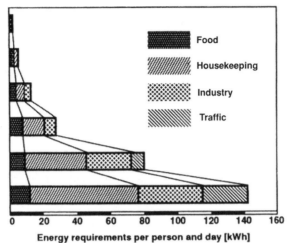

1 000 000 years ago
(collectors, without fire)

100 000 years ago
(collectors, without
hunters)

10 000 years ago
(farmers)

Middle Ages
(Western Europe)

Turn of the century
(Germany)

Present time
(Germany)

Food

Housekeeping

Industry

Traffic

Energy requirements per person and day [kWh]

Figure 4.2 Development of total energy requirements during the history of mankind. © Sebestyen: *Construction: Craft to Industry*, E & FN Spon.

ticated discipline. Over the past 40 years much new knowledge was added to the existing stock of knowledge on meteorology and climate. The most dramatic recognition has been that human activities commenced to influence our climate in a significant way and this would justify new strategies in order to forestall or at least delay serious climatic changes. This has a signal importance for the design of buildings, which in many respects were not designed to cope with certain new conditions.

To acquire a better insight into what is going on, record taking was increased and models have been developed and observations carried out to verify the trends in climate changes. The international umbrella organization, the Intergovernmental Panel on Climate Change, has sponsored substantial research in this area and published much of its results. It has been thought that measurements high up in the atmosphere would eliminate deficiencies inherent in ground-level measurements and contribute to the development of more perfect global and regional models.

The most important climatic change concerns the air around us. Air consists primarily (over 99.9 per cent) of nitrogen, oxygen and argon but it is other gases, primarily carbon dioxide (0.036 per cent volume in the air) that seem to lie at the heart of the changes. Carbon dioxide is important because its absorption and re-radiation of energy helps to main-

tain earth's surface temperature (the so-called greenhouse effect) and it is the source of carbon having a dominant function in various processes of the earth (Berner and Berner, 1996). Atmospheric CO_2 has increased in the course of the last century and this has been caused primarily by the increased burning of fossil fuels (coal, gas and oil) and, to a lesser extent, by the production of cement. Based on this recognition, several international conferences attempted to work out and implement some kind of international agreement binding countries to introduce measures to reduce CO_2 (and methane) in the air. In 1992 in Rio de Janeiro the statement was made that human activities contribute greatly to the warming of the climate. Five years later, in Kyoto, Japan, it seemed that most of the countries would accept certain measures. However, several countries, most notably the USA, disagreed. Their position has been that the essence of the problem lies in the fact that many countries use energy in an inefficient way so that, proportionally, they consume much more energy than, for example, the USA for the production of comparable products. Energy conservation may be best achieved not by imposing restrictions on those countries that already make efficient use of energy, but by improving the situation in other, less efficiently working countries. The hope was that subsequent conferences, in The Hague, 1999 and Bonn, 2000, would yield common views. This turned out not to be the case and the conferences concluded without the much hoped for agreement. The conflict was further aggravated by the presentation of new ideas according to which the main wrongdoer is not so much the CO_2 emission but other substances, primarily methane and soot. The chief proponent of this theory has been James Hansen, the Director of NASA's Goddard Institute for Space Studies in New York and chief advisor to the US government. Then, in 2001, a panel consisting of eleven of America's top atmospheric scientists and oceanographers declared that global warming is still a worsening problem and therefore the USA also should decide to participate in actions to combat it. Finally, recent climatic observations confirmed the continued warming of the global temperature. The warmest years have occurred during the last decade. At the 2001 UN climate conference in Marrakesh this brought nearer an international consensus and agreement on climate and measures to counteract it.

A recent report of the Intergovernmental Panel on Climate Change (IPCC) confirms that the changes in the climate are very much the consequence of human activities: the main causes of the rise in air temperature are the emissions of greenhouse gases and deforestation. Increased concentration of greenhouse gases (CO_2, methane, nitrous oxide and others) causes an enhancement of the greenhouse effect and thus global warming. The European Union decided that the production of 'green energy' should grow by 2010 to 12 per cent of the total. Green energy is understood to be energy produced from all forms of renewable sources: thermal sun-energy, wind, biogas, biomass, biological fuel. Despite much new recognition about CO_2 in the air, its exact movement and transformation are still not fully understood. Air pollution and aerosols (i.e. small solid or liquid particles) also have an impact, which, however, again requires more detailed clarification.

Whilst it has been generally acknowledged that there is (probably) an overall warming of the climate raising the global mean atmospheric temperature, the cause of the climatic warming, the size and the rate of this change, as well as its impact on

wind and precipitation (rain) and the (eventual unevenness of the) regional changes are not clear. In several regions the occurrence of strong winds, rain and cold winters is on the increase. Climatic changes are interrelated with the pollution of atmospheric air, with growing energy consumption and with the greenhouse effect (Ominde and Juma, 1991).

By now, most of the scientists agree that the main cause of the climate's warming is the so-called greenhouse effect, i.e. the increasing emissions of the greenhouse gases, first of all, of CO_2. A decreasing number of scientists, however, accept the warming but still express doubts about the reasons and claim that it is rather caused by certain aerosols, methane and soot. The change of climate may have a drastic impact on certain parameters of our environment and industrial strategies, thereby affecting design values, standards, regulations, design models and programmes for heat, precipitation, wind and other phenomena. We must act to eliminate or at least retard and slow down these changes including weather change. 'We' means in this case institutions (governments, international organizations, research and design institutes) and persons (architects, structural and mechanical engineers, facility managers or institutions having the role of the above-mentioned persons) (OECD, 1993). Policy instruments are manifold (Convery, 1998):

- energy conservation and replacement of fossil fuels by other renewable energy carriers
- grants and subsidies provided to support energy conservation
- information, training, supervision, auditing to promote energy conserving knowledge and methodology
- research and experimentation related to energy conservation including simulation, laboratory tests, architectural and engineering design methods based on up-to-date knowledge (architectural forms favourable from the point of view of energy conservation as, for instance, the design of sunspaces)
- regulation: standards, codes
- demand-side management (DSM)
- institutional development to engender 'bottom up' conservation initiatives.

Architects do not prepare institutional (public or private) strategies but they work within their context and may make good use of such policies: grants, subsidies or other. It is, therefore, their task to study institutional policies and to apply those parts that may have relevance for the building they actually design. Among the actions to achieve the objective are those to reduce energy (fossil fuel) consumption and to reduce greenhouse gas emission, which is a great contributor to climate change. Fossil fuels are globally available although in differing quantities. Coal and natural gas are more plentiful than oil. Among the strategies recommended is to switch from coal to natural gas, which entails the added benefit of reducing carbon dioxide emissions. As far as possible renewable energy sources should be applied: sunshine, wind, geothermal energy, tidal and wave energy, biomass. In particular the use of energy from the sun (solar collectors, photovoltaic cells, louvres, etc.) directly affects the exterior of buildings. Solar collectors are now at a mature stage and there are a number of manufacturers producing and installing them on buildings. Photovoltaic systems are somewhat less common. Even allowing for the fact that the electric energy that they have hitherto produced is more expensive, they do have a bright future. Photovoltaic modules can be designed in any shape; they have no moving components, do not cause pollution, can be adapted to different parts of the building (wall, roof, etc.) and must gradually become cheaper.

Energy-conservation strategies are different for institutions and for individuals. There are numerous advisory services geared up to counsel individuals about energy conservation. This issue, however, lies outside the scope of this book. Nevertheless, architects are frequently approached by individuals seeking advice. With this in mind, we emphasize that usually some 70 per cent or more of energy consumption in homes is spent on heating so that the primary actions to be advised are: increase heat insulation, improve heat equipment, control ventilation and internal air temperature and switch off all equipment unnecessarily consuming energy.

In order to plan optimal strategies and actions for energy conservation, it is necessary to study the composition of energy consumption, the technical appliances affecting such consumption and the ways to achieve energy conservation. In buildings, usually, an increase of heat insulation and top performance windows are among the most important energy-conserving methods (Hestnes et al., 1997, Hensen and Nakahara, 2001). Heating, cooling, ventilation, artificial lighting and electrical appliances make up the main consumers of energy. Measures to improve energy economics in various areas should be continued by integrating measures into a complex energy-related system.

During the past 30 years, a great number of experimental buildings have been erected to measure energy conservation achieved and to serve as lessons for future design (Hestnes et al., 1997). These experiments demonstrated that buildings having a very low energy consumption can certainly be designed and constructed but that this requires adequate knowledge, attention and control.

Decisions concerning energy systems and services affect the design of buildings. Codes, regulations and standards are modified according to new knowledge and these changes have to be reckoned with in architectural design. Climate not only affects individual buildings but also influences phenomena over a larger territory, unbuilt and built. The study of urban climate shows certain peculiarities (such as the heat-island and canyon effect, radiation and pollution distribution, effect of green spaces), which affect architectural design (Santamouris, 2001).

There is a specific danger of which account must be taken and that is the depletion of the ozone layer in the upper stratosphere. Its existence is also essential for many life-support systems to function. This layer shields the surface of the earth against much of the sun's ultraviolet (UV) radiation. The depletion is caused by the increasing use of certain materials (CFCs and HCFCs) in cooling, air-conditioning and refrigerating equipment and containers of sprays. It is catalysing an increase of skin cancers to say nothing of the damage to some ecosystems: land vegetation and the phytoplankton of the oceans. A switch to certain other materials and processes does reduce the harmful depletion process. Whilst this is not a direct task for architects, they have to beware of this problem so that buildings that they design satisfy this requirement.

4.3 Human Comfort, Health and Performance Requirements

Human comfort in buildings comprises appropriate conditions of heat and moisture of the internal air, sound, light and others (e.g. odour, vibration). Developments resulted in a more elaborate system of human requirements or users' requirements and this is also known as the performance concept or the system of performance criteria. These have resulted in the development of technical devices and systems that enable us to control human comfort and avoid human discomfort. Human comfort is affected by unpleasant temperature and moisture conditions (an ambience too hot or too cold, too dry or too wet/moist), too much noise, inadequate lighting (too dark, excessive illumination, strong sunshine, glare disturbing shades and colour effects), vibration (caused by earthquake, strong wind, functioning of elevators or other machines), smells and smoke, some sorts of radiation and any other internal or external conditions that are perceived to cause discomfort or to affect health. Environmental health is a consequence of the natural and man-made environment (Moeller, 1992). The adverse ambience in many buildings resulted in unpleasant and unhealthy conditions for the users, i.e. the so-called 'sick building syndrome'. According to Godish (1995) we have become increasingly aware that human health and comfort complaints expressed by occupants of office, institutional, and other public access buildings are in many cases associated with poor indoor quality. When a building is subject to complaints sufficient to convince management to conduct an IAQ investigation, it may be characterized as a 'problem' or 'sick' building. Health complaints associated with a problem building may have a specific identifiable cause (building-related illness) or, as is true for many problem buildings, no specific causal factor or factors can be identified (sick building syndrome).

Among the various causes contributing to a sick building feeling are:

- people-related risks: health factors, job stress and job dissatisfaction, occupant density, work environment, tobacco smoke, contaminant concentrations

- environmental conditions: thermal conditions, humidity, airflow, air movement and ventilation, lighting, noise, vibration, air ions, electrostatic charges, electric and magnetic fields, radon
- office materials, equipments and furnishings: video-display terminals, computers, copy paper, photocopiers, copying machines, printers, floor covering (carpeting, vinyl floor)
- gas, vapour and particulate-phase contaminants: formaldehyde, volatile organic compounds, dust, asbestos fibre
- contaminants of biological origin: hypersensivity diseases, legionnaires' disease, asthma, chronic allergic rhinitis, allergy and allergens (dust mites), mould, bacteria, microbial products, insects, rodents
- combustion by-products.

Many of the problems listed above and other factors materialize in polluted air, which adversely affects human health. To control air pollution a combination of strategies is applied: ventilation, source removal or substitution, source modification, air purification and behavioural changes. The architect has to tackle the expected air-quality problems and the strategies to achieve adequate air quality.

The multifactor causes of such problem cases are complex but in fact most have been identified and can be eliminated by proper design and functioning of the buildings. In order to achieve agreeable or at the least acceptable ambient conditions, appropriate building materials and structures have to be selected and various measures (for example, heat and moisture insulation, protection against noise and vibration) have to be applied. The range of protective measures against discomfort has become very wide and constitutes components of impact of technical progress on buildings and on architecture and construction in general.

4.4 Heating, Ventilating, Air-Conditioning (HVAC)

The two main groups of heating are direct systems, in which the heating is realized directly within the space to be heated, and indirect systems, in which heating energy is produced outside the space to be heated and then transferred to equipment in that space for use. The nature of the energy source may be solid, liquid, gaseous, or electrical. The terminal heating elements may be primarily radiant or primarily convective.

The leading trends in HVAC are: spreading of central heating (including district and city heating), the switch from some types of fuel (wood) to others (oil, gas and electricity), energy conservation and protection of the environment (reduction of air, water and soil pollution/contamination), introduction of up-to-date control devices and systems (condensing boilers, thermostats, programmable electronic control), automation and integration of systems, reduction of the size of equipment (smaller boilers and boiler rooms), more efficient appliances (consuming less water and electricity). All this is manifested in the cost increase of HVAC equipment relative to the total cost and a need for more intellectual concern in its design, realization and operation. CO_2 emissions and, consequently, energy consumption, may for example be reduced by:

- more effective heat insulation of buildings, including walls, windows and other building parts
- better airtightness and ventilation
- improving the performance of glazing
- enabling façades to react to weather changes by increasing or reducing heat insulation (and daylighting)
- more efficient hot water boilers and household appliances
- use of solar energy (Hestnes et al., 1997)
- economic incentives and management measures (certification of energy consumption, billing of energy on the basis of actual consumption, regular inspection of boilers, energy audits and third-party financing for energy-efficient investment) (Fee, 1994).

The selection of an HVAC system depends on the type of the climate and of the building (Bobenhausen, 1994, Faber and Kell, 1989). Houses usually have individual systems. Large residential buildings may have a central heating plant with individually controlled and metered HVAC systems including mechanical ventilation for interior kitchen and bath areas, or small systems for each res tial unit. The heating may be provided by warm or hot water, steam, air, electricity. Ventilation, cooling and air-conditioning systems may or may not be required. Open fires and closed stoves provide solid-fuel direct heating. Closed stoves and industrial air systems provide primarily convective direct heating. Luminous fires, infra-red heaters and radiant tubes provide primarily radiant gaseous fuel (or radiant electrical direct) heating. Natural convectors, forced convectors, domestic and industrial water air systems are primarily convective gaseous fuel heatings. Quartz lamp heaters, high- or low-temperature panels, ceiling and floor heating are primarily radiant electrical direct heating. Finally, natural convectors, skirting heaters, oil-filled heaters, tubular heaters and forced convectors may serve as primarily convective electrical direct heating. Electrical off-peak storage systems do not fall within the category of either direct or indirect heating systems.Indirect systems comprise a heat distribution system and terminal equipment. Low-, medium-, or high-temperature hot water and steam indirect heating systems have as terminal equipment exposed piping, radiators, metal radiant panels or strips, natural or forced convectors, pipe coils embedded in the structure, metal panels in suspended ceilings, skirting heaters, unit heaters, air/water or heat/air heat exchangers for ventilation systems. Any decision on these will affect the design of buildings.

In order to assist in the design of energy-conserving buildings, various methodologies and computer-based design programs have been worked out. One of these is the Energy Performance Indoor Environmental Quality Retrofit. This was worked out within the framework of a European research programme, supported by the European Commission. Whilst primarily aimed at diagnosing and retrofitting existing buildings, it may also be used in the design process of new buildings (Jaggs and Palmer, 2000) with the objectives to produce a good indoor environment, optimize energy consumption, use renewable (solar) energy and be cost-effective.

A new approach to increasing heat insulation is transparent heat insulation that utilizes the energy of sunshine (Wagner, 1996). It is applied on the

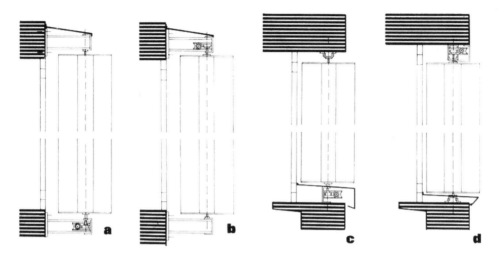

Figure 4.3 External sun-shading elements rotating around vertical axis (Mesconal, Germany). a) rotating mechanism at the bottom, b) rotating mechanism at the top, c) and d) countersunk layout with the rotating mechanism at the bottom and the top respectively. © Sebestyen: *Construction: Craft to Industry*, E & FN Spon.

external façade side, its material is polymethyl-metacrylate (PMMA, Teflon, acryl- or plexiglass) and polycarbonate (PC). A honeycomb or capillary structure made of extruded clear acrylic tubes serves to capture the sunshine's heat.

One should keep in mind that objectives and measures to achieve these may be complex and inter-related. The shading of façades is contributing towards protection against excessive sunshine, to enhancing human comfort by limiting the warming of internal spaces, to reducing disturbing glare and to energy conservation by eliminating or reducing air-conditioning requirements. These objectives are attained by adequate sunshading devices (see also below, under Daylighting). They may be placed on the outside of the façade as independent devices or internally, linked to the windows or as independent curtains or shutters. This exemplifies the complexity of the architect's task in making a decision that will have a profound effect on the look of the building.

Transparent heat insulation equally affects the façade design. The use of translucent fabric roofs has an overall impact on the internal ambience of buildings. Another new factor in the architecture of the exterior of buildings is the use of sunshine for

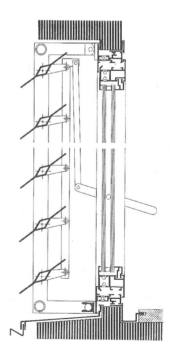

Figure 4.4 Vertically mounted external sun-shading structure rotating around a horizontal axis, with 180 mm wide extruded aluminium lamella. © Sebestyen: *Construction: Craft to Industry*, E & FN Spon.

energy conservation and energy production through the application of solar collectors or photovoltaic cells.

Photovoltaic cells usually produce expensive energy but intensive research promises to improve this. In Japan the application of photovoltaics is increasing and it is expected that by 2020 10 per cent of all energy will be produced by photovoltaics (Yamaguchi, 2001).

The solar collectors may be arranged vertically on the façades, on high- or low-pitched roofs or separated from the plane of the façades and roofs. Solar collectors usually have a black colour all over their surface and the resulting contrast between the black colour of the solar collectors and the envelope's differently coloured surfaces again provides new potentials for architectural design.

Solar systems may be:

- individual collector panels assembled on the roof
- prefabricated large collector modules assembled into complete roofs or other components of the external envelope.

The solar systems may be combined with heat storage systems, which store heat in water or solids (gravel or concrete).

Natural and artificial ventilation are sometimes underestimated because it is assumed that they do not exert any major impact on architectural design and that, being mostly concealed behind surfaces and ducts, their design is primarily the responsibility of mechanical engineers. In real life, however, they may be closely linked to lighting, energy conservation, heat and noise insulation and therefore their technical solution may have important repercussions on overall design. Various solutions may comprise natural or mechanical or combined systems depending on specific circumstances. For example, the Yasuda Academia Building in Tokyo, Japan (architect: Nihon Sekkei Inc., 1994) has an atrium that is naturally ventilated. In warm weather air enters at ground and intermediate levels, rises in the atrium and is expelled through the atrium roof. Air is also drawn to the atrium from the upper-floor bedrooms. A heat-reclaiming plant is located at the top of the atrium (Jones, 1998). A very peculiar solution has been applied to traditional Baghdad homes: inclined towers direct air into the heart of the buildings (Jones, 1998). In the Vice Chancellor's Office, Académie des Antilles et de la Guyane, Martinique, French West Indies (architect: Christian Hauvette and Jérôme Nouel, 1994) the strong winds of the hot, humid climate were utilized for natural ventilation (Jones, 1998). The high-tech Commerzbank Headquarters building in Frankfurt am Main (architect: Norman Foster, 1997) has been mentioned. Where heating requires energy, heat recovery from used air is a resulting economy.

An innovative ventilation system is displacement ventilation, usually combined with cooled ceilings. In this, fresh air is supplied at the lower part of the rooms. Displacement ventilation ensures good ventilation levels, low cost and adequate human comfort and affects the interior design of the buildings. Displacement ventilation may be designed by other arrangements: in Hall 26, Hanover Messe (architect: Herzog and Partner, 1996) the air is introduced via large glazed ducts 4 metres above the ground floor. The fresh air flows downwards distributing itself evenly over the floor. The air then rises upwards transported by the effect of the heat generated in the hall space.

The above examples demonstrate the attention that architects must devote to matters of ventilation. HVAC and other technical services are increasingly integrated into a system, which requires a careful supervision during the design process in order to integrate the technical system with the architectural concept. We will revert to this in Chapter 5.

4.5 The Lighting Environment

The two basic ways of lighting, daylighting and artificial lighting, both progressed enormously during the twentieth century and in doing so they acquired significance in architectural design. Light, both natural and artificial, with its volume, intensity, colour, the control over it and planned changes in its parameters, may become a decisive factor in the design of buildings and in the effect that those buildings have on users and visitors (Millet, 1996). This also explains why the satisfaction with specific types of lighting requirements, such as theatrical lighting, museum lighting, light in religious buildings (see for example, the Ronchamps Chapel by Le Corbusier), and shop lighting has led to special types of light-orienting and shading devices and light sources.

The basic knowledge concerning the visual environment and lighting were put together during the twentieth century (Hopkinson, 1963). It was stated that:

- visual conditions improve with increasing illumination up to a point
- light must be free from damaging or discomforting glare
- various characteristics of bright, contrasting, dull, uniform, colourful, accented or other lighting affect visual conditions. Lighting conditions depend also on the performance of materials and light sources.

All these and further parameters have a major influence on architectural design. In the following the basic stock of knowledge concerning lighting is presumed to be known and we restrict discussion to new objectives. Light is an important source and consumer of energy and, therefore, several lighting design methods assess simultaneously lighting and energy aspects. The Light and Thermal (or LT) method has been developed for the purpose of optimizing both light and energy factors (Baker and Steemers, 1994).

4.5.1 Daylighting

Traditionally, most daylighting (Baker et al., 1994) in buildings was provided through windows with vertical glass panes (sidelighting). Daylighting from above tended to be the exception, for example in the Pantheon in Rome. Shading devices may be positioned on the external or the internal side of windows. External devices that have long been in application take the form of blinds, shutters, louvres, sun breaks, verandas, and new constructions have been developed (Egan, 1983, Ander, 1995, Kristensen, 1994; Verma and Suman, 2000).

Light shelves shade the premises and redirect daylight into the room and up to the ceiling. They (and this is true in general for horizontal linear shading devices) are best suited for southern façades, whereas for eastern and western façades vertical shading elements are more appropriate. Atria are fashionable and by their nature they have special illumination conditions. Heat insulation and shading may be provided by double glass, heat-reflecting (infrared-reflective) and heat-absorbing glass. The optimal design and use of shading devices requires a special knowledge of their optical and thermal properties, including the variations depending on the angle of solar radiation's incidence. Models to predict properties and performance have been developed (Breitenbach et al., 2001).

Daylighting appears in combination with artificial illumination, heat insulation, ventilation and energy control. For this reason, whilst daylighting may be discussed individually, systems and realizations usually can be best described in combination with the other services listed above. This also explains why realizations are discussed only in one of the sections on services even if they also affect other services.

A spectacular daylighting and shading system has been designed and realized for the Arab World Institute Building in Paris (Sebestyen, 1998), designer: Jean Nouvel with partners (Pierre Spria and Gilbert Lézènès). The building has 30 000 shutters, which are activated by an electropneumatic mechanism and photoelectric cells, thereby maintaining natural lighting levels constant. The shutters are placed between the exterior insulating glass and an interior single glass pane. The façade with its 62 × 26 metre surface contains 27 000 aluminium shutter elements. The building took its inspiration from Arabic architecture but technically the traditional type of shading was realized by up-to-date structural solutions and a sophisticated basis.

In the case of the Menil collection in Houston (designer: Renzo Piano) (Figure 4.6) daylight is distributed in the museum premises by means of hanging baffles.

In several buildings daylight is conducted from the top of the buildings' atria: such a situation is to be

Figure 4.5 Town Hall, Emsdetten, Germany, horizontal shading elements. © Courtesy of Shüco, Bielefeld.

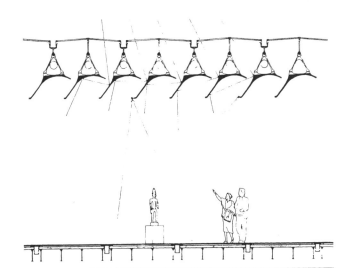

Figure 4.6 The Menil collection, Houston, Texas, USA, 1981–86, architect Renzo Piano. Cross-section of exhibition space with light-directing ceiling components.

101

found in the Berlin Reichstag building (architect: Norman Foster), the Hongkong and Shanghai Bank in Hong Kong and hotels designed by John Portman. Sunshine can be utilized actively, by photovoltaic elements producing electrical energy directly or in a passive way by collecting and storing heat in solar collectors for the purpose of electricity generation or hot water. Passive solar systems and active photovoltaic devices have a conspicuous impact on the appearance of buildings (Hestnes, Schmind, Toggweiler, 1994). The architect may decide whether sun collectors and photovoltaic elements should be integrated and blended with the building or, on the contrary, acquire an important aesthetic impression.

The daylight performance of 60 European buildings has been treated in a publication (Fontoynont, 1999). A selection (about a third) of the buildings described are listed below together with their main characteristics abstracted from the publication cited:

- Galleria Vittorio Emanuelle II, Milan, Italy, a daylit gallery with a glazed roof and a decorated floor.
- Chapel Notre Dame du Haut, Ronchamps, France, a sculptured mastery of daylight designed by Le Corbusier playing with wall thickness, daylight and colours.
- Sainte-Marie de la Tourette Convent, Eveux, France, vivid colours under sparse but focussed daylight.
- Neue Staatsgalerie, Stuttgart, Germany, a glazed attic with a sophisticated control of daylight and sunlight penetration.
- Wallraf-Richartz Museum, Museum Ludwig, Cologne, Germany, more than 1 kilometre of north-facing rooflights filter and control daylight penetration.
- Byzantine Museum, Thessaloniki, Greece, a variety of daylighting solutions.
- Musée de Grenoble, Genoble, France, awnings controlled by 27 light sensors, oriented according to the operation of each daylighting system.
- Waucquez Department Store, Brussels, two-stage daylight transmission admits light to deep areas of the building.
- Modern Art Centre, Lisbon, Portugal, four series of north-facing clerestories designed to bring daylight without sunlight to a museum.

- The 'Sept Mètres' Room, Louvre Museum, Paris, France, three successive translucent layers adjust daylight penetration for display of paintings.
- Sukkertoppen, Valby, Denmark, an atrium serves as a daylight link between new and renovated buildings.
- Domino Haus, Reutlingen, Germany, daylight from a large atrium benefits occupants in surrounding offices.
- EOS Building, Lausanne, Switzerland, 160 metres of aluminium light shelves serve to direct sunlight over one entire façade.
- Reiterstrasse Building, Berne, Switzerland, fourteen courtyards and a network of glazed streets distribute daylight thoroughly in a large-scale office building.
- Kristallen Office Building, Uppsala, Sweden, more than half the windows of the building use secondary daylight for energy conservation.

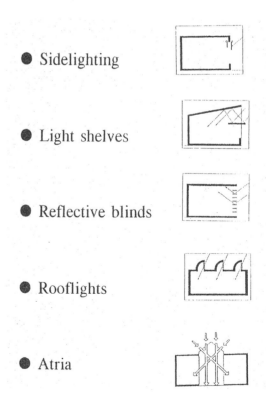

Sidelighting

Light shelves

Reflective blinds

Rooflights

Atria

Figure 4.7 Some daylighting technologies.

- CNA-SUVA Building, Basle, Switzerland, prismatic external panels in double skin can be tilted to deflect sunbeams to the desired angle.
- Gothenburg Law Courts Annex, Gothenburg, Sweden, south-facing clerestory directs sunlight into the atrium on winter days.
- At Dragvoll University Centre, Trondheim, Norway, daylight is directed deep into a university building.
- APU Learning Resource Centre, Chelmsford, Great Britain, a four-storey library lit from a central atrium and façade windows with semi-mirrored indoor light shelves.

These examples illustrate the great variety of clients' requirements concerning daylighting and responses by technologists and architects to these requirements.

4.5.2 Artificial light sources and illumination

Artificial electric light sources and light effects have been available for less than 200 years and in fact many of these only for a quarter of a century (Steffy, 1990). The principal electric light sources are:

- incandescence
- cold cathode
- fluorescence
- high-intensity discharge (HID).

The construction and performance of luminaires provide the effect of light and are powerful tools in architectural design. The light sources (shaped into luminaires) may be combined with architectural components, for example suspended ceilings with the light sources hidden behind them. Light services also play a substantial role in energy conservation. Incandescent lamps emit light from a heated object (bulb, etc.) and therefore convert to light a smaller percentage of energy than other (fluorescent, mercury, metal halide or high-pressure) lamps. Cold cathode lamps have a cathode, i.e. a filament-like device installed in a tubular glass structure, usually filled with some type of gas (argon, neon or another). Fluorescent lamps emit light from an ultraviolet radiated phosphor coating material, while high-intensity discharge (HID) lamps

discharge electricity through a high-pressure vapour.

Different types of lamp render colour in different ways and this enhances the choice of the architect in selecting the lamp type.

The partial or complete reflection of light from a reflective surface (including mirrors and polished metal surfaces) have been used in artificial lighting and illuminating buildings. In the heart of the Berlin Galeries Lafayette (1996, architect: Jean Nouvel) a giant mirror serves to reflect and enlarge everything (Schulz-Dornburg, 2000).

The designer of the extension of the Lyon Opera was also Jean Nouvel. Here a sophisticated light system is connected to a set of cameras. The system controls a range of coloured lights according to the flow of people coming to the performance (designer of the light system: Yann Kersalé).

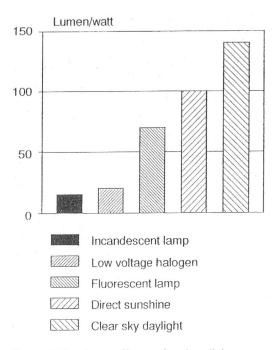

Figure 4.8 Luminous efficacy of various light sources. The selection of light source affects not only the design of illumination but also the design of the façade, the ceiling and the shading devices.

The glass façade of the Central Headquarters of the Affiliated Gas Company Network in Leipzig, Germany, 1997 (architects: Becker, Gewers, Kühn and Kühn) glows as dusk falls in a range of coloured lights (designer: James Turrell).

In the above examples modern computer-controlled lighting systems enhance new architecture.

4.6 The Sound Environment: Acoustics

In our noisy contemporary world sound and noise control is assuming increasing importance (Gréhant, 1996, Cavanaugh and Wilkes, 1999, Chadderton, 2000). Acoustics studies provide comprehensive answers to problems in this field. While it would hardly make sense to attempt to discuss acoustics in a brief section of this book, the significance of acoustics in architectural design must be recognized, so it is necessary to at least draw attention to some salient aspects of building acoustics.

The design of certain types of buildings (manufacturing halls, residential buildings, etc.) and their premises must ensure that noise levels do not exceed specified levels: insulation against the propagation of airborne and impact sounds (airborne sound transmission and structure-borne sound transmission) takes care of this. This can be more easily achieved with heavy surrounding enclosures and it is naturally more difficult with lightweight partitions and floors. Nevertheless solutions are to hand for effective sound insulation in such cases also. Noise may be controlled at the source through different methods of reduction by enclosing it within solid heavy structures, by mounting the noise source on vibration isolators and by installing a resilient floating floor. Open-cell foams (polyurethane, polyester) are efficient sound absorbers, standard polystyrene is a bad sound absorber. Sound moving through walls and floors is reduced by these structures, this reduction being greater if the mass of the wall/floor is higher. This is the so-called Mass Law. Insulation for airborne sound transmission can be improved with composite structures, which are composed from two lay-ers, one from highly absorbent material, the other from a heavy viscoelastic material. Sound insulation reduces the noise along the path from the source to the listener (with particular attention to minimizing flanking noise, e.g. by eliminating cracks and openings) and by protecting the listener in some form (Harris, 1994). Recently considerable attention has been paid to noise control from moving equipment (window shutters, sunshading devices) and motorized or other noise-generating equipment. In particular mounting them on the inner surface of external walls may cause disturbing noises but this is the case also specifically with HVAC and plumbing equipment.

In some buildings the task extends far beyond merely preventing excessive noise and takes in the prime requirement of ensuring the reproduction of sound with certain qualitative characteristics. This is the objective in concert halls, auditoria, lecture and music halls, recording studios and others. In concert halls appropriate sound reverberation and diffusion are the basic criteria for good enjoyment of classical music. Combined multi-purpose halls are more widespread in our time. Their design is possible through a combination of realistic simulation and accurate calculation (Sendra, 1999). Up-to-date electro-acoustical means comprise better digital equipment and better transducers, i.e. loudspeakers and microphones. To achieve good acoustics adequate sound absorption has to be ensured. For this purpose sound-absorbing materials (granular or fibrous porous materials) or resonant materials are used and sound absorbers in the enclosures (air, people, seats) have to contribute. Acoustical panels (resonators) have been developed. These are made up of an airtight material fixed at a distance from a rigid surface, thereby forming an airtight gap between the two layers. The resulting sound heard by listeners in concert halls and auditoria is defined by the strength of relative sound level, which can be measured at individual measurement positions or calculated as a mean value. In addition there is also an element of personal judgement including the level of 'auralization' of the sound (3-D sound) which counts. Whilst it is still a matter of conjecture as to how in ancient times spaces with good acoustics could be created, nowadays large spaces with high acoustical requirements are designed by utilizing all knowledge available. Some such large halls are:

- Boettcher Hall, Denver, volume 42 450 cubic metres
- Salle Wilfried Pelletier, Montreal, volume 32 100 cubic metres
- Philharmonie Am Gasteig, Munich, volume 31 000 cubic metres.

The foregoing does illustrate some of the problems in the architectural design of spaces with high acoustical performance.

4.7 Revolution in the Technology and Control of Services

Services and the technology of information and telecommunications have developed since the nineteenth century. Early progress was achieved by the invention and general introduction of a central supply of hot and cold water, heating, cooling, electricity, gas, telephone and radio. Later came the telegraphic, telex and fax service, black and white and colour television, the thermostat and others. The next step was to integrate the various existing and new services and to build up integrated electronic systems such as the Internet, telecommanding of home services, work from the home, telefinancing and the widespread application of computers and robots. As has been noted in previous sections, modern equipment in buildings is integrated into functional computer-control systems. These control heating, ventilating, air conditioning, refrigerating and other equipment (Newman, 1994). Most of the controls are performed digitally, some by pneumatic or electronic analog controls. Sensors measure actual data or changes of electrical or physical properties, such as temperature and pressure and issue commands to components of the system, usually through actuators. The brains of control systems are computers and microprocessors and it is these that make up the hardware for the system. The software, consisting of components sometimes called modules, tells the hardware what to do.

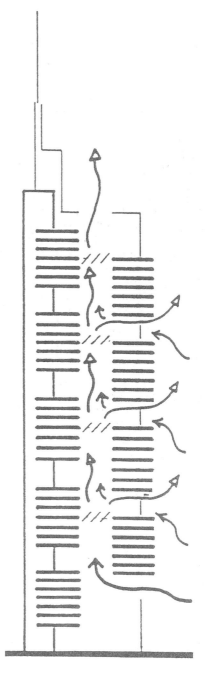

Figure 4.9 Commerzbank Building, Frankfurt/Main, Germany, architect: Norman Foster. A tall office building with natural air ventilation encouraged through the centre of the building.

Architects do not design technical equipment systems but they must be fully aware of their implications and cooperate with those responsible for designing the systems. Architectural design has to provide adequate space and location for the hardware of the system including the communications network. The operator(s) also must have a suitable workplace in order to be able to establish ongoing contact with these systems. In view of the rapid development of technical equipment systems, potentials for changes have to be foreseen in the design of the building.

Home automation has the objective to build 'smart homes' that not only require an integrated system but also appliances capable of responding to and acting on remote control and commands. Most progress in home automation has been attained in the USA, Japan and France. In France the expression *domotique* is used for 'home automation' and, usually, a distinction is made between several systems (Chemillier, 1992):

- the security system: surveillance of homes, detection of intrusions and technical faults, surveillance of people (children, elderly people), medical advice from a distance
- the control system monitoring operating parameters of HVAC, gas, electricity
- the domestic help system to facilitate cleaning, washing clothes, cooking, watering, opening and closing shutters and blinds
- the communication and information system related to the telephone and other telecommunication media, audiovisual equipment.

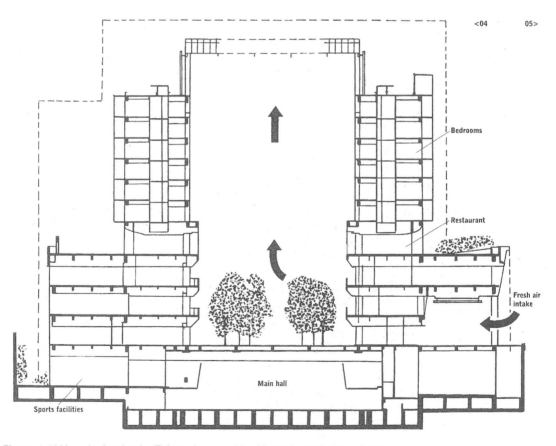

Figure 4.10 Yacuda Academia, Tokyo, Japan, 1994. Natural ventilation of atrium.

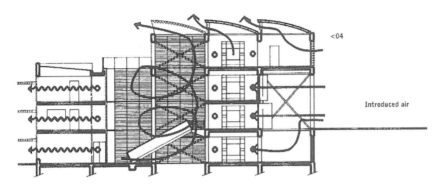

<04

Introduced air

Figure 4.11 Académie des Antilles et de la Guyane, Vice Chancellor's office, Martinique, French West Indies, 1994. Ventilation of atrium in a hot, humid climate with strong winds, air from wind is used for ventilation without causing irritating draught.

A special system concerns administrative tasks: rent payments, etc.

The latest developments aim at introducing remote control appliances. The Swedish Electrolux company has brought on to the market the Screen-Fridge refrigerator which, with its flat computer monitor affixed to its door, will serve as the control centre for household management including operating as the interface between appliances and services in the home and external services such as the Internet, building management and control from outside the home. A similar development is under way at the Japanese Panasonic and the US Frigidaire companies. Other appliances, such as the vacuum cleaner, the microwave oven, the CD player, will be equipped with electronics enabling users to control them from a distance. The technical problems are solved; the basic question remains one of affordability.

Smart or intelligent buildings are built first of all for the handicapped and the elderly, that is for those people needing care. Among the buildings already constructed, let us mention a building with 126 flats in the Kungsholmen district of Stockholm equipped with basic information technology services:

- the front door can be checked, opened or locked by care staff without a key and by finger pressure by the user
- central switch for cooker and iron
- leakage alarm plus automatic disconnection of water or gas
- videophone
- lighting can be turned off with a switch from the bed

- guide lights come on when the person gets out of bed, etc. (*Swedish Building Research*, 2000).

Bibliography

Climate, energy, HVAC

Ahuja, Anil (1997) *Integrated M/E Design Building Systems Engineering*, Chapman & Hall

Aspinall, P.A. (2001) Building Behaviour, *Building Services Engineering Research and Technology*, Vol. 22, No. 1, pp. 34–46

Baker, Nick and Steemers, Koen (2000) *Energy and Environment in Architecture: A Technical Design Guide*, E & FN Spon

Berner, Elizabeth Kay and Berner, Robert A. (1996) *Global Environment: Water, Air, Geochemical Cycles*, Prentice Hall

Bobenhausen, William (1994) *Simplified Design of HVAC Systems*, John Wiley & Sons, Inc.

Born, F.J. et al. (2001) On the Integration of Renewable Energy Systems Within the Built Environment, *Building Services Engineering Research and Technology*, Vol. 22, No. 1, pp. 3–13

Capello, R., Nijkamp, P. and Pepping, G. (1999) *Sustainable Cities and Energy Policies*, Springer

Cavanaugh, William J. and Wilkes, Joseph A. (Eds) (1999) *Architectural Acoustics: Principles and Practice*, John Wiley & Sons, Inc.

Chemillier, P. (1992) The Home of Tomorrow: Communication and Control, In: W.A. Allen, (Eds) E & FN Spon

Convery, Frank J. (Ed.) (1998) *A Guide to Policies for Energy Conservation: The European Experience*, Edward Elgar

Faber, Oscar and Kell, J.R. (1989) *Faber and Kell's Heating and Air-Conditioning of Buildings*, 7th edn rev. P.L. Martin and D.R. Oughton, Butterworth

Fee, Derek (1994) *'SAVE' Programme Proposal to Limit Carbon Dioxide Emissions, European Directory of Energy Efficient Building*, James & James (Science Publishers)

Flynn, John E., Kremers, Jack A., Segil, Arthur W. and Steffy, Gary R. (1992) *Architectural Interior Systems: Lighting, Acoustics, Air Conditioning*, 3rd edn, Van Nostrand Reinhold

Godish, Thad (1995) *Sick Buildings: Definition, Diagnosis and Mitigation*, Lewis Publishers

Hensen, J.L. and Nakahara, N. (2001) Energy and Building Performance Simulation: Current State and Future Issues. Preface, *Energy and Buildings*, Vol. 33, No. 4, pp. vii–ix. Special Issue. Building Simulation '99, Proceedings of IBPSA Conference, Kyoto, Japan, 13–15 September 1999 (in total: 183 papers)

Hestnes, Anne Grete, Hastings, Robert and Saxhof, Bjarne (Eds) (1997) *Solar Energy Houses: Strategies, Technologies. Examples, International Energy Agency (IEA)*, James & James (Science Publishers)

Jaggs, M. and Palmer, J. (2000) Energy Performance Indoor Environmental Quality Retrofit: A European Diagnosis and Decision Making Method for Building Refurbishment, *Energy and Buildings*, Vol 31, No. 2, Feb

Jones, David Lloyd (1998) *Architecture and the Environment: Bioclimatic Building Design*, Laurence King

Levenhagen, J.J. and Spethmann, D.H. (1993) *HVAC Controls and Systems*, McGraw-Hill

McQuisaton, F.C. and Parker, J.D. (1994) *Heating, Ventilating and Air Conditioning: Analysis and Design*, John Wiley and Sons

Moeller, Dade W. (1992) *Environmental Health*, Harvard University Press

Newman, H. Michael (1994) *Direct Digital Control of Building Systems: Theory and Practice*, John Wiley & Sons, Inc.

OECD (1993) *International Economic Instruments and Climate Change*, OECD

Ominde, S.H. and Juma, Calestous (Eds) (1991) *A Change in the Weather: African Perspectives on Climate Change*, African Centre for Technical Studies

Pritchard, D.C. (1995) *Lighting*, 5th edn, Longman Scientific & Technical

Santamouris, M. (Ed.) (2001) *Energy and Climate in the Urban Built Environment*, James & James (Science Publishers)

Wagner, Andreas (1996) *Transparente Wärmedämmung an Gebäuden*, Fachinformationszentrum Karlsruhe, TUV Rheinland

Wise, A.F.E. and Swaffield, J.A. (1995) *Water, Sanitary and Waste Services for Buildings*, Longman Scientific & Technical Publications

Yamaguchi, M. (2001) Present Status and Prospects of Photovoltaic Technologies in Japan, *Renewable and Sustainable Energy Reviews*, Vol. 5, No. 2, pp. 113–37

Lighting

Ander,G.D. (1995) *Daylighting Performance and Design*, Van Nostrand Reinhold

Baker, N.V., Fanchiotti, A. and Steemers, K. (1994) *Daylighting in Architecture: A European Reference Book*, James & James (Science Publishers)

Breitenbach, J., Lart,S., Längle, I. and Rosenfeld, L.J. (2001) Optimal and Thermal Performance of Glazing with Integral Venetian Blinds, *Energy and Buildings*, Vol. 33, No. 5, pp. 433–42

Crosby, Michael, J. (Ed.) *The Passive Solar Design and Construction Handbook*, John Wiley & Sons, Inc.

Egan, David (1983) *Concepts in Architectural Lighting*, McGraw-Hill

Fontoynont, Marc (1999) *Daylight Performance of Buildings, European Commission*, James & James (Science Publishers)

Hestnes, Anne Grete, Passive Solar Systems; Schmind, Jürgen, Integrated Photovoltaics in Architecture; Toggweiler, P., Building-Integrated Photovoltaics; all three in: Lewis, Owen and Goulding, John (Eds) (1994) *European Directory of Energy Efficient Building*, James & James (Science Publishers)

Hopkinson, R.G. (1963) *Architectural Physics: Lighting*, Her Majesty's Stationery Office

Kristensen, Poul E. (1994) Daylighting Technologies in Non-Domestic Buildings, In: *European Directory of Energy Efficient Building*, James and James (Science Publishers) (and other papers in the same publication)

Millet, Marietta, S. (1996) *Light-Revealing Architecture*, Van Nostrand Reinhold

Schulz-Dornberg, Julia (2000) *Art and Architecture: New Affinities*, Gustavo Gili

Sebestyen, G. (1998) *Construction: Craft to Industry*, E & FN Spon

Steffy, Gary R. (1990) *Architectural Lighting Design*, Van Nostrand Reinhold

Verma, V.V. and Suman, B.M. (2000) Simple Method for Design of External Shading for Windows in Air-Conditioned Buildings, *Architectural Science Review*, 43.1, March, pp. 37–44

Sound

Cavanaugh, W.J. and Wilkes,J.A. (Eds) (1999) *Architectural Acoustics: Principles and Practice*, John Wiley & Sons, Inc.

Chadderton, David V. (2000) *Building Services Engineering*, 3rd edn, E & FN Spon

Gréhant, Bernard (1996) *Acoustics in Building*, Thomas Telford (French original: 1994)

Harris, Cyril M. (1994) *Noise Control in Buildings: A Practical Guide for Architects and Engineers*, McGraw-Hill, Inc.

Sendra, J.J. (1999) *Computational Acoustics in Architecture*, WIT Press

Swedish Building Research (2000), 3–4, p. 5

5

The impact of invisible technologies on design

5.1 Some General Considerations

Architectural design has acquired and retained certain common features since earliest times. Indeed some architects go about their business in virtually the same way as did their colleagues in former days. On the other hand tremendous changes have also occurred. Some architectural firms number their staff in the hundreds and operate globally, perhaps with design teams or complex practices in several cities in various regions of the world.

Contemporary architects cooperate with designers active in other fields: structural, HVAC and other engineers, with manufacturers of building materials, components, equipment and clients, who sometimes themselves have competent teams producing briefs for controlling, supervising and engaging in design and construction. In the previous chapters we have looked into the impact of technology on architectural design. In the following sections we will examine other factors, for example, research, application of computers – the so-called 'invisible technologies'.

5.2 The Changing Image, Knowledge and Cooperation of Architects

When studying the oeuvre of an architect, a certain image may become apparent. Often each design by a specific architect reveals common features that enable the viewer to identify that architect. A similar process of recognition is well known in other branches of art; one may pick out, purely from the style, the music of Tchaikovsky or a picture by El Greco. For certain architects, however, this is not the case; each design is quite different and is itself largely determined by the actual circumstances of the project. I.M. Pei when asked in an interview whether his designs comprise some common features, replied that the only common feature was the fact that he was the designer. On the other hand, Richard Meier is well known for his strong preference for clear, simple forms and white metallic cladding sheets. Other examples are abundant. We can state that the designs of certain architects may have an individual image solely characteristic of that particular architect, although this image itself does change over time, with its specificity occurring in given periods.

The individual image is developed by the architect himself. However, another type of image is the corporate image, which is developed by large national or international companies, for example, IBM, Philips and others. These large companies are clients for a number of buildings and complexes of buildings and wish to project a common corporate image through each of their buildings. Such major clients usually have their own architectural and construction organization and these, though not carrying out the full design, take care to require that the architects working for their company actually incorporate the corporate image in their design. This is, for example, expressed for railway station design, by the following (Edwards, 1997: p.128):

*To achieve consistency four conditions
need to apply:
The client (the railway company) needs to
value design and be conscious of the
benefit of corporate image
A single coordinating architect is required,
armed with the ability to produce design
guides and influence briefs
All design skills (from graphics to
structural layout) need to subscribe to the
same basic aesthetic ideals
Over time, the changes required of
stations need to be carried out in
sympathy with the original aesthetic aims.*

The corporate image may allow the architect sufficient freedom to shape a building quite different from others built for the corporation. For small buildings, with a strictly defined function, the entire building may be more or less standardized: kiosks for fast food chains, petrol (fuel) stations of big oil companies (Shell, etc.).

A common image may also have other sources, such as the influence of a style, of a domestic tradition of construction, or of a metaphor.

The overall lesson to be drawn from all this is that architectural design must in one way or other permit the influx of various factors and aspirations but the final outcome must be that any decision concerning those external factors being allocated a place in the design process should be an independent one.

Many architects practise on their own or in a purely architectural firm; others, however, are active in architectural-engineering firms or are employed by 'design-build' or engineer-construction companies. Such combinations certainly influence the management of architectural design and may also be favourable for the cooperation of architects with engineers and construction practitioners, but they should not have any adverse impact on the creativity and inventiveness of the architects.

In the family-home market, catalogues of houses on offer have long been in use. With the assistance of the computer the different house types may be visualized on the monitor screen and as a result individual wishes may be incorporated in the design directly on the monitor. The designs of such catalogue houses may be worked out by an architect independently or by one related to a homebuilder or the services of an architect may be dispensed with entirely. Understandably, architectural associations are not in favour of design work executed without an architect, concerned by eventual aesthetic or technical deficiencies in the designs. This is increasingly becoming a bone of contention in the field of private housing, which in many Western European countries nowadays accounts for more than half of all housing bought and sold. To many people the low quality of this stock provides compelling proof of the inability of society to comprehend architecture.

Architects build up for themselves through their work a certain degree of recognition. This can develop into national or even global fame and celebrity status. The components of such fame have been discussed in various ways (Dunster, 2001) and, understandably, to achieve such fame is part although not the final objective of an architect's career. Celebrity status helps the architect in winning new important commissions.

An equally important change in the practical professional life and position of architects is that their expertise now increasingly comprises the results of science and research. Building design in the past was primarily based on empirical experience. Since the scientific and industrial revolution during the seventeenth and eighteenth centuries, construction acquired a stock of new knowledge, partly in basic science (mathematics, physics, etc.), partly in specific building science (structural design, building physics, etc.). This progress affected architectural design. Without the knowledge acquired during the last centuries, skyscrapers, long-span bridges and many other buildings could not have been built. The advances in mathematics (finite elements method, etc.), strength of materials, analysis of structures and the appearance of computers contributed to a more accurate analysis of structures and their design.

The new methods in mathematics and computing have been increasingly applied in structural analysis and also in studying other engineering problems: in building physics, heat and moisture transfer, acoustical problems, fire and smoke propagation and control. Progress in mathematics was combined with enhanced potentials in computation, for example in structural dynamics (Buchholdt, 1997), aerodynamics, fluid dynamics and the new analysis methods were applied in structural design, airflow control, design of heat and ventilation systems. The new knowledge and methods require that when involved in complex problems the architect broadens his or her knowledge and cooperation with experts in various engineering disciplines.

The architect in our time must have the ability to cooperate constructively with other specialized participants in the design process. This applies first of all to the structural designer but also to those working on the services, acoustics, lighting and others. A special word is needed for the structural design. There have been and are engineers who themselves design buildings and structures, such as stadiums, grandstands, railway terminal canopies, which satisfy users' requirements. Engineers who fall into this category are Nervi, Torroja, Candela

and, more recently, Calatrava. Another set of engineers is willing to enter into cooperation with the architect and to contribute to the architectural design by innovative structural solutions. Among these Peter Rice and Anthony Hunt merit mention. The former was a major initiator of the structural glass systems. The latter has been an important author of present-day steel frames and masted structures with cable structure. The work done by Hunt and others contributed to replacing riveted and bolted steel structure joints by welded connections and cast steel couplers. New and future architecture has gained and stands to gain much by creative cooperation between architects and structural engineers (Macdonald, 2000).

Whilst the work of architects retains many of its historical features, contemporary design processes have become more abstract and experimental. However, one of the recognizable results of computers has been to accelerate the rate of reaction of architecture. The representation of the design has been sometimes transformed into conceptual diagrams developed with the aid of high-end

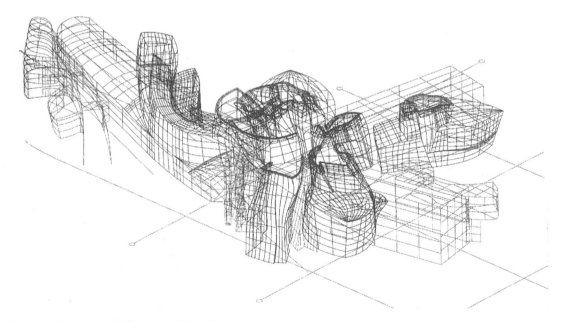

Figure 5.1 Guggenheim Museum, Bilbao, Spain, architect: Frank O. Gehry. The complex forms of the 'metal flower' envelope could be designed only with the assistance of a computer: the CATIA software developed by the French aircraft company Dassault was used; the material of the envelope is thin titan sheet.

computer software packages (Contemporary Processes in Architecture, 2000). The participation of the client and future users, as well as the interim review of design is taking new forms (Jones, 2001). Although design reviews are not expected to select, and even less to create, an optimal design, they may prevent serious mistakes. At the same time there is a risk that they themselves may become sources of errors.

The changes concerning the knowledge requirements of architects must be reflected in their education as is proven by a number of publications on this subject (Denès, 1996, Harris, 2001).

Modern education for architects must reconcile seemingly contradictory requirements: a reasonable selection from increasing traditional and new knowledge (artistic, technical, economic, environmental, social, information and computing technologies) and assistance to creative, artistic work, comprising also modern methods of assistance in design work.

5.3 Fire Engineering Design

Research established the new discipline of fire science and fire safety engineering (Bickerdike Allen, 1996). At the present time there exists a solid stock of knowledge on fire in and around buildings and the design principles to ensure safety. This includes knowledge of internal and external growth and spread of fire and smoke, requirements concerning the means of escape in case of fire and access and facilities for the fire service.

The essence of fire safety engineering lies in the knowledge of the movement of fire including gases and smoke created by fire. This was helped by progress in fluid dynamics and advances in the mathematics of complicated computational problems. Much of the theoretical analysis of fire behaviour has been represented by zone modelling, which incorporates modelling of heat transfer and fluid flow in different zones in premises and buildings. It is now possible to compute in advance what could happen in a fire and by using the results of the analysis, to design buildings with a predetermined safety. This must also comprise a sufficient number of safe escape routes that are accessible,

clearly recognizable and usable when needed.

Fire catastrophes have often been caused by incorrect management methods, e.g. unauthorized closing of exits. Management and foresight deficiencies were the underlying causes of a major recent fire in Volendam, Netherlands with attendant high mortality. Clothing has also been the subject of intensive study to clarify the differences in ignitability of different textiles and flame spread.

The extreme importance of fire safety obliges architects thoroughly to master matters of fire safety and to allocate adequate attention to it in the architectural design of buildings.

5.4 New Methods in Structural Analysis – Design for Seismic Areas

Structural analysis underwent a tremendous development during the twentieth century (Sebestyen, 1998). Probability-based models were offered in order to perfect deterministic models.

Strictly elastic and linear models gave way to plastic or partly plastic and non-linear models. Macromolecular structural models remained to dominate structural analysis but fracture mechanics commenced investigating better models of structures. More accurate models were also introduced to analyse the impact of dynamic actions, the impact of earthquakes, wind and other forms of vibration. Devices to reduce the damages to buildings during earthquakes have now reached the position when they include structural and dynamic tools for passive and active dampening. The structural design that formerly was carried out with models of permissible stresses has been succeeded by ultimate stress models in which the structure was presumed likely to fail when it could no longer meet either the ultimate limit states causing failures, or the serviceability limit states comprising deformations. Ultimate limit states correspond to the following adverse states:

- loss of equilibrum of the structure or a part thereof
- attainment of the maximum resistance capacity

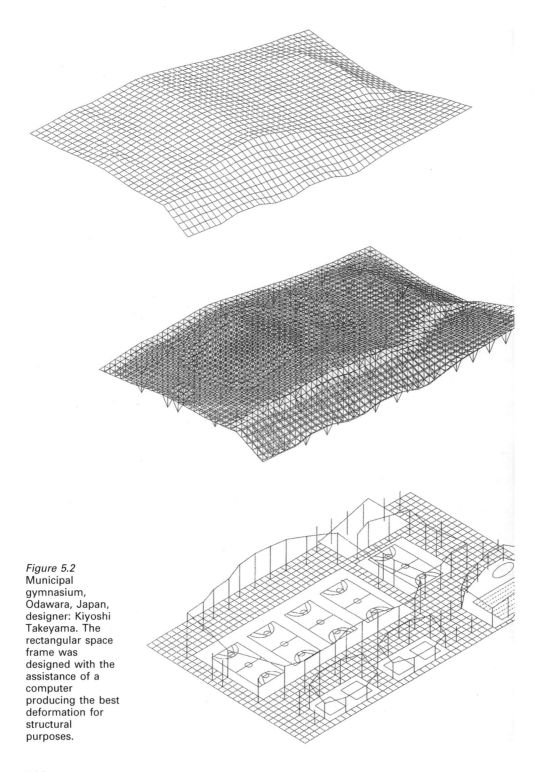

Figure 5.2
Municipal
gymnasium,
Odawara, Japan,
designer: Kiyoshi
Takeyama. The
rectangular space
frame was
designed with the
assistance of a
computer
producing the best
deformation for
structural
purposes.

of sections, members, or connections by rupture, fatigue, corrosion, or excessive deformation

- transformation of the structure or part of it into a mechanism
- instability of the structure or part of it
- sudden change of the assumed structural system into a new system
- unacceptable or excessive deformation.

The two basic models for structural analysis are the partial factor method and the full probabilistic method, the first being considered as a simplification of the second. Whilst both models may be applied (as stated, for example, in the ISO 2394 International Standard), in practice it is the partial factor method that finds practical application, this being abundantly supported by calculation methods, characteristic values, partial factor values and load combinations. Research is faced with the clear task to elaborate all necessary help for the full probabilistic method in order to make it also operational.

The most important progress in structural analysis has been the advent of electronic computation. Eminent civil engineers (Torroja, Nervi, Arup, Iyengar, Rice and many others) and architect-engineers (Frei Otto, the late Ted Happold) figure in the list of structural designers who have contributed to the development of innovative structures (Rice, 1993). Various forms of cooperation between architects and structural designers were experienced and such cooperation was often a decisive factor in progress, for example, in the cooperation among several of the designers listed above. Special computer-based methods were developed for protection against earthquakes, wind, fire, smoke and building physics (heat, moisture, light, noise). Electronic computation enabled designers to solve large-size calculations and design new types of structure, such as skyscrapers, long-span bridges and wide-span roofs.

Earthquakes are attributed to fault movement within the earth's crust. They are a natural phenomenon occurring as a result of sudden rupture of the rocks, which constitute the earth (*Dynamic Analysis and Earthquake Resistant Design*,1997). Throughout the history of mankind they have brought catastrophic results in their wake. It was not so long ago that scientific research into their

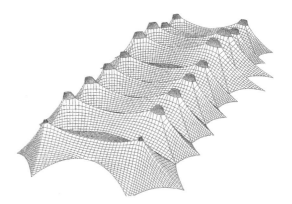

Figure 5.3 Denver International Airport, USA, designer: Severud Associates, New York (Edward M. DePaola, principal), principal design consultant: Horst Berger. The tensile roof structure covers 428 000 square metres, it consists of a series of tent-like modules, supported by two rows of masts: the roof mesh's design was generated by computer using non-linear analysis methods to take account of possible maximum deformations.

causes commenced, which has evolved into a solid science over the last hundred years. Vibrations, surface waves and ground motion of differing magnitude and intensity are generated by an earthquake. Serious earthquakes cause damage to or failures of buildings and structures and can also result in heavy loss of life. Strong motion observations have been recorded since the last century. By now much data on strong motion is available and theoretical models of strong motion could be calculated. As a consequence, earthquake hazard can be analysed, risk indices can be calculated and seismic zones; in which construction should be avoided or at the least special design guidelines should be applied, could be established. Building design profited from this progress so that currently design can assess in advance probable seismic force. For this purpose dynamic analysis methods were worked out.

The behaviour of a structure in an earthquake hinges on the intensity of the earthquake and the quality of the structure (Jeary, 1997). The quality of the structure in turn depends on the configuration of the building (very much a result of architectural

115

intentions), the characteristics of the building materials, the architectural and structural design solutions and the quality of the construction's execution (Penelis and Kappos, 1997).

The seismic design principles comprise the following guidelines:

- Structures must resist low-intensity earthquakes without suffering any structural damage, which means that during such earthquakes all structural elements should remain in the elastic range.
- Structures should withstand moderate-intensity earthquakes with very light and repairable damage.
- Structures should withstand high-intensity earthquakes (whose frequency of occurrence should not exceed calculated periods) without collapsing.

The above-listed principles are formulated in EC8 'Earthquake Resistant Design of Structures' by some fundamental requirements, compliance requirements and some specific measures. Earthquake-resistant structural analysis and design are based on the requirements. Methods based on structural dynamics are necessary for important buildings with a considerable height, wide span or other sensitive characteristics. For simpler buildings static analysis may be satisfactory (Browning, 2001). In well-defined and limited cases seismic design may be restricted to structures with controlled inelastic response, assuming primarily elastic behaviour in earthquakes (CEB, 1998).

Traditionally, seismic design relied mostly on the ductile behaviour of the structure. The ductility of an element is its ability to sustain inelastic deformations without substantial structural reduction in strength and the capacity to absorb and dissipate seismic energy (Penelis and Kappos, 1997). Modern design comprises the (static or dynamic) analysis of the superstructure and, very often, seismic isolation and passive and/or active dampening (Kelly, 1997, Soong and Dargush, 1997; Wada et al., 2000). The essence of the concept of seismic (or base) isolation is that uncoupling the superstructure by some type of support would allow the building to slide in the event of an earthquake. The

isolation system may be a system of elastomeric bearings (usually natural rubber) or sliders. The low horizontal stiffness of the seismic base isolation reduces the superstructure's fundamental frequency below its fixed base frequency and the predominant frequency of the ground. Most often, multi-layered laminated rubber bearings with steel reinforcing layers are used for seismic isolation. It is also possible to combine sliders with elastomeric bearings. Excessive displacement of the structure may be controlled by active damping counteracting the forces during the earthquake.

The seismic design is different for tall buildings and for light wide-span structures. Rubber-metal laminated bearings as seismic isolation proved to be a good solution for tall buildings and, therefore, find increasing application for such structures. Space structures do in general perform outstandingly when subject to severe earthquakes (Moghaddam, 2000). Translational pendulum and paddle isolators provide a better protection for wide-span structures (Tatemichi and Kawaguchi, 2000). However, they are difficult to apply for lightweight structures.

Structural dynamics is applied also when designing buildings and structures to withstand strong winds (Simiu and Scanlan, 1996).

Seismic design, especially of important, tall or wide-span structures, requires specialized knowledge and experience, which means that the architect's and the structural engineer's skill and work should be combined.

5.5 Heat, Moisture and Air Quality Affecting Architectural Design

In a limited way architects have always been confronted with the need to solve problems of physics such as (not counting statics and dynamics of structures): natural light and shading, acoustics in theatres, heat and moisture in public baths, etc. The complexity and sophistication of such problems have grown enormously in our time. Together with this, it was recognized that the expression 'building physics' does not cover all problems related to human comfort, internal and external ambience and behaviour of structures and buildings. The new term 'environmental design' has been coined covering also, chemical and biological problems (corrosion, fire, mould, etc.) but building physics (heat, moisture, sound, light) remains an important component of knowledge (Thomas, 1996).

The traditional way of designing and constructing buildings took care in some empirical way of heat, moisture and air quality problems. However, human comfort conditions have not been altogether favourable. At the present time, despite stricter requirements the heat and moisture conditions of buildings have often deteriorated. Even with increased heat insulation, mould, surface and interstitial condensation appeared and only following widespread damage and extensive research have we arrived at the position where we have the capability to develop adequate means to ensure appropriate heat, moisture and air quality conditions. Architects must be aware of the measures that need to be taken to ensure adequate internal ambience. In particular, multi-layer external envelopes of buildings give rise to concern. In these, heat and moisture find their way through the structure from the inside to the outside. The temperature sinks from the inside towards the outside. The lower-temperature air can retain a smaller quantity of vapour than the warmer inside air. Where the vapour pressure reaches the dew point, i.e. the saturation level, condensation occurs. An obvious requirement is that the resistance to vapour penetration should be greater at the inside part of the structure where the temperature is relatively higher. A more refined analysis not only investigates static temperature and moisture conditions but examines whether a relatively limited amount of condensed vapour lacks the possibility of evaporating during drier and warmer periods.

Serious defects of the innovative façades assembled from large-size prefabricated reinforced concrete panels became evident. Driving rain penetrated through the joints between the panels and so a new detailing was developed. Instead of trying to stop the driving rain at the outside of the envelope, a 'decompression space' was inserted behind the wind barrier. The water barrier was placed behind the wind barrier and the decompression space. The horizontal joint received a threshold to

prevent the wind attempting to force the water through the joint. The new solution became generally applied and proved to be successful. Another example of a new technical solution, this time to prevent surface or interstitial condensation, was

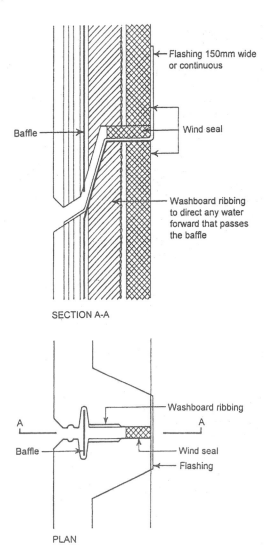

SECTION A-A

PLAN

Figure 5.4 The standard new solution of a façade joint between large-size pre-cast concrete panels. Decompression space in the vertical joint reduces the pressure of the driving rain; a threshold in the horizontal joint has a similar influence on upwards-oriented driving rain. © Sebestyen: *Construction: Craft to Industry*, E & FN Spon.

the inverted low-pitched roof in which the heat insulation (polystyrene with closed cells) was placed above (and not, as was usually the case, below) the water insulation. The general practice for multi-layer structures (walls, ceiling or roof) is to place a vapour-resistant layer on the inside and the heat insulation more on the outside. Technologically, however, this may cause problems, which in common with other factors may finally determine the order of layers (Bojic et al., 2001).

Heat and moisture transfer has been elucidated already in the course of the first half of the twentieth century but with some major limitations, assuming stable conditions and simple geometric parameters. The second half of the twentieth century saw an expansion in analysis of dynamic conditions and complex geometric parameters. In order to deal with these, new models and advances in mathematics and computation capacities were needed.

The finite elements method, the boundary conditions analysis and the use of computers enabled progress in analysis as much in structural theory and analysis as in branches of building physics: heat and moisture analysis, airflow, sound and light.

The heat flows through the external envelope not in parallel straight lines but is more intensive where there are thermal bridges, i.e. places with reduced heat insulation (window frames, reinforced concrete or steel girders). This increases the total amount of heat (or energy) losses. The actual flow can now be analysed thanks to progress in mathematics and computing. The architect must be aware of such problems in order to avoid subsequent damage.

5.6 Technical Systems of Buildings: 'System Building'

The development of technical systems goes back a very long way in construction. Systems were developed for timber houses, steel members and others. In modern times, the industrialization of building induced designers to create systems. Jean Prouvé, Buckminster Fuller, and others attempted

this during the first half of the twentieth century but in general met with only limited success. The failures meant that the expression 'system building' was brought almost totally into disrepute. During the third quarter of the twentieth century another step towards industrialization and systems yielded more durable results but they were still only on a restricted scale. The various attempts comprised:

- school building systems: in the UK CLASP, SCOLA and others; in the USA the Californian school building systems
- industrial hall and agricultural building systems initiated by steel and steel structure manufacturers and constructors (Butler, etc.) but also by the concrete prefabrication industry
- industrialized housing systems including the reinforced concrete large-panel systems: Larsen-Nielsen, Camus, Coignet, the systems in the Eastern European countries
- systems of building components: windows, doors, ceilings, floors, partitions
- systems of services: HVAC, elevators, bathroom units, etc.

As an example let us have a glance at the systems of the Butler Manufacturing Company:

- Widespan structural system: single-storey buildings with steel frame, straight or tapered columns, several alternatives for the frame, cladding and roof
- Landmark 2000 structural system: single-storey steel frame, open web truss purlins, single or double slope and offset ridge roof, straight or tapered columns
- Multi-storey structural system: steel frame for low-rise buildings
- Hardwall structural system: a combination of masonry or concrete walls and steel structure
- Self-storage building system
- Re-roof system: for repairs
- MR-24 roof system: steel panels joined with a double-lock standing seam and fastened to the purlins with clip formed into the seam
- CMR-24 roof system: as MR-24 but with a layer of rigid heat insulation
- YSR roof system: a standing-seam roof system for high-level appearance of buildings

- Butlerib II roof system: for wide-span structural system buildings
- Butler wall or fascia systems: for cladding of buildings.

The selected list of technical systems is only an example. Many others exist, and the decision on which one to accept depends on many circumstances.

The most devastating critics of systems remark that most of the systems for complete buildings ended up with an unattractive architectural appearance, often low-quality housing slums, and in addition brought with them no real economic advantages. System thinking, however, retains advantages, which should not necessarily be downgraded by the deficiencies in the systems themselves. In particular it is worth considering systems of individual services (heating, elevators, fire control, etc.) and structures (partitions, ceilings), which have been discussed in previous chapters.

Many recent buildings, however, have been designed with integrated systems of services and such buildings are sometimes referred to as 'high-tech' buildings. Let us take one building as a model. The building selected is the RWE Headquarters, Essen, Germany, 1996 (architects: Ingenhoven, Overdiek, Kahlen and Partner). The company itself is engaged in energy-conservation strategies and this is reflected in its headquarters building. The building comprises 30 storeys and is 163 metres high. Internal environmental conditions are managed by Building Management Systems (BMS). In every room there is a single control panel through which light, temperature and sun protection can be controlled. The building is encased in a double glass skin with the external skin being made from strengthened safety glass. The material used as inner glazing is heat-insulated Climaplus white glass. The 50 centimetre void between the two glass layers functions as a thermal buffer. Electronically controlled aluminium lamellae provide protection from the sun. Air baffle plates control the inflow and outflow of air in the glass corridor. The concrete floors contribute to heat storage thereby reducing energy consumption. Some of the building's energy is generated by photovoltaic panels incorporated into roof-level loggia elements (Jones, 1998).

This brief account of just one building's integrated service system is evidence of the growing importance of the design of service systems within the overall architectural design of buildings.

5.7 Computers and Robots in Architecture and Management

Complexity characterizes architecture and construction. This is an inevitable result of the diversity of their products but it also stems from the complications inherent in the commissioning of different designers, manufacturers and contractors. Complexity is defined in different ways by various authors (Jencks, 1997).

Following the Second World War the computer gradually penetrated all the traditional fields of architecture, construction and management of buildings. Moreover, it created new activities and enabled architects, structural and other designers and managers in the building industry and facility management to carry out new types of activities (Sanders, 1996, Howard, 1998). For architects the use of computers initially meant no more than assistance in their work. Over the recent past this has been extended to providing new design potentials. One new field worthy of mention is structural shape-finding of long-span structures, such as for bridge tensile structures, shells and others. Programs been either of an architectural character o bined with structural analysis and other tasks (structural and architectural morpho

Architectural and engineering designers aware of the many codes, standards an ulations affecting their work. In ord them, special search programs have b out.

Computer-assisted architectural desi ,n may be open-ended or system-oriented. In open-ended design, programs have to be applied that enable the architect to create any possible form. In system-related CAD, the program is restricted to forms and structures that have been designed earlier, enabling the architect at a later stage to design individual buildings that fit into the overall structure of the system. Understandably, present-day systems, for example, school and hospital building systems, contain computer-assisted design systems. For hospitals a complex CAD system was worked out at the Architectural Faculty of Leuven University, Belgium. Another hospital designing system, the GADES system, is described by Bentley (1999).

Computers provide the new possibility of design through creation of Virtual Reality (VR) (Bertol and Foell, 1997). Virtual Reality is the computer-generated representation, visualization and simulation, in which the architect or other players can participate in real time interaction.

'Animation' is yet another new method for visualizing and representing architectural work. To animate means to impart life and vitality to something. For this purpose cinematographic technologies are applied (More, 2001). A common application is for the purpose of so-called 'walk-throughs' within a building or in the city. A notable example is the Walk Thru Project, which is executed by a team of computer scientists at the University of North Carolina (*National Science Foundation News*, 2001). This helps architects and engineers to create extremely detailed virtual structures that designers can 'walk through' and thereby eliminate potential problems before any work starts. The project is developing new algorithms and software for advanced prototyping with the aim of producing safer and more cost-efficient buildings and spaces.

One author, Tim Cornick gave the following answer to the rhetorical question that he had himself posed:

> *The architect working at his or her CAD station and electronically linked to other co-designers (which now include the client and construction manager) generates alternative building forms and material concepts. Immediate access to cost, time and performance standard data, as well as regulations and standards, gives immediate feedback on how targets are met. The total project process is now under control without architectural creativity and innovation being impaired. (Cornick, 1996: p.123)*

Predicting the future has always been a risky business but in this case, undoubtedly, the future has been correctly assessed. Small practices may still be able to stay in business without the use of computers but the trend is towards a general acceptance of a certain role for computers and, for large practices, computer-assisted design has become a natural part of the work. For architects, the use of computers is, and increasingly will be, a normal part of life and an important impact of modern technology on architectural design.

Computers are increasingly finding application in urban life. Information technologies are applied in city urban management such as urban transport, municipal services and public and private residential management. Information networks are provided for telework and other telecommunications services, including services for the aged and handicapped, anti-burglary, fire protection and defects announcement services (OECD, 1992). Some of these networks are integrated in homes ('smart' or 'intelligent homes'), others are serving institutions only and some have an interface, for example, between individual users and housing organizations. There is no need to prove that this development affects the design of buildings. .

Research is in progress for the use of new glass fibres that would help to establish an all-optical regional or metropolitan-area network.

One of the fields in computer research is the modelling of architectural and engineering activities by adaptation of neural networks. Artificial neural networks (ANN) have the ability to learn from experience and examples to adapt to changing situations and to be used where input data is fuzzy, discontinuous or incomplete (Rafiq et al., 2001). ANNs are computing systems made up of a number of simple, highly interconnected processing elements that process information by their dynamic state response to external inputs (Rafiq et al., 2001). Several applications have been published (El-Kassas et al., 2001). Neural networks and other computing innovations affect architectural and engineering design.

5.8 Architecture and Industrialization of Construction

Various parts of this book demonstrate the enormous influence of construction's technical progress on architecture. This technical progress is often described as the industrialization of construction, which encompasses, in addition to the already discussed introduction of new building materials, structures, services and the use of computers and new knowledge, the mechanization, prefabrication and automation of construction (Bock, 2001). Automation is also referred to as the appearance of robots (i.e. robotization) in construction.

Warszawski defines the industrialization process 'as an investment in equipment, facilities, and technology with the purpose of increasing output, saving manual labour, and improving quality' (Warszawski, 1999). Whilst we would agree with the components listed, the application of up-to-date knowledge about achievements of science and research may be added. This might also complete the features listed by Warszawski as being prerequisites to successful industrialization:

- Centralization of Production
- Mass Production
- Standardization
- Specialization
- Good Organization
- Integration (Warszawski, 1999).

One should not forget that in the subtitle Warszawski defines his book as being a managerial approach. This book, on the other hand, discusses even industrialization from the point of view of architecture and, as far as possible, the entire building process .

Mechanization is to a limited extent a concern of the architect. Provided it strives towards a more efficient execution of the ideas of the architect, it causes no problem. However, it may interfere with the design process, require a change to the architectural concept and the details due to some kind of restriction of the machines. Prefabrication also affects the design, and particularly so when the prefabricated parts are not concealed but visible on the surface. The distances between emphasized joints on the surface form a different scale from that of joints between bricks or other building blocks destined for manual handling. The properties of joints are also different. The great distances between them cause deformations due to shrinkage or other causes and the design has to foresee

these. Architects have to learn to design with prefabricated components. While this situation confronts them with new problems, it also furnishes them with new design potentials.

Industrialization enhances the possibilities for creative design but it also imposes restrictions. It is the responsibility of the architect and the engineer to reconcile seemingly contradictory requirements. This has been solved by most architects and engineers through amicable professional cooperation and by reaching mutually acceptable designs.

The use of robots is also not without its difficulties. These arise to only a slight extent with single-task robots (concrete finishing robots, spray-painting robots, inspection robots, material-handling robots, etc.) but extensively when it comes to automated construction methods. It is primarily in Japan where such systems have been developed and where a number of individual buildings were constructed by these methods. Without going into detailed discussion, we list the companies and their 'automated' systems below (Cousineau and Miura, 1998):

Takenaka	Push-Up
Shimizu	SMART
Obayashi	ABCS
Taisei	T-Up
Maeda	MCCS
Fujita	Akatsuki 21
Kajima	AMURAD

Several automated and robotized production methods were devised for family homes, such as Sekisui and others (Kashino, 1992).

While it is obvious that robotized construction of buildings will only claim a relatively small share of total construction, at least in the foreseeable future, it is certainly a field that also calls for attention on the part of architects.

5.9 Management Strategies

Architecture (and construction itself) has become an important branch of human activities. In our time a great variety of architectural practices function, some quite large. Not surprisingly, certain studies and publications devote their attention to architectural firms and their management (Lods, 1976, and Gauch and Tercier, 1980). One publication describes the activities of almost 40 important architectural practices (Zabalbeascoa, 2001).

Management is an umbrella term for widely different types of activity such as:

- management of design: architectural, structural, interior, engineering, urban
- management of construction including activities of clients, designers, builders, contractors and subcontractors
- management of the use of buildings, facility management
- management of economic and financial affairs in architecture and building feasibility studies, quantity surveying, cost control
- management of information matters: data storage, communications, computer applications.

Management forms and methods have changed together with technological progress. The architect's position in management affairs depends on the size and type of the architectural practice and on the way in which the various activities are contracted, i.e. the procurement methods. Whereas in traditional procurement the architect receives his contract from the client to whom he is responsible, in new procurement methods his position may be different. The main new procurement systems are:

- Design and Build (or Design and Construct)
- Turnkey Method (or Package Deal)
- Build – Operate – Transfer (BOT)
- Management Construction (in management construction a contractor is appointed at the pre-construction stage and is paid a fee to manage and deliver the project)
- Construction Management (construction management is a particular form of project management; the construction manager acts as the client's agent, issuing contracts for a fee)
- Project Management
- Relational Contracting, Partnering.

According to their function in the design process, firms can have different orientations. In the USA design firms may be classified as engineer-constructors, engineer-architects, architect-engineers and architects. Builders, contractors, developers and other firms may also assume a design function.

In each of the procurement and design methods, the architect may be able to identify for himself a professionally acceptable position, but in general preference should be given to those forms that guarantee in practice a sufficient degree of integrity for the architect. In all forms the architect bears a high degree of professional responsibility, which may be regulated in different ways and in each form its scope should be clear and unambiguous. Splitting the architectural responsibility between the client, the contractor and its subcontractors and the architect, may put the very quality of the architect's work at risk.

Architects have always had to manage their own affairs. In modern times this obligation has altered less for small but more for large architectural practices (Kaderlan, 1991). The tasks have been expanded for major design practices, which may have a staff of a hundred or more (in some cases over a thousand) persons (Harrigan and Neel, 1996). The architect must himself or herself be prepared to assume management tasks or liaise in some way with a manager. Some large architectural practices have become more sophisticated by taking on a number of additional tasks.

Large practices may take the legal form of partnership. Partners in an architectural practice may be responsible for a certain area in which each partner bears the responsibility for a number of projects, eventually with the owner of the partnership or a senior partner overseeing all work. In large practices there may also be a professional specialization, with partners or sections specialized in certain disciplines, for example, structural engineering, services, heat insulation, acoustics, or others. Architectural practice may be combined with engineering design and/or contracting activity. Globalization results in establishing regional offices, sometimes in partnership with local practices.

Some architectural practices also accept project management commissions (Tavares, 1999). Project management would not in general be considered as a responsibility of an architect but frequently it does become one and indeed there are architects who specialize in project management. Anthony Walker writes that this involves:

> The planning, co-ordination and control of a project from conception to completion (including commissioning) on behalf of a client, requiring the identification of the client's objectives in terms of utility, function, quality, time and cost, and the establishment of relationships between resources, integrating, monitoring and controlling the contributors to the project and their output, and evaluating and selecting alternatives in pursuit of the client's satisfaction with the project outcome. (Walker, 1984: 124)

The burgeoning but already well-established discipline of facility management includes system development for various types of buildings and therefore provides basic information to the architect within the design process. Offices may be cited as an example: earlier a new idea was to have a large office space, but more recently the concept of interlinked workgroup spaces (such as Hertzberger's Centraal Beheer in Apeldoorn and the NMB Bank Building in Amsterdam, both in The Netherlands) has gained favour (Boyd, 1994).

Several authors have attempted to predict the future forms of building design and construction procurement. These prophesies endeavour to define the role of modern information technologies, networking, partnering, up-to-date technologies and other factors. Whilst these predictions do describe evolving methods and procurement forms, it is easy to realize that any possible future form will not be without its antecedents. In the past also relations of client, architect, contractor and others took various forms although they lacked the experience of current and future technologies.

The core of purely architectural design work may at first sight seem unchanged, but the new stock of knowledge and management requirements certainly affects various aspects of the work of architects. Architects have always the dual task of producing optimal designs for their clients and others and, on the other side, functioning in an optimal way for their own firm. This dual task may even be considered as constituting a dilemma, which, however, must be solved in a complex way (Spector, 2001).

Bibliography

Bentley, Peter (1999) *Evolutionary Design by Computers*, Morgan Kaufmann Publishers

Bertol, Daniela and Foell, David (1997) *Designing Digital Space: An Architect's Guide to Virtual Reality*, John Wiley & Sons, Inc.

Bickerdike Allen Partners (1996) *Design Principles of Fire Safety*, HMSO

Bock, Thomas (2001) Potenziale Erkennen, *Deutsche Bauzeitschrift (DBZ)*, special issue: Elementiertes Bauen, No. 5, pp. 36–9

Bojic, M., Yik, F. and Sat, P. (2001) Influence of Thermal Insulation Position in Building Envelope on the Space Cooling of High-Rise Residential Buildings in Hong Kong, *Energy and Buildings*, Vol. 33, No. 6, pp. 569–81

Boyd, D. (Ed.) (1994) *Intelligent Buildings*, Alfred Waller in association with UNICOM

Browning, JoAnn (2001) Proportioning of Earthquake Resistant R.C. Building Structures, *Journal of Structural Engineering*, Vol. 127, No. 2, February, pp. 145–51

Buchholdt, H. (1997) *Structural Dynamics for Engineers*, Thomas Telford

CEB, Comité Euro-International du Béton (1998) *Seismic Design of Reinforced Concrete Structures for Controlled Inelastic Response*, Thomas Telford

Contemporary Processes in Architecture (2000) *Architectural Design*, special issue, Vol. 70. No. 3, June

Cornick, Tim (1996) *Computer Integrated Building Design*, E & FN Spon

Cousineau, Leslie and Miura, Nobuyasu (1998) *Construction Robots: The Search for New Building Technology in Japan*, American Society of Civil Engineers Press

Denès, Michel (1996) *Le Fantome des Beaux-Arts: L'enseignement de l'architecture depuis 1968*, Les Editions de la Villette

Dunster, David (2001) Some Thoughts on Fame and the Institution of Architecture, *Architectural Design*, special issue: Fame + Architecture, Vol. 71, No. 6, November, pp. 6–11

Dynamic Analysis and Earthquake Resistant Design, Volume I (1997)

Edwards, Brian (1997) *The Modern Station: New Approaches to Railway Architecture*, E & FN Spon

El-Kassas, E.M.A. et al. (2001) Using Neural Networks in Cold-Formed Steel Design, *Computers and Structures*, Vol. 79, No. 18, July, pp. 1687–96

Gauch, Peter and Tercier, Pierre (Eds) (1980) *Das Architekten-Recht, Le droit de l'architecte*, Universitätsverlag Freiburg, Schweiz

Harrigan, John E. and Neel, Paul R. (1996) *The Executive Architect: Transforming Designers into Leaders*, John Wiley & Sons, Inc.

Harris, Jonathan (2001) Fame and Fortunes in Architectural Pedagogy, *Architectural Design*, special issue: Fame + Architecture, Vol. 71, No. 6, November, pp. 71–4

Howard, Rob (1998) *Computing in Construction: Pioneers and the Future*, Butterworth-Heinemann

Huybers, P. and van der Ende, C. (1994) *Prisms and Anti-Prisms*, IASS

Jeary, Alan (1997) *Designer's Guide to the Dynamic Response of Structures*, E & FN Spon

Jencks, Charles (1997) Nonlinear architecture: New Science = New Architecture?, *Architectural Design*, Vol. 67, No. 9–10, September–October, pp. 7–9

Jencks, Charles (2001) Fame versus Celebrity, *Architectural Design*, special issue: Fame + Architecture, Vol. 71, No. 6, November, pp. 12–17

Jodidio, Philip (1998) *Contemporary American Architects*, Volume IV, Taschen

Jones, David Lloyd (1998) *Architect and the Environment: Bioclimatic Building Design*, Laurence King

Jones, Robert A. (2001) Design, Communication and Aesthetic Control: Architects, Planners, and Design Review, *Journal of Architectural and Planning Research*, Vol. 18, No 1, spring, pp. 23–38

Kaderlan, Norman (1991) *Designing Your Practice: A Principal's Guide to Creating and Managing a Design Practice*, McGraw-Hill, Inc.

Kashino, N. (1992) Housing and Advanced Technology: Towards a Total Housing System, In: W.A. Allen, et al., (Eds) *A Global Strategy for Housing in the Third Millennium*, E & FN Spon

Kelly, James M. (1997) *Earthquake-Resistant Design with Rubber*, 2nd edn, Springer

Lods, Marcel (1976) *Le métier d'architecte*, Editions France-Empire

Macdonald, Angus (2000) *The Engineer's Contribution to Contemporary Architecture: Anthony Hunt*, Thomas Telford & RIBA

Moghaddam, Hassan A. (2000) Seismic Behaviour of Space Structures, *International Journal of Space Structures*, Vol. 15, No. 2, pp. 119–35

More, Gregory (2001) Animated Techniques: Time and Technological Acquiescence of Animation, *Architectural Design*, special issue: Architecture + Animation, Vol. 71, No. 2, April

National Science Foundation News, 22 May 2001, NSF PR 01–46

Nooshin, H., Disney, P. and Yamamoto, C. (1993) *Formian, Brentwood, Eng.*, Multi-Science Publishing Co.

OECD (1992) *Cities and Technologies*, OECD

Penelis, George G. and Kappos, Andreas J. (1997) *Earthquake-Resistant Concrete Structures*, E & FN Spon

Rafiq, M.Y. et al. (2001) Neural Network Design for Engineering Applications, *Computers and Structures*, Vol. 79, No. 17, July, pp. 1541–52

Rice, Peter (1993) *An Engineer Imagines*, Ellipsis

Robbin, T. (1996) *Engineering a New Architecture*, Yale University Press

Sanders, Ken (1996) *The Digital Architect: A Common-Sense Guide to Using Computer Technology in Design Practice*, John Wiley & Sons, Inc.

Sebestyen, G. (1998) *Construction: Craft to Industry*, E & FN Spon

Simiu, Emil and Scanlan, Robert H. (1996) *Wind Effects on Structures: Fundamentals and Applications to Design*, John Wiley and Sons, Inc.

Soong T.T. and Dargush G.F. (1997) *Passive Dissipation Systems in Structural Engineering*, John Wiley and Sons

Spector, Tom (2001) *The Ethical Architect: The Dilemma of Contemporary Practice*, Princeton Architectural Press

Tatemichi, Ikuo and Kawaguchi, Mamoru (2000) A New Approach to Seismic Isolation: Possible Application in Space Structures, *International Journal of Space Structures*, Vol. 15, No. 2

Tavares, L. Valadares (1999) *Advanced Models for Project Management*, Kluwer Academic Publishers

Thomas, Randall (Ed.) (1996) *Environmental Design*, E & FN Spon

Wada, Akira, Huang, Yi-Hua and Iwata, Mamoru (2000) Passive Damping Technology for Buildings in Japan, *Progress in Structural Engineering and Materials*, Vol. 2, No. 3, July–September, pp. 335–50

Walker, Anthony (1984) *Project Management in Construction*, Blackwell Science

Warszawski, Abraham (1999) *Industrialised and Automated Building Systems: A Managerial Approach*, E & FN Spon

Zabalbeascoa, Anatxu (2001) *Les architectes et leur atelier*, Editions du Seuil Gustavo Gili (Spanish:1996,)

6

The interrelationship of architecture, economy, environment and sustainability

6.1 Urban Development

One must turn the pages of ancient history to find out just when construction activities first exercised a pivotal role in influencing human society. They shaped human settlements, villages and cities, residential, industrial, commercial, leisure and cultural buildings and architecture played an active role throughout.

The first groups of buildings for human social life appeared at the least some 5000–10 000 years ago and some towns in the Middle East date back 5000

years. Most of the population continued to live for a long time in rural communities but some of the great cities that we know today (Xian in China and Rome) had already developed into major conurbations one to two thousand years ago. For a long period the population growth was slow but then it accelerated. As industrialization proceeded some towns grew to large mega-cities: London, Paris, New York, Chicago, Tokyo, Los Angeles, others became large or medium-sized cities: Manchester, Lyon, Marseille, Frankfurt/Main, Miami, Madrid. Urbanization spread from the industrialized to the

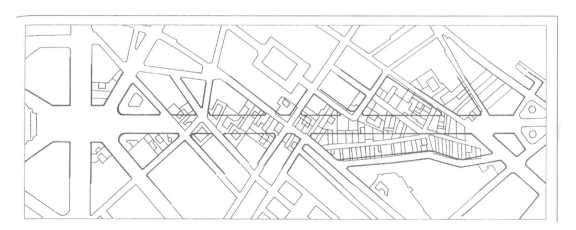

Figure 6.1 Avenue de l'Opéra, Paris, cut through the Paris street structure, according to the city plan by Georges Eugène Haussmann. Radical transformation of medieval Paris street structure into one of a modern metropolis.

developing countries with the result that Mexico City, São Paulo, Cairo, Bombay, Calcutta, Buenos Aires, Seoul, Shanghai, Singapore, Bangkok, Jakarta, qualified for inclusion in the category of the largest cities of the world. Indeed, most of the large towns are already now located in developing countries and this shift towards mega-cities in developing countries is inexorable.

Their success, their equally obvious degradation problems and finally their future have been the focus of much attention (Geddes, 1997, Duffy, 1995). New concepts were worked out, for example, the garden cities and the self-sustained satellite towns but as time went on it became evident that their capacity to alleviate the problems of urban growth and large cities was limited (UN ECE, 1996).

Global population growth has pushed ahead only during the last 200–300 years. Urban population in some industrialized countries reached more than half of the total and even touched 75–90 per cent in some. The spontaneous growth of urban settlements has been gradually replaced by conscious urban planning, which liaised with the profession of architecture. In our time architects contribute in a massive way to the renewal and development of cities.

The growth of cities was primarily caused by population growth but also by development of certain functions (administrative, touristic, cultural, commercial, industrial) of individual settlements. Political power, geographical location, commercial importance and other factors exercised differing degrees of importance for settlements. As a result cities came into existence, partly with similar, partly with different characteristics within the regions of the world.

Investment in buildings and infrastructure, their maintenance and renewal, necessitated an active input on the part of architecture and construction. In our time new functions and moving forces have joined the old ones. Industrialization was one of the great causes of urban development. The demographic explosion was another. The appearance of nation states and their administration contributed to the establishment of administrative (government and municipal) centres. More affluence, higher pro-

ductivity, education, culture, more free time for leisure were all factors that stimulated the construction of buildings serving the demand for new forms of buildings. Cities with specialized functions – harbour and transport hub cities and tourist settlements – were built. The shift from earlier economic sectors, such as mining and heavy manufacturing, towards light industries, such as information technologies and biogenetics, led to new types of clusters: technopoles and science parks. Services, including health care and telecommunications and media services, all oriented the development of cities and the structure of the built environment in new directions (Hall and Hay, 1980).

The new functions called for new technical and architectural characteristics, such as super-clean air and controlled internal ambience. Technopoles and science parks are typical for such new characteristics. Following the first ones in Silicon Valley in California and Sophia Antipolis in France, very many more were established in numerous countries (Bailly et al., 1999, Quéré, 1998, Scott, 1998, Lacour and Puissant, 1999, Horvath, 2000, Dunford and Kafkalas, 1992). Technopoles and science parks attract smaller businesses ambitious in high-tech fields, various forms of structural fragmentation of larger firms, organizations availing themselves of the facility to outsource activities to larger firms. Science parks through the firms investing in them have operational links with university and research centres.

In many countries concerns about unemployment increased the desire of city administrations to attract to their territory firms offering employment. Globalization increased the size of multinationals and thus turned them into important employers. Through subsidies or the offer of other advantages, cities seek to induce multinationals to select them for new locations of their factories.

Urban life inevitably became complex and this brought with it new disciplines: urban economics and urban public policy emerged (Heilbrun, 1987).

In the late 1920s architectural functionalism or rationalism became the modern movement in European architecture and the International Style in American architecture. It was confidence in human progress that inspired Le Corbusier to visions like the Ville Radieuse and Plan Voisin, and Hilber-sheimer to his New City (Le Corbusier, 1935, Hilber-sheimer, 1944). The Athens Charter, initiated with others by Constantinos Doxiades, an international planner, was an outstanding document that set out the vision of future architecture and urban development. Eminent architects and town planners were well to the fore in the production and its paragraph 92 self-confidently proclaims that architects preside over the destiny of the city and that architecture holds the key to all within the development of human settlements. In Europe the modern movement already had a significant impact before the Second World War, but in America where individual housing units and low-density residential suburbs continued to be dominant, only during the post-war period.

The over-optimism as regards architecture's omnipotence was gradually shattered by the crisis of cities. The book by Jane Jacobs, *Death and Life of Great American Cities* (1961) had a massive influence. Whilst her proposed solutions were not always of the optimal calibre, her critical analysis compelled many to rethink the situation. Interdisciplinarity emerged, in which while architecture and city planning did not have a monopolistic function, they did nevertheless fill a relevant and significant role.

A new wave of thinking was ushered in with the environmental movement. It also brought a reassessment of history, which modernism rejected. Whereas the modernists were inclined to discard the architectural heritage, the recognition of the continuity in urban development paved the way for contemporary new architecture and urban conservation and rehabilitation.

Adaptation of old buildings to new functions, for example, the transformation of the old railway station of La Gare d'Orsay into a museum, the modernization of old warehouses at the London Docklands, Hamburg, Marseille (Villes portuaires, 2001), combinations of old and new, as in Nîmes at the Maison Carré, by Foster (Plate 25) or the Lyon Opera, by Jean Nouvel, were great successes. For new constructions, size ('megastructures') was thought to be the new magic panacea. Kenzo Tange was one of the pioneers, others followed including Rem Koolhaas, John Portman and Cesar

Pelli. Not that megastructuralism is the solution for all ailments of cities; it is one possible approach but in its proper place.

Architecture is moving towards balanced and enhanced approaches where design can avail itself of different and tried solutions but it has always to evaluate what is best suited to actual circumstances. It also has to adapt itself to the ups and downs of economic conditions. During the past decades architects and clients were sometimes faced with relatively abundant funds for construction; at other times they had to operate under severe constraints.

World cities or mega-cities are characterized by certain indices, such as population, number of vehicles, headquarters of international organizations and multinationals, international air and other transport connections, good urban transport, research and higher education institutes, major cultural, leisure and health care establishments, high-tech networks of telecommunication, information technology, media services and sophisticated infrastructure for services. The quality of life in mega-cities is increasingly coming under scrutiny: green areas, parks, security, air and water quality (Knox and Taylor, 1995, Timberlake, 1985). It would be quite unrealistic, however, to confine attention to mega-cities given that the urban system is made up of large, medium-sized and smaller cities. In addition, dispersed small communities merit attention also. The quality of life in all types of human settlements may and frequently does go into decline. Urban pollution is increasing; dirtiness, lack of greenery and of health care institutions, noise, waste and the absence of cultural, education and leisure facilities contribute to this deterioration. There is a demand for improvement in all types of communities. Social conditions also must be tackled: the elimination of slums and squatter settlements should be the objective, and that part of the building stock that is in bad condition should be repaired. Urban transport that is in poor condition should be modernized. The recognized deficiencies led in many cities to massive renewal programmes getting under way.

Architecture is considered as a profession responsible for the design of buildings. One cannot forget, however, that buildings do not stand separated from their environment and it is the responsibility of architects to take care of everything related to their buildings: open spaces around and between the buildings, together with vegetation, external structures and the interior equipment of the buildings. All this is part of human perception and architects must be concerned as to how people perceive their internal and external ambience, and indeed with environmental human psychology. This has led to the birth of a new field: environmental psychology and perception of the environment (Rapoport, 1977 and 1986, Duncan and Ley, 1993). Methods of becoming acquainted with the needs and requirements of future users of buildings are more or less familiar to clients and architects. The matter is vaguer when it concerns open spaces. Architects often recognize this only when working under conditions with which they are unfamiliar: foreign countries, developing regions, specific ethnic minorities. In developing countries with hot climates open spaces are simultaneously places of work, family and social life. Technology and life-pattern changes create new uses for common or public spaces. Take, for instance, the new sports facilities: ski slopes in flat land areas, tropical baths in moderate or cold climate regions; these also serve various requirements in the context of social life. Architects, therefore, have to work out methods that will provide an insight into the requirements of the future within and outside buildings. With advances of urbanization, theoretical work on cities developed also (Heilbrun, 1987, Henderson, 1985). This included city sociology and mathematical methods to optimize complex urban problems.

In our era the impact of construction has gained in intensity and speed. The size of certain new buildings has grown together with the number of their occupants and visitors. This in turn has given rise to new social circumstances both in and between buildings including a spectacular increase in urban and long-distance travel. Architects always participated through their work in shaping the framework of human social life. However, whereas the transformation of urban and rural communities used to be a somewhat tardy process, today the rate of change has speeded up and the consequences of construction are very soon apparent (Law, 2000).

As was highlighted earlier, some cities have become active in attempting to attract important new buildings, which generate attention, income and development by their design. Attention-grabbing, famous architects (such as Niemeyer for Brasilia, Le Corbusier for Chandigarh) were eagerly sought after. This phenomenon is by no means without precedent, it has historic parallels. What is new is that it is no longer emperors, popes, or similar dignitaries who nurture the ambition to develop their capital, but rather (representatives of) cities or regions. Architects who have already proved their capability to design impressive buildings are well positioned for commissions of this kind. Other not as yet famous architects must at first provide evidence of their potentials.

All this boils down to the recognition that if an architect is to pursue a successful career he or she may need to hone up on their marketing skills. We have seen that air and rail authorities, tourism, culture, education, entertainment, public authorities, science, multinationals have all developed into powerful clients. Hence, architects must win their confidence and with it their commissions. Architects have to acquire knowledge in various branches with important building programmes and also the marketing ability necessary to become credible participants in the realization of development programmes.

The new Guggenheim Modern Art Museum in Bilbao designed by Gehry has been mentioned in this book on several occasions. Since its opening in 1997, it has become a catalyst in the renewal of the city. Other investments in Bilbao – the new Metro designed by Sir Norman Foster, the design by Santiago Calatrava of the new airport and a footbridge – all reflect the strategy of Bilbao's developers to use the attraction of spectacular new constructions designed by the world's best architects for accelerating the renewal of the city. This strategy is being applied in many other cities by urban leaders, economists and business strategists. It also stimulates architects to achieve such effect with their design.

Another strategy aimed at similar objectives is to develop a city's 'cyberspace', that is, its information infrastructure (Dodge and Kitchin, 2001, Mitchell, 1995, Wilbur, 1997). However, it would be an oversimplification to recommend to all cities simply the building of a new museum or the expansion of the city's information infrastructure. The solution appropriate for any city has to be found following specific studies. The only general conclusion can be that often innovative ideas are needed to push urban renewal to a new speed (Experiment Stadt, 2001).

Utopias for the 'ideal city' were formulated in several countries over recent centuries, for example, during the period of the Renaissance, by Filarete (the utopian town of Sforzinda) and Francesco di Giorgio Martini and, later, by Thomas More.

Utopias never materialized completely though they did have an impact on cities, still on occasion visible today (e.g. in Karlsruhe). Various plans were put into practice. 'New towns', 'satellite cities', 'urban villages' and others are some of the catchwords for the future built environment. These brought a response to some problems while raising new ones (King, 1996). The ideal solution was not and will never be found. Instead architecture, urban and regional development will have to cope with the changing conditions and ambitions. Architecture will remain a challenging discipline. Physical planning, the discipline comprising urban planning, has aspects extending beyond the scope of architecture: geography, demography, territorial statistics, urban economy, various forms of urban and inter-urban transport, municipal services (water, gas, electricity supply, telecommunications). Architects would be guilty of complacency if they believed that they could master all these adjacent or distant disciplines. Cooperation is the only solution to grasp such diverse areas of knowledge and research.

Nevertheless, even if architecture may not act alone, it does remain an important partner in urban development. Technological progress is not an enemy of architecture; rather it is an ally, enhancing the potentials of architects in contributing to the renewal of cities.

6.2 Economy

Economic considerations always had an impact on investment and building decisions. On occasions these were disregarded, with different, sometimes even ominous consequences. As there are no Pharaohs or other omnipotent clients unfettered by economic constraints, these considerations in most cases do have a restricting influence. In exceptional cases, the influence may be indirect only, for example, for prestige buildings of rich multinationals, for whom the image radiated from their luxurious buildings may have an indirect economic value. In our time, economic assessments of buildings and their design have undergone radical changes. First of all, the modelling of consequences of investment and their subsequent benefits has been elaborated. Cost versus benefit, pay-back analysis, internal return rate calculation, assessment of risk and inflation, all are now standard tools in feasibility assessment.

Whilst architecture is not governed by purely financial calculations, these do impact on the design.

Obviously, economic calculations and feasibility studies receive substantial back-up nowadays from computer programs. These comprise models of the calculations and incorporate data for the inclusion of changing parameters, such as interest rates, inflation rates, risk exposure, risk attitude and others.

Architects are frequently compelled to insist on their design in the face of economic objections. There is no general rule about when and to what extent extra costs may be justified. Architects must learn to live with economic influences and eventually to fight for the realization of their ideas and, in other cases, to accommodate the necessary adjustments or revisions. The economic modelling and computing of economics has fairly recently been obliged to accept the intrusion of new problems: protection of the environment, climate changes, energy conservation and sustainability. They may also have to cope with economic parameters of the functioning of the building, which certainly requires an input from the client or its representative.

In addition to full-scale economic calculations, there exist a number of indicators or indices that are easy to calculate and which provide a quick reflection on certain economic aspects of designs. Several of these have been mentioned in Chapter 3, when discussing housing, schools, hospitals and

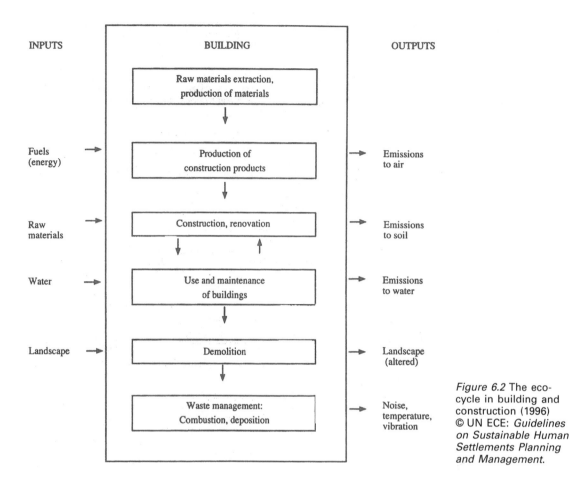

INPUTS | BUILDING | OUTPUTS

Raw materials extraction, production of materials

Fuels (energy) → Production of construction products → Emissions to air

Raw materials → Construction, renovation → Emissions to soil

Water → Use and maintenance of buildings → Emissions to water

Landscape → Demolition → Landscape (altered)

Waste management: Combustion, deposition → Noise, temperature, vibration

Figure 6.2 The eco-cycle in building and construction (1996) © UN ECE: *Guidelines on Sustainable Human Settlements Planning and Management.*

offices. Some of them are purely technical and objective, such as the number of flats on one level of a staircase, floor space per hospital bed, relation of office space to property land surface. Others have a cost factor, for example cost of residential building per square metre of useful floor space, cost of building per hospital patient, or per office worker or student. Finally, there exist macroeconomic indicators, for example the number of dwellings in the housing stock per 1000 head of population. Architects working on the design of a certain building should be acquainted with such indices or indicators and use them when presenting or revising their design.

6.3 Environment

The population density and the total population have grown enormously. An increasing part of the population is now living in concentrated settlements. More and more of the earth's surface is taken up by buildings and public works, roads, railways and public services, and much of it including the soil, air and water has become polluted (contaminated). The natural environment is shrinking as are forests and the areas of agricultural and cultivated land. Human life and activities affect our environment: vegetation, animals, biodiversity, climate, soil, water, geomorphology, atmosphere

(Goudie, 1993, Takeuchi and Yoshino, 1991). It is important that we understand the present conditions, the factors affecting and changing the environment and finally that we formulate strategies to influence these changes in a desirable orientation.

When modelling environmental conditions, pressures on the environment (e.g. economic growth and population change), the state of the environment (e.g. pollution concentrations) and the response of society (government policies, etc.) must be appropriately reflected. This is by no means an easy task when we consider, for example, the quantification of health costs caused by environmental damage. There is some progress on establishing resource, pollutant and other environmental accounts ('green national accounts'). The result of determining indicators of environmental changes (e.g. of the depletion of natural resources) may serve as a basis to introduce the information into economic indicators (GNP per capita or others) and thereby to obtain a picture about the changes in the environment.

Architects must and in fact do design buildings with suitable ideas as to how their building will fit into the environment. This can be done by harmonizing with the environment or by consciously creating some accentuated relationship to the environment. Some outstanding realizations exist that reflect the different faces of combining architecture and nature or the earlier built environment. Other important responsibilities of the architect are to design buildings that withstand natural forces (wind, earthquake), ensure stability and an adequate lifespan of the building, its structures and materials, and healthy and pleasant internal ambience: appropriate temperature, air quality, good light and sound conditions. It is important to halt and even reverse the deterioration of the environment and architects have to regard this as very much within their responsibility. This requirement has been identified as ensuring sustainable development.

6.4 Sustainability

The study of the global and local environment and the recognition of its degradation led to studies on sustainability. An important early step in this direction was the study on 'the limits of growth' (Meadows et al., 1972). A great number of studies followed, ultimately consolidating a new discipline (Capello et al., 1999, Pugh, 1996). Sustainability was defined in the Brundtland Report of the World Commission on the Environment and Development in 1987 and this particular definition remains authoritative to this day. 'Sustainable development is the development that meets the needs of the present without compromising the ability of future generations to meet their own needs' and, according to Brown (Bartelmus, 1994), 'if we fail to convert our self-destroying economy into one that is environmentally sustainable, future generations will be overwhelmed by environmental degradation and social disintegration'.

Sustainability is a macroeconomic phenomenon and has only a macro-social validity. It makes no sense to economize resources within a given region if this harms the stock of resources in another. Whilst this is self-evident, its implementation is difficult. Based on various studies, the following contemporary global environmental concerns, affecting sustainability, may be listed (Haughton and Hunter, 1994):

- threatens biodiversity, desertification and deforestation
- increase of various hazardous substances
- changes in global and regional climate, greater weather instability, rises in sea levels
- rise in air, water, land and noise pollution and in transfrontier pollution
- inappropriate aid for developing countries, deprivation of indigenous people of their homes and means of living, obliterating scarce fertile agricultural land
- resource-base depletion
- overpopulation, rising and non-sustainable consumption
- harmful side effects of modern technology, including biotechnology
- uneven terms of trade, ethnic, economic, religious and cultural conflicts and, as a consequence, military conflicts.

The economy and the natural environment interact. Economic activity is based on the continued

...ability of sufficient material and energy resources and an environment that is acceptably clean and attractive. Sustainability indicators reflect the reproducibility of the way in which a given society utilizes its environment (Kuik and Verbruggen, 1991). Whilst not easy to calculate and a task rather for macroeconomic researchers, environmental and sustainability indicators may serve as an objective towards which construction and architecture must strive. A precondition for any numerical expression of environmental values and changes in the level of sustainability, is the ability to quantify 'public goods' or 'public commons' (like the atmosphere) which hitherto have usually been at our disposal free of charge. The absence of a price for a public good or a global resource leads to a waste of that good: no one is interested in saving it. Economists have proposed the introduction of a price or a tax for the use of public goods, which should serve as an incentive for their conservation (Pearce, 1995). The introduction of such taxes, levies or incentives is necessary because the normal market mechanism is insufficient to ensure the protection of global environmental values. Global-missing markets can be corrected by creating global environmental markets (Pearce, 1995). These can function because substantial economic value resides in the protection of the global environment and mutually profitable trades can emerge so as to capture economic value. Whilst the creation of such markets is still in its infancy, the first bilateral and multilateral agreements and international protocols are up and running and look promising. The international community has made some additional funds available for this purpose and has established a new international institution (the Global Environmental Facility) to put into practice a mechanism that provides incentives for the protection of global environmental commons and by that means come nearer to a sustainable world economy.

One of the measures is the trading of emission reductions. In any case, prices may become a powerful instrument in the pursuit of environmental policies needed for sustainable development (UN ECE, 1996).

The whole area of international joint implementation of the principles worked out for the protection of global commons is very much on a macroeconomic global level, and of no direct concern to individual architects. Nevertheless, the implementation will have repercussions on prices and on technological strategies. This will in the end inevitably affect the choice of building materials, structures and other factors of architectural design. The global programme will have an influence on architecture as a whole, as well as on individual projects and designs.

Population growth and increasing consumption (the so-called 'over-consumption') are factors in the depletion of some environmental assets (for instance, deforestation), but it would be quite wrong to advocate a reduction in the real income level of people. Sustainability should be achieved without recourse to such unacceptable goals. Whilst architecture and construction must proceed with these in mind, they do have their own specific concerns.

Implementation of sustainability would necessitate establishing global (or at least, regional or national) models, containing information not only about production and consumption with the usual restrictions but also about the stock of resources and their changes. Earlier global models were focussed on economic optimalization without considering sustainability. Any attempt to introduce sustainability into a global model must inevitably face the conflict between short-term economic optimization and maintaining sustainability over a prolonged period of time. Despite the difficulties, attempts have been made to quantify (absolute or partial levels of) sustainability and these provide a methodology for assessment and defining preferences (Anink et al., 1996; Woolley and Kimmins, 2000, Faucheux et al.,1996).

When assessing construction sustainability the following components have to be evaluated (Anink et al., 1996):

- prevention of unnecessary use of land and the avoidance of unnecessary construction
- restricting the brief for construction to the necessary minimum
- selection of the most efficient use of building materials
- optimal exploitation of natural resources and the

efficient use of energy in production and use of buildings, i.e. throughout the entire integrated life cycle of the building

- assurance of optimal new construction and sustainable refurbishment.

When making a selection between alternative building materials, which is part of an overall assessment of sustainability, the following basic environmental issues have to be evaluated:

- damage to ecosystems
- scarcity of resources
- emissions
- energy use
- waste
- reuse
- lifespan and repairability
- impact on the environment.

When drawing up the list of alternative materials, local materials and by-products must also come into the reckoning (Elizabeth and Adams, 2000). In this book our attention is focussed on (but not restricted to) materials entailing industrialized construction methods.

If the changes in wealth were customarily described by indices of Gross National Product (GNP) and Gross Domestic Product (GDP), we would now like to construct indicators that also reflect data having an impact on sustainability. This would enable us to measure sustainable development (Atkinson et al., 1997). For such a purpose we would need information on economic and social factors, wealth, consumption and international trade in resources, ecological indicators, investment in human capital and technological progress. Much of the information required is not at present available and when it is it is far from definitive. However, these difficulties have not thwarted work being initiated in this direction. To measure sustainable development quantifiable models must be determined, which means constructing appropriate systems. Work has been carried out on system theory and global economic and environmental models (Forrester, 1968 and 1971, Meadows et al., 1972). A more recent study has been authored by Clark, Perez-Trejo, Allen (1995). Whilst sustainability cannot be measured accurately on a micro level, i.e. related to the design of

a single building, it is necessary to do

For architects, structural engineers engaged in construction, building and indicators are to be calculated that refle. ... well as possible the impact on sustainability. Such factors are: energy consumption, water, land and other natural resources.

Sustainability requires the conservation of the world's resources – sources of energy, fossil fuels, minerals, forests, land; and safeguarding the quality of the environment – clean air, soil and water. Various aspects have been defined by special expressions, for example green architecture, energy conservation, whole-building concept, ecological design, bio-architecture, etc. Bioclimatic architectural design has been defined as 'an approach to design which is inspired by nature and which applies a sustained logic to every aspect of the project, focused on optimising and using the environment. The logic covers conditions of setting, economy, construction, building management and individual health and well-being, in addition to building physics' (Jones, 1998). A book published on architecture and the environment reviews 44 recent buildings, which in one way or another address environmental issues and nature in a cogent and imaginative manner (Jones, 1998). These buildings reflect the two long-term basic trends in architecture: the design of buildings that blend into nature and environment (one example being the Westminster Lodge, Hooke Park, Dorset, UK, architect: Edward Cullinan, 1996), and buildings based on up-to-date technologies, which intentionally are conspicuous in their environment (an example is the Menara Mesiniaga building, Selangor, Malaysia, architect: Ken Yeang, 1992). The two trends may or may not be fundamentally antagonistic; various mixtures have always existed and continue to co-exist also as products of ecological and sustainability-oriented buildings. Another publication equally demonstrates various cases in which sustainable architecture has been the leading objective (Melet, 1999). The demonstrated examples comprise glazed thermal buffers and atria (e.g. the Commerzbank Headquarters, Frankfurt, Germany), green roofs and application of plants in the building (e.g. the Technical University Library in Delft, The Netherlands), smart buildings

Figure 6.3 Hotel du Département Des Bouches-du Rhone (nicknamed 'Le Grand Bleu'), Marseille, France, 1994, architects: Alsop and Störmer. A complex building with premises for different purposes, post-modern geometry: flattened cylinder, cigar-shaped wing, contributing to city centre renewal.

(e.g. the Law Courts, Bordeaux, France), buildings as energy generators and various plans for future buildings.

Ecological architectural design encompasses appropriate design of architectural form, airtightness, optimum ventilation, selection of building materials from the category of least scarce resources ('green building materials'), energy conservation, HVAC control, good heat insulation and shading, thermal storage, replacing ozone layer-depleting heat insulation and cooling equipment by others, protection of air, soil and water purity, recycling of wastes, increased attention to maintenance and renewal of buildings (Stratton, 2000) and much more. On the level of city (public) policies, energy strategies enjoy a high priority and complete the strategies for energy conservation in buildings. Municipal energy conservation policies may support sustainability by the following policies:

conscious land-use policy, regulatory and energy policies aimed at energy conservation, financial incentives and information activities, market-based energy policies, encouraging technological innovations. Although not in itself ensuring energy sustainability, for architects and engineers the promotion of renewable energy technologies should have a high priority. In some countries (USA, Germany, Denmark, The Netherlands) wind energy has been installed on a remarkably high level but it still justifies further development elsewhere.

Photovoltaics has also progressed some way but much more will have to be achieved. The same applies to biomass, biogas, solar water heating, district heating combined with hot water supply and refuse incineration. Economic feasibility naturally is important but this has to be examined in a time-dependent way because some investments may become feasible with future fluctuations in prices. This applies at the institutional level also: in certain cases individual investments provide the optimum solution, in others integration of some energy systems is the answer. A relatively new instrument in environmental policy is marketable and tradeable emissions. These are not directly aimed at energy conservation but primarily towards a reduction of pollutants. All this means that the architect must be ready to participate in complex studies in order to determine for the architectural design the criteria for optimal energy conservation (Capello et al., 1999).

According to a book authored by Spiegel and Meadows (1999):

> Green building materials are those that use the Earth's resources in an environmentally responsible way. Green building materials respect the limitations of non-renewable resources such as coal and metal ores. They work within the pattern of nature's cycles and the interrelationships of ecosystems. Green building materials are non-toxic. They are made from recycled materials and are themselves recyclable. They are energy efficient and water efficient. They are 'green' in the way they are manufactured, the way they are used, and the way they are reclaimed after use. Green building materials are those that earn high marks for resource management, impact or indoor environmental quality (IEQ), and performance (energy efficiency, water deficiency, etc.).

The book poses the following hypothetical questions to which it thereupon seeks to respond: What are green building materials? Why use green building materials? How does the production selection process work?

Within this context it is interesting to mention an annual architectural competition that began in Japan in 1999 in which an alliance of non-profit public foundations participate. The objective is to encourage contemporary architects in Japan to give serious consideration to the idea of a 'house returnable to the earth', which has its origins in the traditional way of building Japanese houses using wood and renewable materials that could be returned to the earth. The fact that in 2000 the competition attracted 250 proposals demonstrates that the concept found a ready response among architects (*Sustainable Building*, 2001).

A deeper acceptance of environmental and sustainability aspects is justified but caution should be exercised lest it lead to utopian ideas. A vision of future architecture envisages a synthesis of biology and architecture with its ideals finding expression in charming villages and hill towns.

Communities incorporating bio-shelter technologies being self-reliant for food and energy, factories converted to solar food barns, whole villages or neighbourhoods having a single envelope roof, are envisioned but, with each one bearing a striking resemblance to the others, the utopia produced is somewhat disquieting (Todd and Todd, 1994: 115–18). Land use and urban form policies should envisage sustainability but never to the detriment of environmental quality. Even so, many cities today plan or implement identification strategies whose essence is the realization of all building activity within existing built-up areas thus achieving more effective land exploitation. Whilst overall land use policies are a responsibility of municipalities, the architect has to be conscious of these policies and as far as possible, contribute to their implementation.

The strategies for a sustainable city have been summarized among others in the following (Haughton and Hunter, 1994):

> The sustainable city is developed to respect and make the most of natural environmental aspects, to conserve resource use and to minimise impacts on the local and wider natural environment.
> The sustainable city is a regional and global city: no matter how small or how large, its responsibilities stretch beyond the city boundaries.
> The sustainable city involves a broadly based, participatory programme of radical change, where individuals are encouraged to take on more responsibility for the ways in which their cities are run.
> The sustainable city requires that environmental assets and impacts are

135

...buted more equitably than at present.

The sustainable city is a learning city, a sharing city, an internationally networked city.

The sustainable city is not rooted in an idealised version of past settlements, nor is it one given to a radical casting-off from its own particular cultural, economic and physical identity in the name of the latest passing fad for wholesale urban change.

The sustainable city will seek to conserve, enhance and promote its assets in terms of natural, built and cultural environments.

The sustainable city presents tremendous opportunities for enhancing environmental quality at local, regional and global scales.

To sum up: sustainability and protection of the environment consist of a great number of specific design and management approaches, all interlinked and together forming a total concept. Architectural design has a major function in realizing these ambitions. It naturally directs attention towards urban environmental and urban development problems and is a factor in their solution.

Finally, a word of warning. 'Green building' and 'sustainable building' are commercial labels in the sense that they have a marketing and promotion value. This is not in itself harmful so long as they express genuine characteristics of the design. However, the use of such labels is to be rejected out of hand if all that they do is to make unjustified claims. Naturally, uncertainties are still rife as to what precisely is 'green' or 'sustainable'. As far as possible, given the level of present-day knowledge such labels should always be substantiated by serious efforts to attain green and sustainable qualities.

Bibliography

Anink, David, Boonstra, Chiel and Mak, John (1996) *Handbook of Sustainable Building: An Environmental Preference Method for Selection of Materials for Use in Construction and Refurbishment*, James and James (Science Publishers)

Atkinson, Giles et al. (1997) *Measuring Sustainable Development: Macroeconomics and the Environment*, Edward Elgar

Bailly, A. and Huriot, J.-M. (Eds) (1999) *Villes et croissance: Théories, modèles, perspectives*, Anthropos/Economica

Bartelmus, Peter (1994) *Environment, Growth and Development: The Strategies of Sustainability*, Routledge

Berge, Bjorn (2000) *The Ecology of Building Materials*, Architectural Press (Norwegian edition: 1992)

Capello, Roberta, Nijkamp, Peter and Pepping, Gerard (1999) *Sustainable Cities and Energy Policies*, Springer

Clark, Norman, Perez-Trejo, Francisco and Allen, Peter (1995) *Evolutionary Dynamics and Sustainability: A Systems Approach*, Edward Elgar

Cornick, Tim (1996) *Computer Integrated Building Design*, E & FN Spon

Dodge, M. and Kitchin, R. (2001) *Mapping Cyberspace*, Routledge

Duffy, Hazel (1995) *Competitive Cities: Succeeding in the Global Economy*, E & FN Spon

Duncan, James and Ley, David (Eds) (1993) *Place/Culture/Representation*, Routledge

Dunford, Mick and Kafkalas, Grigoris (Eds) (1992) *Cities and Regions in the New Europe: The Global-Local Interplay and Spatial Development Strategies*, Belhaven Press

Elizabeth, Lynne and Adams, Cassandra (2000) *Alternative Construction: Contemporary Natural Building Methods*, John Wiley & Sons, Inc.

Experiment Stadt (2001) *Deutsche Bauzeitung (db)*, special issue, Vol. 135, No. 6

Faucheux, Sylvie, Pearce, Davis and Proops, John (1996) *Models of Sustainable Development*, Edward Elgar

Forrester, J.W. (1968) *Principles of System*, MIT Press

Forrester, J.W. (1971) *World Dynamics*, Wright-Allen Press

Frieck, Dieter (Ed.) (1986) *The Quality of Urban Life: Social, Psychological and Physical Conditions*, Walter de Gruyter

Geddes, Robert (Ed.) (1997) *Cities in Our Future: Growth and Form*, Environmental Health and Social Equity

Goudie, Andrew (1993) *The Human Impact on the Natural Environment*, 4th edn, Blackwell

Hall, Peter and Hay, Dennis (1980) *Growth Centres in the European Urban System*, Heinemann Educational Books

Haughton, Graham and Hunter, Colin (1994) *Sustainable Cities*, Regional Studies Association, Jessica Kingsley Publishers

Heilbrun, James (1987) 3rd edn, St. Martin's Press

Henderson, J. Vernon (1985) *Economic Theory and the Cities*, 2nd edn, Academic Press, Inc.

Hilbersheimer, L. (1944) *The New City: Principles of Planning*, P. Theobald

Horvath, Gyula (Ed.) (2000) *Regions and Cities in the Global World*, Centre for Regional Studies, Pecs

Jacobs, Jane (1961) *Death and Life of Great American Cities*, Vintage Books

Jones, David Lloyd (1998) *Architecture and the Environment: Bioclimatic Building Design*, Laurence King

King, Ross (1996) *Emancipating Space: Geography, Architecture and Urban Design*, The Guilford Press

Knox, Paul, L. and Taylor, Peter J. (Eds) (1995) *World Cities in a World-System*, Cambridge University Press

Kuik, Onno and Verbruggen, Harmen (Eds) (1991) *In Search of Indicators of Sustainable Development*, Kluwer Academic Publishers

Lacour, C. and Puissant, S. (Eds) (1999) *La métropolisation: Croissance, diversité, fractures*, Anthropos/Economica

Law, Christopher M. (2000) Regenerating the City Centre through Leisure and Tourism, *Built Environment*, Vol. 26, No. 2

Le Corbusier (1935) *La Ville Radieuse: Architecture d'Aujourd'hui*,

Meadows, D.H. et al. (1972) *The Limits to Growth: A Report for the Club of Rome's Project on the Predicament of Mankind*, Potomac Books

Melet, E. (Ed.) (1999) *Sustainable Architecture: Towards a Diverse Built Environment*, NAI Publishers

Mitchell, W.J. (1995) *City of Bits: Space, Place and the Infobahn*, MIT Press

Pearce, David (1995) *Capturing Global Environmental Value. Blueprint 4*, Earthscan Publications

Pugh, Cedric (Ed.) (1996) *Sustainability, the Environment and Urbanisation*, Earthscan

Quéré, M. (Ed.) (1998) *Les technopoles en Europe*, France Technopoles

Rapoport, Amos (1977) *Human Aspects of Urban Form*, Pergamon Press

Rapoport, Amos (1986) The Use and Design of Open Spaces in Urban Neighbourhoods, In: Dieter Frick (Ed.) (1986) *The Quality of Urban Life: Social, Psychological and Physical Conditions*, Walter de Gruyter

Scott, A.J.(1993) *Technopolis: High-Technology Industry and Regional Development in Southern California*, University of California Press

Scott, A.J. (1998) *Regions and the World Economy: The Coming Shape of Global Production, Competition and Political Order*, Oxford University Press

Spiegel, Ross and Meadows, Dru (1999) *Green Building Materials: A Guide to Product Selection and Specification*, John Wiley & Sons, Inc.

Stratton, Michael (2000) *Industrial Buildings Conservation and Regeneration*, E & FN Spon

Sustainable Building. Issue 02-2001, A.E. Kluwer, Amsterdam

Takeuchi, K. and Yoshino, M. (Eds) (1991) *The Global Environment*, Springer-Verlag

Timberlake, Michael (Ed.) (1985) *Urbanisation in the World-Economy*, Academic Press, Inc.

Todd, Nancy Jack and Todd, John (1994) *From Eco-Cities to Living Machines: Principles of Ecological Design*, North Atlantic Books

UN ECE (1996) *Guidelines on Sustainable Human Settlements Planning and Management*, United Nations

Villes portuaires (2001), *L'Architecture d'Aujourd'hui*, special issue, January–February

Wilbur, S.P. (1997) An Archeology of Cyberspaces: Virtuality, Community, Identity, In: D. Porter (Ed.) *Internet Culture*, Routledge, pp. 5–22

Woolley, Tom and Kimmins, Sam (Eds) (2000) *Green Building Handbook*, Volume 2, E & FN Spon

7

Architectural aesthetics

7.1 Introduction

Among the many components that make up architectural design a special importance must be attached to construction technology. The availability of certain building materials, such as clay, stone, timber and others, has influenced building technology as is evident for example in masonry, vaulting, timber framework, and this had an impact on architectural style. This book has focussed attention on this relationship but it is important to see that this is not the only component of architectural design. The result of the impact of various technological and non-technological factors and the design process itself is architecture. What architects are doing to attain the objective of designing pleasing buildings makes up the study of architectural aesthetics, an applied part of overall aesthetics.

Aesthetics, i.e. the science concerned with beauty, was originally a part of philosophy. It has now become elevated to the rank of an independent scientific discipline but leading scientists on aesthetics even today are also philosophers (e.g. Lyotard, Derrida). The main fields of aesthetics have always been literature, art, music. In modern times it is very much engaged with film, industrial design and leisure crafts. A notable early publication about architectural aesthetics was authored by the Roman Vitruvius. Indeed Michael Hawley notes that Vitruvius's order – and remember this was more than 2000 years ago – has *finitas* (buildings should be structurally sound shelters), *utilitas* (they should accommodate human needs) and *venistas* (they should be beautiful like Venus). There followed in the renaissance period, Palladio, in the first half of the twentieth century, Le Corbusier,

and during the period 1960–2000, a host of theoreticians, architects and non-architects: Zevi, Venturi, Jencks, Eisenman and others.

Following the Second World War, some authoritative publications subjected urban life and architecture to critical analysis. They were authored by Jane Jacobs (*The Death and Life of American Cities*), Robert Venturi, Paolo Portoghesi. Postmodernism was introduced and architecture was among the early fields where post-modernism was studied and initiated. The 'meaning' and 'signs' of architectural forms were investigated together with the application of the theory of semiotics (i.e. the study of signs) as well as of linguistics. One of the outputs of such scientific work was the creation of deconstructivist architecture. In general one may postulate that if architectural aesthetics has developed into an independent discipline, then right at the forefront of that discipline is the topic of historical architecture. New architecture has created its aesthetics only very recently.

Modern architecture (which may be thought of as basically spanning the period from 1920 to 1960) held fast to the tenet that it did not need to attain its aims by means of the ornamentation and decorations of historical styles and that the use of up-to-date structures (structuralism, constructivism) would suffice also for its aesthetic objectives. This rationalism changed in about 1960. Irrationalism and sometimes mysticism regained a place, ornaments and decorations were no longer 'taboo'. Philip Johnson declared that whilst the moderns hated the history and the symbolism, we (i.e. the post-moderns) are fond of them; the moderns built without consideration for the site, we are seeking

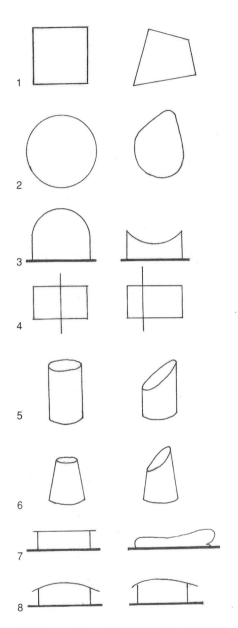

Figure 7.1 Comparison of some preferred design approaches. Left column: historical-traditional. Right column: post-modern and other new trends. 1) square – irregular quadrilateral; 2) circle – irregular curve; 3) vault – suspended roof; 4) symmetry – asymmetry; 5) regular cylinder – irregular cylinder; 6) regular cone – irregular cone; 7) flat low-pitched roof – irregular curved roof; 8) vaulted roof – roof with irregular shape.

for the *genius loci* to receive inspiration from the spirit of the site.

Modernism's scarce use of decorative forms metamorphosed into an abundance of forms. This sometimes led to 'supermanierism' or 'supermannerism' and 'façadism'. Some of the early buildings designed by Robert A.M. Stern, Ricardo Bofill, Charles Moore and Michael Graves belong in such a category. The use of metaphors, direct similes and the evocation of various forms of association have been mentioned in the first chapter of this book, along with some examples. One further example is the Fujisawa Municipal Gymnasium, Kanagawa Prefecture, Japan, designed by Fumihiko Maki, which is reminiscent of a warrior's helmet (Figure 3.30), but the list is endless.

Some structures, such as bridges, towers, silos and others, have their own aesthetics (Heinle and Leonhardt, 1989, Leonhardt, 1982). In the case of buildings, however, the matter of the components of aesthetics is more complex. During the twentieth century, repeated attempts were made to define the aesthetic principles of new architecture. As an example, the principles summarized in a book on tall buildings are quoted below (Beedle, 1995: 231):

1. *Seek harmonious geometric relationships in the overall structural arrangement. Study of geometry, classical architecture, fundamentals of music, and the basics of light and colour will reveal the presence of harmonious and disharmonious relationships. Harmonious relationships may be sought in the structure geometries and geometric proportions of the various parts of the structure. A rich source for learning classical rules in modern design is the study of classical architecture.*

2. *Omit all superfluous and unnecessary items. Avoid merely decorative items. If an item is omitted and the design is still complete, then omit that item.*

3. *Avoid superficial sculpture. To attempt sculpting may pamper one's ego but the results of such efforts will be worthless, even to its designer. If, in certain situations, sculptural elements are desired, those should be developed by an accepted and respected artist who exercises good common sense and restraint.*

139

4. *Flat, large, unexpressive, and overbearing surfaces, such as long and high walls, are unattractive, and should be broken up with clear geometric subdivisions or figures.*

5. *For concrete structures, many designers, in search for aesthetic expression, have treated the hard concrete externally to soften its looks.*

6. *The most honest forms for load-bearing elements are those related to the character of Greek, Doric, Tuscan, or Ionic columns and related framing arrangements.*

7. *If a choice is to be made between some expected aesthetic expression or a particular geometric configuration, and structural and functional capacity, the latter should be chosen for the design. Further, if meeting the structural design objectives should result in a structure that is questionable in appearance, then the structural design has not been successfully completed.*

Whilst many of the above principles retain validity, several important ones have lost it. Modernism, as has been seen, negates decorations and in particular historical style forms. Post-modernism revives decorations but its ideas on harmony and disharmony and on sculptures are quite different.

The aesthetic characteristics of new architecture often demonstrate the influence of technical progress but sometimes, partly or fully, cannot be derived from technology and are consequences of purely architectural considerations. In analysing general design principles, we may state that whilst earlier designers sought to achieve a situation where their buildings radiated harmony, post-modern architects consciously aim at dynamism. Symmetry is replaced by asymmetry, smooth linkages by hard contrasts. The hierarchy of parts is not necessarily an aim; solutions may seem arbitrary. Sizes and scales may be different from those on historical buildings. The historical buildings express some sincerity, post-modern (and deconstructivist) buildings may mislead the spectator. This explains why sometimes new architecture buildings do not reveal the number of levels or the internal function of buildings. Scales are selected in new ways, a vivid illustration of which is the Chiat/Day-Main Street building of F.O.

Gehry which has a huge binocular 'sculpture' in front of its façade. Architectural exteriors and interiors sometimes look like a huge scene from a show.

The past achievements in aesthetics have provided a foundation on which to build the aesthetics of new architecture. However, this has been achieved only in part and such aesthetic principles as hierarchical ordination, harmony, disharmony, articulation, rhythm, scale, repetition, contrast, contour, light, colour, texture, relief and many others, have been interpreted from the viewpoint of new architecture to a limited extent. There is also a subjective response to the built form and the psychological factors inherent in the appreciation of built form change in time. As has been the case for many innovations in art in the past, and is still so today, arriving at an understanding and acceptance of new architecture is not an instant process. The aesthetic assessment of an object is determined according to the way that it exists in the world and is undertaken in the context of a given environment only. The fact that changes are continually taking place in our world and in the environment must inevitably have an influence on aesthetic assessment.

In addition to identifying general trends, one should not lose sight of the important fact that architecture, being also an art, is very much the result of individuals. Eminent architects have left the imprint of their own individual taste and choices on those general trends. This may be exemplified by some characteristics of the 'style' of certain present-day Japanese architects:

• Shin Takamatsu: his buildings have a dark belligerence and a somber aggressiveness, an architecture bristling with weapons and with metallic clothing
• Kazuo Shinohara: new graphic architecture, 'zero-machines'
• Itsuko Hasegawa: preference for spheres, pyramids, simulating trees, mountains, artificial landscapes
• Hiroshi Hara: perforated buildings in motion.

'The relativity, the arbitrariness of all aesthetic propositions, of all value-judgements is inherent in human consciousness and in human speech. Anything can be said about anything' (Steiner, 1996) and, further:

> Aesthetic philosophies, critical theories, constructs of the 'classic' or the 'canonic' can never be anything but more or less persuasive, more or less comprehensive, more or less consequent descriptions of this or that process of preference. A critical theory, an aesthetic, is a politics of taste. It seeks to systematise, to make visibly applicable and pedagogic an intuitive 'set', a bent of sensibility, the conservative or radical bias of a master perceiver or alliance of opinions. There can be neither proof nor disproof ... No aesthetic proposition can be termed 'right' – 'wrong' either. The sole appropriate response is personal assent or dissent. (Steiner, 1996: 150)

New architecture cannot have one single set of aesthetics because new architecture itself is composed from buildings with different functions and stylistic trends, some of whose aesthetic ideals not only differ but are even contradictory.

A significant number of contemporary buildings have a simple geometric box-like form: witness residential, office, school and other buildings. For these, the external form, the envelope, is of primary aesthetic significance and the most important part of the envelope is the façade.

Façade walls may have a uniform appearance without any dominant articulation and without windows or other openings, or have dominant vertical, or horizontal lines, or a chessboard-like articulation, again with or without dominant vertical or horizontal lines. Surfaces may also be articulated by some regular pattern of point-like interruptions. Even uninterrupted surfaces may be decorated or differentiated by texture, or colour or lighting. Whilst this book does not deal with the architectural and structural detailing of various types of façade, these obviously have to be developed together with the objectives for a certain aesthetic appearance. Buildings with wide-span roof, masted structures and air-supported structures have their own aesthetics. Many buildings have forms designed specifically for them. The forms may be derived

from geometric shapes or from nature, or imagination. In earlier chapters a number of designs in these categories were discussed. The deconstructivist, metaphoric and organic trends use such forms. Some of these, especially deconstructivist designs, have on occasion been stigmatized as eccentric, although they may be responding to certain special requirements in a quite sober way. Let us mention here three examples.

The Planet Hollywood in Walt Disney World, Orlando, USA, 1994 (architect and interior designer: Rockwell Group) (Plate 26) contains entertainment restaurants. The building itself is a translucent blue globe, over 30 metres high and at night is illuminated all over with shimmering coloured lights.

The Trocadero Segaworld, Piccadilly Circus, London, 1996 (architect: RTKL UK Ltd, Tibbatts Associates) (Plate 27) is a futuristic pleasure dome, with neon-lit escalators leading to the top floor. It has its background in the Japanese Sega computer game manufacturer and the idea in the design is to make computer games a cyberspace adventure.

The new Guggenheim Museum in Las Vegas, which was unveiled in October 2001 (architect: Rem Koolhaas and his firm DMA) has exterior and internal walls made of Cor-Ten steel. The material with its velvety rusted surface was chosen as being evocative of the velvet-covered walls in the eighteenth century classical galleries at the Hermitage in St Petersburg, Russia. The exhibition space is partitioned by three Cor-Ten walls, which can be rotated by means of a pivot system. This provides different exhibition configurations such as a single gallery with a long central wall or four symmetrical galleries. A striking effect has been achieved by installing opaque glass panels beneath the steel walls on the front perimeter of the building. The steel walls give the appearance of floating above the floor.

The three above examples display innovative (the first two also futuristic and eccentric) internal environments. The design of internal spaces equally reflects all those possibilities that have also been discussed in the context of the external envelope. New architecture works also with sculptured or relief forms both in the exterior and interior of the

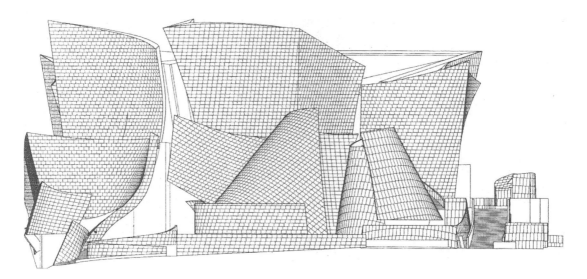

Figure 7.2 Walt Disney Concert Hall, Los Angeles, California, USA, architect: Frank O. Gehry. Deconstructivist architecture; design based on computer program, cladding from titan sheet.

buildings. The Fish Lamp, 1984 (Plate 28), by F.O. Gehry, made from Colorcore Formica, is an enigmatic sign, not having any deep meaning. However, it does acquire a practical meaning in front of fish restaurants. The standing glass fish, 1986 (Plate 29), designed by Gehry, has become an art object and is on display at the Walker Art Gallery, Minneapolis. Its materials are wire, wood, glass, steel, silicon, plexiglas, rubber and it is 6.70 metres high.

The envelope of the added volume on top of a restored and modernized office building in Budapest, Hungary 1995 (architect: Erick van Egeraat) is designed in the shape of a whale. The boardroom of the bank occupies a place in the ribbed belly of the whale.

These executed projects do go a long way to proving just how diverse are architectural design and aesthetics.

7.2 Size, Scale, Proportion

The subject of size, scale and proportion is discussed at various places in this book. Here we draw attention to some general aspects concerning which there are no universal aesthetic rules in art. A short poem or a miniature painting may be of the same high aesthetic value as monumental creations, like *War and Peace* by Tolstoy, the paintings in the Sistine Chapel by Michelangelo. This applies to architecture also. The Il Tempietto in Rome by Bramante is just as much a masterpiece as the Saint Peter Basilica also in Rome. Driven to the extremes of small or huge size, a work may be admired not so much for its aesthetic value as for the expertise in producing it in such minuscule or enormous dimensions. At the one extreme small elaborate sculptures in ivory or miniature paintings may serve as models. At the other extreme skyscrapers, pyramids, long-span suspension bridges, may serve as models. The opposite of what was previously said is also true: size in itself may not disqualify any art object from aesthetic appreciation.

Size, and other related characteristic categories – such as scale, proportion – must harmonize, however, in some measure with the actual expectations of people, or, on the contrary, be convincing with their new, and possibly revolutionary, characteristic features. Technological aspects have a function here. The cathedrals from the fifteenth to the eighteenth centuries utilized to the full the technological potentials of their period. Cathedrals with a similar stylistic approach but built in the nineteenth century (St Vlasius in the Black Forest region, Germany) or in the twentieth century (Notre Dame de la Paix in Yamassoukrou, Ivory Coast) evince admiration for their sheer size but the anachronism between style and the period of design and realization acts adversely. As has been stated earlier (see Chapter 3) new architecture has very much altered perception of size: skyscrapers and wide-span structures have been widely accepted.

Similar statements as for size may be made for scale and proportion. Absolute size and relationships of size may be very different from what was generally acceptable in historical styles.

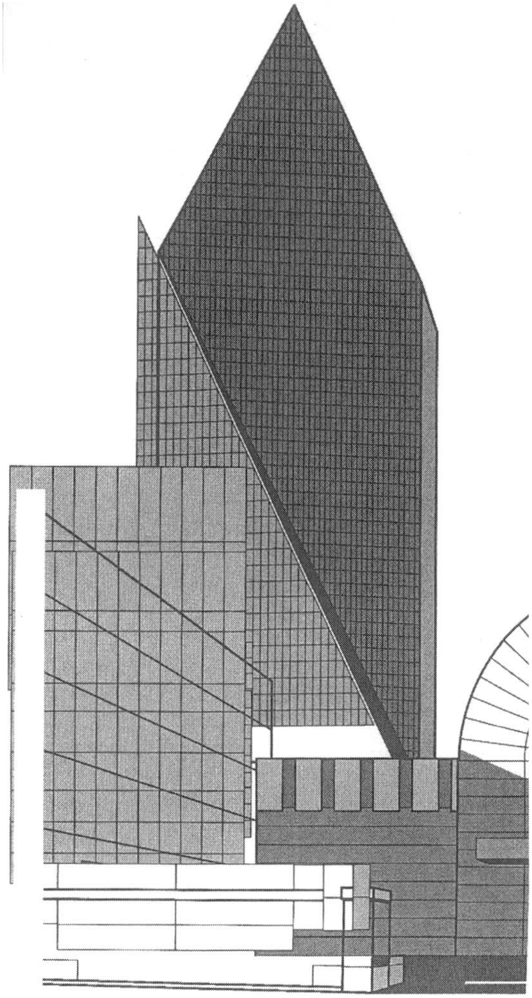

7.3 Geometry

Many authors, with widely different professional backgrounds, believed in the existence of certain systems of proportion, scale and numbers.

Alberti wrote:

> It is manifest that Nature delights in round figures, since we find that most things which are generated, made or directed by Nature are round ... We find too that Nature is sometimes delighted with figures of six sides; for bees, hornets, and all other kinds of wasps have learnt no other figure for building the cells in their hives, but the hexagon ... The polygons used by the Ancients were either of six, eight or sometimes ten sides. (Leone Battista Alberti, Ten Books on Architecture, Florence, 1485, cited in March and Steadman, The Geometry of Environment).

The various series of numbers (the Cantor set, the Fibonacci series), of curves (the Koch, the Minkowski and the Peano curves), the system of fractals, the golden section, Le Corbusier's 'modulor' (based on repeated golden rectangle proportions) are but a few examples (Van Der Laan, 1983, Mandelbrot, 1983, Bovill, 1996). It has been assumed that certain such systems must be applied in architecture also (Padovan 1999, Salingaros, 2000). Geometric systems (as for example the module system) are transformed into number systems and vice versa (as for instance the Van Der Laan scale) (Van Der Laan, 1983). Certain styles and some architects did introduce various systems of proportions, scales, rhythms and mea-

Figure 7.3 First Interstate Bank Tower, Dallas, USA, 1985, architect: Henry N. Cobb. Uninterrupted large-scale slanting glass facade (unknown in historical architecture).

New Architecture and Technology

Figure 7.4 National Assembly, Dacca, Bangladesh, 1962–83, designer: Sher E. Banglaganar. Geometric patterns (triangle, etc.) may be dominant on a façade.

sures. Palladio designed the plans of his villas on rectangles with whole number proportions: 1:1, 1:2, 2:3, 1:4, 3:8 (Elam, 2001, Padovan, 1999).

Architecture, after all, is a manifestation of geometry applied for the purpose of the design of buildings. Research attempted to create geometric systems for structural or architectural design, as has been seen already when discussing space frames, shells, domes and membranes. Some of the systems are of a pure mathematical or geometric character, in others structural or architectural design forms the basic background. There are attempts to develop fully automated structural design systems with geometric representation for structural domains, using automated techniques for finite element modelling, coupling self-adaptive integration of optimization techniques with geometry models (Kodiyalam, and Saxena, 1994). 'Solid modelling', meaning representation design, visualization, and analysis of three-dimensional computer models of real objects, finds application in the design of buildings but in other quite different fields also.

The attributes of symmetry and harmony gained favour in historical architecture: asymmetry, however, was appreciated only to the extent that it achieves harmony. On the other hand Viollet-le-Duc, a nineteenth-century architect, wrote: 'Symmetry – an unhappy idea for which in our homes, we sacrifice our comfort, occasionally our common sense and always a lot of money' (quoted by March and Steadman). Rhythm meant either repetition or variations with pleasing relationships. In modern and post-modern aesthetics, sometimes seemingly arbitrary deviations from repetition and disharmonic alterations became welcome. So, for instance, the memorial colonnade by Oscar Niemeyer was designed with variable column distances.

However, even the most sophisticated systems do not prevail forever, and invariably change over time. Styles and architectural design have to cope anew repeatedly with this transience and must devise their own solution for attaining pleasing appearances of buildings. What, however, is 'pleasing', is in itself a dynamic concept and the history of art and architecture continuously reports new design concepts that initially were judged to be ugly but as time went on were considered to be agreeable (Kroll, 1986).

The geometry of new architecture buildings may also display new features. Straight lines become curves, verticals and horizontals may be slanted and cut into each other at odd angles. Curves that

144

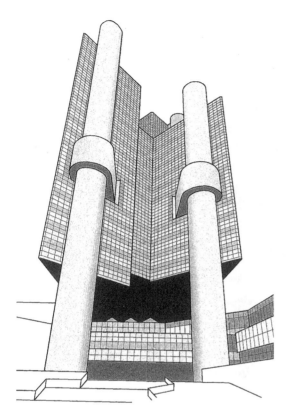

Figure 7.5 Hypo Bank Headquarters, Munich, Germany. Façade with out-of-size proportioned components.

traditionally featured in gothic, renaissance and baroque architecture are ignored; partly regular curves (circle, etc.) and individually designed curves take their place.

Naturally, the foregoing does not apply to all new buildings. Neo-classicist and late-modern buildings may adhere much more closely to the old rules.

Japanese architects have been ingenious in their application of geometric forms. Tadao Ando, for instance, favours a grid derived from traditional rice straw tatami mat with dimensions of 90 by 180 centimetres. Ando designs concrete walls with an exposed surface and each of his moulding boards (with the size of a tatami) has six holes through which the boards' screws are driven. Arata Isozaki accords preference in his geometry to the square

and the circle. In some designs he uses segments of curves and curved surfaces. On occasion grids are applied combined at slanted angles.

Size, scale and measure are changing. Large-size surfaces are articulated and contain uniformly spread identical small-scale elements or forms. In such cases a certain uniformity of the surface may be achieved and the contours of such surfaces can be selected almost at random.

It was pointed out that new architecture often extends components to the outside of buildings and sometimes into the air space. This is typical for suspended structures with external masts and cable systems but it can occur in other cases too, see, for example, Himmelblau's office extension in Vienna. An innovative architectural component is the tall atrium often applied in large hotel buildings and office buildings. The internal height of such atria may reach up to 40 or more levels and poses a fresh challenge for their internal design (see the interiors of the hotels designed by John Portman).

7.4 Recesses, Cavities, Holes, Canted/Slanted Lines and Planes

Although energy conservation and control over cost would call for simple contours and building volumes, in new architecture recesses and cavities in the building volumes are frequent. This ensures deep shadows and picturesque buildings. Some authors call buildings with recesses, cavities or holes 'eroded' volumes. Buildings with volumes pushed into each other at irregular angles, are referred to as 'crashed' volumes.

Cavities and holes in a building, in particular at some height, are new in architecture (not counting arches) and also give rise to new technical problems, such as the wind blowing through the aperture.

Canted or slanted planes, façades, columns and other components cause particular difficulties for the architect, the structural and services engineer and in addition require special skill from the construction team. Many architecturally impressive tall buildings have been designed and constructed

Figure 7.6 Residential Building, Berlin Friedrichstrasse, Germany, architect: Aldo Rossi. Large-size cylindrical column and cut-out of building.

with such geometry. A notable realization is the Dongba Securities Headquarters, a 35-storey tower in Seoul, Korea and there are several others. In some historic buildings (for example, at the Winter Palace in St Petersburg, Russia), an arch in the building opens a throughway. In modern times, reinforced concrete and steel structures enable the designer to cut through a building in different spectacular fashions. Examples are abundant.

7.5 Colour, Light and Shadow

In historical architecture the range of colours was limited and depended on available natural materials and paints. In new architecture the range of colours is much broader and harsh colours are feasible through the application of paints, enamels and anodized colouring (Couleur, 2001).

Colour, light and shadow have always had an impact on the appearance of buildings and structures and nowadays these factors may be used in new ways (Franck and Lepori, 2000). The choice of colours, in particular on external surfaces, was limited also by weathering requirements. Research has built up a vast knowledge on colours comprising the phenomena of brightness, lightness, blackness, greyness, whiteness, contrast, hue, shade, colour systems, combining and mixing of colours, colour harmonization and patterns, changing colour impressions and interaction between colour and people (Rihlama, 1999).

New chemical processes have created new types of paints and colours. Architects are willing to design the exterior or interior of buildings with new colour effects. To mention one realization only: the new Luxor Theatre in the Kop van Zuid district of Rotterdam has a leading red colour on the surfaces (architect: Bolles and Wilson AIT, 2001). Strong colours on buildings evince a similarity with the colouring of machines (cars, electrical appliances, furniture, etc.) and electrical cables. There are some architects who have opted to make certain colours their design trademark, e.g. Richard Meier

with his steel panels enamelled to a white colour. Others, e.g. some Japanese architects, prefer the dominance of grey.

Lighting has grown into an important factor in architectural design, as can be seen from this statement from Le Corbusier (Sebestyen, 1998): 'Architecture is the learned, correct and magnificent play of masses under light.' Building with light has been applied ingeniously by architects and studied in great detail (Building with Light, 2001). Artificial illumination provides new visual effects. The New York LVMH tower designed by the Frenchman Christian de Portzamparc is illuminated nightly by a warm golden colour that gradually changes into a deep green. Colour may be applied over a surface or focussed on a spot or on several spots. If light is concentrated over several small points and applied to a dense pattern, it becomes a tool of articulation. This approach was applied by

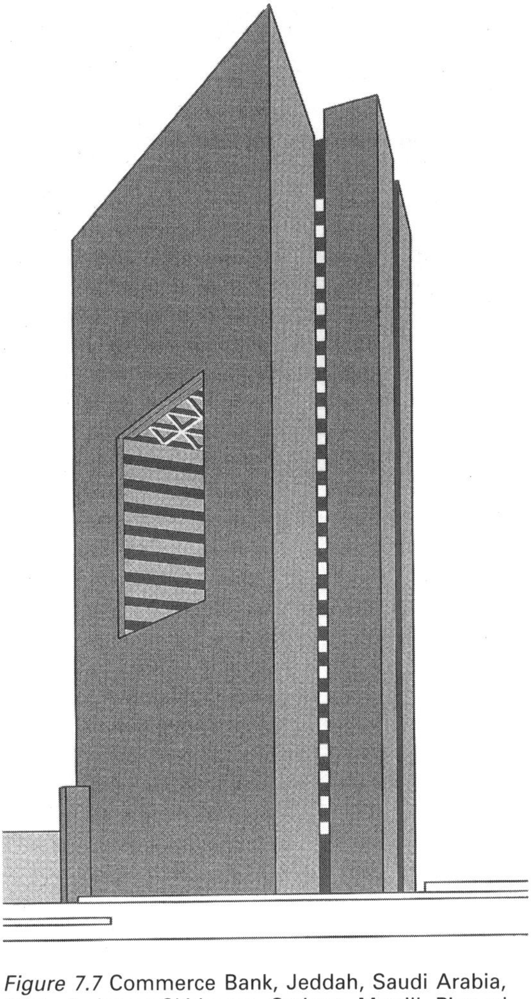

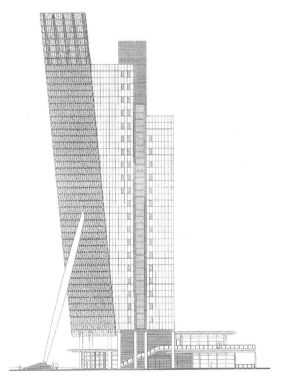

Figure 7.7 Commerce Bank, Jeddah, Saudi Arabia, 1984, designer: Skidmore, Owings, Merrill. Pierced-through volume in a tall building.

Figure 7.8 The new Dutch KPN Telecom building, Rotterdam. Articulation may be realized through light spots.

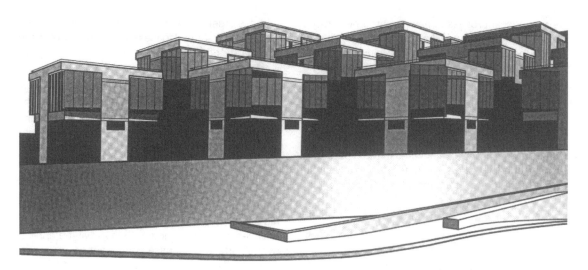

Figure 7.9 Centraal Beheer Office, The Netherlands, architect: Herman Hertzberger. Articulation of building volumes: separated but interconnected workplaces.

Renzo Piano at one façade of the KPN Telecom Office Tower in Rotterdam (Figure 7.8). Green lamp elements are set on this façade in a grid pattern. The lamps are individually switched on and off and are controlled by a computer program.

7.6 Articulation

In Beedle (1995: 149) articulation is defined as follows: 'Action or manner of jointing or interrelating architectural elements throughout a design or building.' This definition is of general validity and it includes articulation of a ground plan to rooms, the division of a façade by repetitive decorations and/or dividing lines of floors or panels. Articulation of building volumes and of the urban space has acquired special meaning. Dutch architects (Aldo Van Eyck and Herman Hertzberger) designed buildings with strongly articulated premises and provided theoretical justification for this kind of articulation: 'Things must only be big as a multiple of units which are small in themselves, for excess soon creates an effect of distance, and by always making everything too big, too empty, and thus too distant and untouchable, architects are producing in the first place distance and inhospitality'

(Hertzberger, in Lüchinger, 1981). However, articulation of the building volume (anti-block movement) and of the urban fabric does not exclude bigness. Articulation in our time is specifically used as a decorative (and constructive) subdivision of a surface (a façade or a ceiling) into uniform small decorative elements where there exists a complete neutrality regarding the size and shape of that surface. This led to the development of various 'systems' or 'subsystems' for façades, ceilings and other surfaces (Ornement, 2001).

Articulation of the space is achieved among other means by space divisions. In deconstructivist architecture (e.g. by Frank O. Gehry) spaces may be divided by quasi-virtual components, for instance, chains and grids.

Historical styles articulated the surface by a variety of flat or relief decorations. In modern architecture big flat surfaces, not articulated in any way, were employed.

Then in some designs large flat surfaces received an articulation of large sub-surfaces, frequently by marking these in specific colours. This type of 'decoration' may be applied in some cases but it never becomes a basic way of articulating and decorating surfaces.

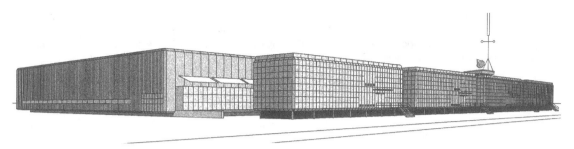

Figure 7.10 CENG industrial building project, Grenoble, France, architect: Jacques Ferrier. Example of façade building articulation with emphasis on parallel vertical lines.

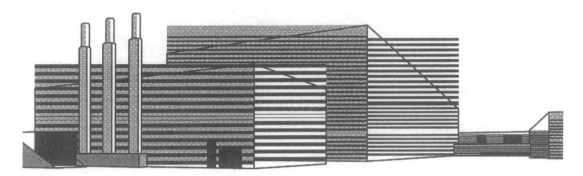

Figure 7.11 IBM factory office, Basiano, near Milan, Italy, 1983, architect: Grino Valle. IBM company design model.

7.7 Theory and Praxis

The aesthetics of new architecture has spawned many publications, essays, theories. Ultimately, however, architecture is concerned with buildings and not theories. Ben van Berkel, a young Dutch architect (designer of the Rotterdam cable-stayed bridge) insisted 'that he is of a different generation, implicitly criticising them [meaning educators of young architects] for designing buildings to suit their theories' (quoted from Philip Jodidio (1996) *Contemporary European Architects*, Volume IV, Taschen).

Bibliography

Beedle, Lynn S. (Ed.-in-Chief), Armstrong, Paul J. (Ed.) (1995) *Architecture of Tall Buildings*, Council on Tall Buildings and Urban Habitat, McGraw-Hill, Inc.

Benjamin, A. and Norris, C. (1988) *What is Deconstruction?*, Academy Editions

Bofill, Ricardo (1989) *Espaces d'une vie*, Editions Odile

Bovill, Carl (1996) *Fractal Geometry in Architecture and Design*, Birkhäuser

Broadbent, G., Bunt, R. and Jencks, C.A. (1980) *Signs, Symbols and Architecture*, Wiley

Building with Light (2001) *Deutsche Bauzeitung (db)*, special issue, Vol. 135, No. 1

Canter, D.V. (1977) *The Psychology of Place*, Architectural Press

Couleur (2001), *L'Architecture d'Aujourd'hui*, special issue, No. 334, May–June

Dufrenne, Mikel (1st and 2nd Vols: 1976, 3rd Vol.: 1981) *Esthétique et philosophie*, Kleinsieck

Elam, Kimberly (2001) *Geometry of Design*, Princeton Architectural Press

Engineering News-Record, 12 March 2001, p. 16

149

Franck, Karen A. and Lepori, R. Bianca (2000) *Architecture Inside Out*, Wiley-Academy

Giorgini, Vittorio (1995) *Spatiology: The Morphology of the Natural Sciences in Architecture and Design*, Arca Edizioni

Heinle, E. and Leonhardt, F. (1989) *Towers: A Historical Survey*, Butterworth Architecture

Holgate, A. (1992) *Aesthetics of Built Form*, Oxford University Press

Ibelings, H. (1998) *Supermodernism: Architecture in the Age of Globalization*, NAI

Jencks, C. and Baird, G. (Eds) (1969) *Meaning in Architecture: Barrie and Rocklift*, The Cresset Press

Johnson, P.-A. (1994) *The Theory of Architecture: Concepts, Themes and Practices*, Van Nostrand Reinhold

Johnson, Philip and Wigley, Mark (1988) *Deconstructivist Architecture*, The Museum of Modern Art

Kodiyalam, S. and Saxena, M. (1994) *Geometry and Optimisation Techniques for Structural Design*, Computational Mechanics Publications & Elsevier Applied Science

Kroll, Lucien (1986) *The Architecture of Complexity*, B.T. Batsford

Leonhardt, F. (1982) *Brücken/Bridges*, Deutsche Verlags-Anstalt

Lucan, Jacques (1990) *OMA: Rem Koolhaas*, Electa Moniteur

Mandelbrot, Benoit (1983) *The Fractal Geometry of Nature*, W.F. Freeman

Michelis, P.A. (1974) *L'esthétique de l'architecture*, Kleinsieck

Ornement (2001) *Techniques and Architecture*, March–April

Padovan, Richard (1999) *Proportion. Science, Philosophy, Architecture*, E & FN Spon

Prak, N.L. (1968) *The Language of Architecture*, Mouton

Rihlama, Seppo (1999) *Colour World*, The Finnish Building Centre

Robbin, T. (1996) *Engineering a New Architecture*, Yale University Press

Rossi, Aldo (1981) *A Scientific Autobiography*, MIT Press Institute for Architecture and Urban Studies

Salingaros, Nikos A. (2000) Hierarchical Cooperation in Architecture and the Mathematical Necessity for Ornament, *Journal of Architectural and Planning Research*, Vol. 17, No. 3, autumn, pp. 221–35

Scruton, R. (1979) *The Aesthetics of Architecture*, Methuen

Steiner, George (1996) *No Passion Spent, Essays 1978–1996*, Faber and Faber

Toy, M. (Ed.) *Minimal Architecture*, AD Profile No. 139, Academy Editions

Van Der Laan, Dom H. (1983) *Architectonic Spaces*, E.J. Brill

Zevi, B. (1978) *The Modern Language of Architecture*, University of Washington Press

8

The price of progress: defects, damages and failures

Before analysing the problems arising from technical progress, let us glance at the sources of architectural-technical development, which may be defined in terms of scientific discoveries, innovations and improvements. It can be readily perceived that whereas in industry research is a main source of technical progress, it is much less so in architecture.

Research in building has developed later than in industry, although this is not to say that construction did not always make good use of research results achieved elsewhere. The introduction of new materials such as steel, concrete, plastics and of modern equipment in construction resulted from applications of industry's technical progress. The creative new ideas in architecture originated from inventive architects and structural designers. Building research concentrated its efforts on consolidating these new ideas and rendering them capable of being applied by all practitioners. Inventions and patents play a more restricted role in building than in most other branches of industry (Kronz, 1977). Intellectual property matters in architecture are for the most part regulated by legal restrictions on plagiarism, which is understandable given that patents are there to protect inventions applicable in industry. Publications about the sources of invention rarely, if at all, accord architecture a mention, although case studies on prestressed concrete, geodesic domes, suspension and cable-stayed bridges would surely deserve documentation (Jewkes, 1958). Nevertheless, there do exist problems about protecting new ideas in architecture and construction and such problems merit study.

The dilemma of technical progress also faced in construction is that whilst innovations are desirable, the great number of factors affecting the built products frequently cause unforeseen defects, damages, failures, catastrophes and this commands caution in introducing novelties. In historical periods approaches by trial and error did provide some, but by no means sufficient, protection. Currently the use of small-scale models, laboratory tests, visualization through models, simulation, experimental and demonstration projects assist the designer, but the most significant contribution to design is the application of widened research, its results and methods. Despite such measures, damages and failures cannot be avoided completely but they should be kept to a minimum. Where symptoms of defects become apparent, the causes should be clarified as soon as possible and measures taken to prevent further deterioration.

The study of defects and damages has become an independent discipline, which is often called 'building pathology' (Watt, 1999, Blaich, 1999, Hinks and Cook, 1997, Marshall et al., 1998). Certain individuals and institutions specialize in the study of defects and damages and appear as expert witnesses before courts as well as devising remedies for individual cases. Indeed some architects themselves include in their portfolio of activities the function of expert in various cases of damages and defects.

In any case, an architect must be equipped to tackle problems of building pathology and conflicts. This is a safeguard against loss of prestige and eventual legal and financial responsibility. Liability may affect the architect's work and he may be called upon to prove that defects and damages have not occurred as a consequence of his own work, negligence or inadequate knowledge (Knocke, 1993).

Building pathology comprises various activities, such as:

- assessment of the technical condition of buildings and structures
- identification, investigation and diagnosis of defects in existing buildings
- scientific and practical study of abnormalities in materials, components and equipment of buildings, classification of abnormalities and their development in time, methods of prognosis of various forms of degradation
- developing investigative methods with the purpose of ascertaining in advance eventual future abnormalities, identifying already occurred degradation and prognosis of future degradation
- establishing typical categories of abnormalities, preparing statistical studies on occurrence, study of economic impact of degradation also as a basis to define what strategies to follow concerning these abnormalities
- exploring methods of repair and other remedial work
- preparing recommendations, codes and principles of improved design, contributing to the future prevention of defects.

Defects, damages and failures can be classified in different ways. One of these is the classification based on the field of activities in which they occur (Feld and Carper, 1997):

- Fundamental errors in concept
- Site selection and site development errors
- Programming deficiencies
- Design errors
- Construction errors
- Material deficiencies
- Operational errors.

Other classifications are based on:

- the place where the defects occur (foundation, wall, floor, roof, etc.)

- classes of disciplines in which the failure has been caused (failures due to errors in structural analysis, building physics, etc.)
- the agents causing the degradation, such as mechanical agents, electromagnetic agents, thermal and moisture agents, chemical agents, biological agents
- classes of failure consequences (inadequate human comfort, deformation, structural collapse, etc.).

Such a classification has been detailed for the case of low-rise housing (Marshall et al., 1998):

- Building Movement, Foundations
- Building Movement, Walls
- Brickwork and Stonework
- Ground Floors
- Upper Floors
- Pitched Roofs
- Flat Roofs
- External Rendering
- Plastering and Plasterboard
- Internal Walls
- Timber Pests
- Condensation
- Damp
- System Building
- Services.

Work directed towards the investigation of damages, failures and catastrophic events is also referred to as forensic engineering investigation (Carper, 2001, Noon, 2001). Behind each of the above headings a vast stock of knowledge is concealed, so that the list serves only as a pointer for further literature search.

Specific categories of structures (such as foundations, walls, roofs, etc.) display specific types of damages and failures. For example, the principal degradation categories for metal sheet cladding have been classified as follows (Ryan et al., 1994):

- Chalking, loss of gloss or colour change
- Crazing or flaking
- Corrosion of galvanizing (steel cladding)
- Base metal corrosion.

For typical types of damages and degradation processes repair technologies have also been worked out.

During the post-Second World War period and subsequently technical progress accelerated. New materials, components, structures, equipment have been introduced and unfortunately, together with this, damages, some causing substantial loss of human life and financial loss, have occurred more frequently. Particularly vivid descriptions were provided by the late William Allen (Allen et al., 1995). He recorded the most widely occurring diseases, veritable epidemics in housing in the United Kingdom following the Second World War. These included: condensation in the external walls, flat roof membrane destruction, degradation of plastics for roofs, thermal pumping, dimensional conflicts and rain screen technology.

Many catastrophes are caused by natural forces in the form of earthquakes, extreme wind, flooding, fire and subsoil collapse. Some of these are dealt with as appropriate elsewhere. Whatever the cause, however, we are intentionally refraining from a discussion of the failures of civil engineering structures: bridges, tunnels, dams, and instead we are confining our attention to failures in buildings.

Certain major catastrophes have become so well known as to require no more than a simple listing (together with a short description of what happened):

- Ronan Point, London, 1968: progressive collapse in a 22-storey residential building with factory-manufactured load-bearing walls, caused by an accidental gas explosion.
- Civic Center Coliseum, Hartford, Connecticut, USA, 1978: a 9700 square metre building's steel space truss roof collapsed under moderate snow load, due primarily to design deficiencies.
- West Berlin Congress Hall, (former West) Berlin, Germany, 1980: collapse of one-third of a reinforced concrete shell structure, due to dynamic stress and corrosion in the prestressing tendons.
- John Hancock Tower, Boston, Massachusetts, USA, a 241 metres-tall office building, defects appearing during the period 1971–80: dramatic fractures of the glass façade, unacceptable dynamic response in the wind.
- Hyatt Regency Hotel Pedestrian Walkways, Kansas City, Missouri, USA, 1981: 114 deaths

and 185 injuries resulted; the collapse was the consequence of a number of mistakes in the design and execution of the walkway suspension.

A special note, however, must be inserted as regards certain violent cases of catastrophe: suicidal and terrorist actions. Whilst at first sight this may appear to be too broad an issue to be discussed just within the context of structural design, it does regrettably seem to be a problem to be confronted by politicians, managers and engineers, with obvious repercussions on architectural practice. A number of catastrophic events have over several years served as a warning. One of these was the terrorist bombing of the Alfred P. Murrah Federal Building in Oklahoma City on 19 April 1995, which resulted in 168 deaths and over 500 wounded. The bomb attack on the World Trade Center in New York on 16 February 1993 caused six deaths and well over 1000 wounded. The most tragic event, however, was the terrorist attack on the twin towers of the New York World Trade Center and the Pentagon Building in Washington DC on 11 September 2001 when the number of fatalities ran into thousands. Whilst it is true that systematic early detection and prevention is the main issue, there are inevitable consequences on codes and design practices.

Although each failure may have individual characteristics, many may be considered as having certain common causes. One group of defects has a structural engineering background, others are of a non-structural character. Whilst the responsibility of the architect takes in every type of defect, the responsibility for structural failures rests primarily with the structural designer. For non-structural defects the architect's responsibility is direct although it may be shared with specialist experts and companies having a responsibility in a given restricted field of the design and execution. What follows is an (incomplete) listing of some common failure/defect categories.

Foundations of buildings may fail due to changes in the properties of the subsoil: undermining or unsafe support of existing structures, lateral soil movement, down-drag and heave, vibrations, water content fluctuations, landslides, land subsidence. The inadequacy of connections is a frequent cause of timber structures' failure. Timber and steel frequently deteriorate as a consequence of insufficient protection against corrosion and (in the case of timber) fungi, termites, insects. Errors in erection and assembly mistakes (e.g. in bolting, welding, etc.) cause failures of steel structures. A major cause of damages in concrete and reinforced concrete structures are mistakes in the composition of the concrete, corrosion due to inadequate cover of reinforcement and excessive amount of admixtures (calcium chloride, etc.). Design defects (through faulty evaluation of, for example, shear, buckling or ductility) may also result in failure of reinforced concrete structures.

In the field of non-structural damages new techniques sometimes led to damage in the initial period of their application, for instance, in the external envelope, surface and interstitial condensation. After the Second World War new types of multi-layer external walls were introduced: curtain walls, prefabricated reinforced concrete large-panel walls and framed light walls for family houses. In these the weather-resistant hard layer was on the external side with the soft heat-insulating layer to the inside. The transmission of vapour across the wall was impeded. An additional frequent source of trouble was that at the connection of wall and floor a reinforced concrete beam further reduced heat insulation. This gave rise to vapour condensation especially in the upper external corners of rooms. Inadequate ventilation, better insulating windows and too many persons in small flats all contributed to increased partial vapour pressure and humidity of the air. Vapour-resistant claddings were one cause of spalling of façade tiles and stone slabs. A vapour barrier on the inside of the wall and better ventilation helped to eliminate humidity. One group of frequently occurring damages were those in flat roofs. The membrane materials used in the 1960s and 1970s (asphalt and felt) tended to become brittle with age (Stratton, 1997). Vapour control was often inadequate resulting in internal condensation and mould. Perimeter details were deficient thereby allowing the penetration of water. The experience collected during the study of damages led to the introduction of new materials and principles (for example, the inverted roof) as a means to prevent future occurrence. The use of lightweight multi-layer external walls and various types of façade claddings proved to be a source of damages. Tile spalling became one of the adverse consequences, interstitial condensation another. The introduction of the decompression cavity in joints of external wall panels halted the penetration of driving rain through the wall. The application of proven new technologies has become essential to avoid new architecture being brought into disrepute.

When reviewing defects, damages, failures and, above all, catastrophic events, one reaches the inescapable conclusion that technical progress itself has not put a complete stop to the occurrence in any of the above categories. It is also to be admitted that in most cases it is not the absence of knowledge that can be blamed but rather carelessness and even superficiality.

In the Netherlands a fireworks storage and manufacturing plant blew up as a consequence of unlawfully stored material. The last two days of 2001 saw two further catastrophic fires in fireworks factories: one in Lima, Peru with a great number of deaths and another in China. In Israel guests at a marriage ceremony fell as the reinforced concrete floor under them gave way, following an earlier dismantling of supporting columns. In Budapest, Hungary, in 2001, a large-panel building was partly destroyed after an explosion, caused by stored chemicals on the third floor ignited with criminal purpose. In Quezon City, near Manila, the Philippines, a hotel fire in August 2001 caused the deaths of 75 people who could not escape because all exits including windows were shut and blocked.

Better education, more care and attention, stricter control for ensuring safety and security, are needed. New architecture and, together with it, modern technology, provide an overwhelming majority of splendid new buildings yet caution must always remain.

The responsibility of the architect is first and foremost to design faultless buildings and structures. He cannot take on responsibility for the negligence or ignorance of others: the contractor, user, facility manager and others. Nevertheless it is the mission of architects to draw attention to potential problems and eventually (if so authorized) to serve as adviser and educator in the course of construction and exploitation of his buildings. An important responsibility lies with authorities in carefully controlling a building throughout its life. It can be expected that if the above conditions are met, disaster prevention will be effective (Allen et al., 1992) and the spin-off will be praise rather than criticism for the architect's work.

Whilst repeating the statement that most damages and failures do not lie in a lack of knowledge but are derived from personal ignorance, negligence and mismanagement, there still are fields where additional research is required. For a long time, in fact for more than a century, suspension bridges were in this category. Major and smaller failures were numerous, among such spectacular ones as the collapse of the Tacoma Narrows Suspension Bridge, USA (spanning over a mile with a combination of a cable-supported suspension structure and steel-plate girder approach spans) in November 1940. In-depth research into their behaviour under dynamic action resulted in seemingly safe bridges.

Recently, however, some disquieting experiences have surfaced with swinging and buckling of suspension and cable-stayed bridges. One such new bridge has been the one over the Maas in Rotterdam where excessive swinging necessitated the addition of members to make the cables more rigid. The pedestrian bridge between St Paul's and the Tate Modern Gallery in London and the designed, but as yet to be constructed, pedestrian bridge between Pimlico and the former Battersea power station required similar reinforcement. This seems to confirm the thesis that scientific progress is a precondition for technological progress and for construction without damages.

Bibliography

AIT (Architectur, Innenarchitektur, Technischer Ausbau) (2001) No. 7/8, pp. 69–77

Allen, William (1995) The Pathology of Modern Building, Building Research and Information, Vol. 23, No. 3, pp. 139–46

Allen, W.A., et al., (Eds) (1992) A Global Strategy for Housing in the Third Millennium, E & FN Spon

Blaich, Jürgen (1999) La détérioration des batiments, EMPA (in German: Bauschäden. Analyse und Vermeidung)

Carper, Kenneth L. (2001) Forensic Engineering, 2nd edn, CRC Press

Feld, Jacob and Carper, Kenneth L. (1997) Construction Failure, 2nd edn, John Wiley & Sons, Inc.

Hinks, John and Cook, Geoff (1997) The Technology of Building Defects, E & F N Spon

Jewkes, J., Sawers, D. and Stillerman, R. (1958) The Sources of Invention, Macmillan

Knocke, J. (1993) Post-Construction Liability, E & FN Spon

Kronz, Hermann (1977) Patentschutz im Bausektor, Mitteilungen der Deutschen Patentanwälte, February, Jahrgang 68, Heft 2

Levy, M. and Salvadori, N.M. (1992) Why Buildings Fall Down, W.W. Norton

Marshall, Duncan, Worthing, Derek and Heath, Roger (1998) Understanding Housing Defects, Estates Gazette Defects, School of Land and Property Management, UWE Bristol

Noon, Randall K. (2001) Forensic Engineering Investigation, CRC Press

Ransom, W.H. (1981) Building Failures, E & FN Spon

Richardson, B.A. (1980) Remedial Treatment of Buildings, The Construction Press

Ryan, P.A. et al. (1994) Durability of Cladding, WS/Atkins and Thomas Telford

Salvadori, M. (1980) Why Buildings Stand Up, W.W. Norton

Stratton, Michael (Ed.) (1997) Structure and Style: Conserving 20th Century Buildings, E & FN Spon

Watt, S. David (1999) Building Pathology: Principles and Practice, Blackwell Science

9

Conclusion

Architecture has undergone continual change from time immemorial but these changes have multiplied during the twentieth century. A plethora of styles, trends and approaches have come and gone. However, as Mies van der Rohe stated: 'one cannot have a new architecture every Monday morning'. We have reached a position where we can identify certain characteristics of new architecture, but there does not exist as yet any leading, dominant architecture. We may appreciate the position that we have reached and now we must sit back and wait to see where further development will lead us.

New (contemporary and future) architecture has retained many of its historical antecedents, but along the way it has also acquired some exciting new components. One of these is the impact of modern technology. This itself has a dual character: the changing technologies in the sectors that are clients and users of buildings and the changing technology of the construction process including changes of design and execution. The first of these two changes resulted in new requirements for and in buildings. The second altered the technology of design and architecture. The function and relations of participants in the construction process changed. The new pattern of the client supported by an expert staff for the buildings that that client requires and operates, and general and specialized designers and contractors exerted strong pressure for the emergence of new procurement methods. All this is intimately interwoven with the new technologies in information, telecommunication and management.

The new materials and composites introduced, such as steel and aluminium alloys, titanium, high-performance concrete and plastics, are powerful new components of present-day design. The same applies to new structures: domes, shells, vaults, space trusses, masted, suspended, stressed and air-supported structures and new functions of buildings. A particularly conspicuous new step in technological progress has been the large-scale introduction of tall buildings, wide-span structures and the much broadened scope of the technical services in buildings. These upgraded the role of structural and other (HVAC, acoustical, fire, heat and moisture, etc.) engineers as partners of the architects in the design process. Increased importance has been given to new aesthetic effects and new requirements: light, shade, sound, security, transparency, clean air, new forms, cooperation with other branches of art.

A new feature of the scene for architecture is the reshaping of city centres, which offers new perspectives to new construction and the renewal of buildings.

It is fair to admit that progresses in science and applied research are by no means the sole factors to have an impact on architecture. Overall changes in society, the economy and culture and demographic changes will become increasingly relevant to architecture and the development of human settlements. Considerations for conservation of natural resources, such as land, energy, timber, minerals, protection of our environment, prevention of contamination and pollution of soil, air and water and retaining or creating conditions for sustainable human life and wealth will all take on increasing significance for future architecture.

The great masters of modernist architecture felt imbued with a mission to shape the future of society. They thought that by designing buildings and cities with new ideas, they would also be able to devise future social structures. Post-modernist and present-day architects seem to nurture less ambitious ideas. They want to design good and appealing buildings although they do have certain visions as to how these will affect future human and social life. The impact of function on form has undergone a change. Modernist architectural theory claimed that function is the most important factor in determining architectural form and rejected any interference with this relationship. Function has remained important in our time but the architect's form-finding has regained a notable measure of liberty. Greater liberty in artistic creative work, however, goes hand in hand with an increased respect for the participation of technical engineering designers.

These developments have resulted in new systems of users' requirements and, in order to satisfy these, new performance of materials, structures and buildings. These changes ultimately transformed the appearance of buildings.

The architecture of the twentieth century commenced with the last historical styles: eclecticism and secession. Then the powerful thrust for modernism brought with it a wish for a new global style. This movement was crowned by the success of the 'International Style'. During the second half of the century the situation that saw buildings appearing that were independent from characteristics of the region, the traditions and the place, and the total abandonment of all ornamentation, evinced dissatisfaction. Post-modernism stepped on the scene but this, however, was no longer a 'style'. Some of the trends during the post-modernist period even went so far as to reject the label of post-modernism. Deconstructivism, organic-regional and metaphoric thinking and other trends all vied for a place in architecture. Now, having entered the twenty-first century, it must be recognized that there is ample justification to offer freedom for the architectural solution of individual design problems. This freedom, however, is not without certain constraints. The diversification of the buildings, a renewed wish for some kind of artistic ornamentation and the need to incorporate into the designs the most recent results of technological progress all proved to be components of the work of the architect.

Together with the technological changes, the principles, morphology and ornamentation of architecture have been transformed.

This book has focussed on the impact on architecture. It has mentioned, but not in any detail, such subjects as architectural education, the new position of architectural practice and many others. It is also fair to point out that architecture, during the twentieth century and at the present time had and has at its pinnacle eminent figures who usually also have been in the vanguard as regards applying modern technology. There are no restricted lists of such top architects but, for example, Le Corbusier and one or some of the designers of modern structures (Kenzo Tange, Paolo Nervi, etc.) would certainly justify inclusion on the list covering the first 60-odd years of the twentieth century; Norman Foster and Frank O. Gehry would be on the list covering the last 30 years or so and into the present. In the meantime a new generation of architects has entered the scene and in our century we shall be certain to see further names figuring in the catalogue of top architects. Fame and celebrity in themselves are not the ambition of any professional, including architects, but it certainly is a help in receiving important commissions of architectural design. In parallel to a list of outstanding architects each period selects its candidates for a list of the most outstanding realizations, which also enhance the stock of the most outstanding products of human activities. At the same time one should not forget that the total architectural product of any period comprises various types of building and their overall quality is of paramount importance.

The manifold tasks of architecture have broadened the scope and history of architecture. No longer can one point to a well-defined architectural style and this plurality will probably manifest itself in the future also. Common fashion trends will appear and disappear but will be accompanied by local or individual approaches. To sum up: architecture as affected by modern life will be rich and many-sided.

Human society never stands still. What has long been a matter for debate is the extent to which technical progress is also progress in the quality of life. Time and again architects have come forward who believed that they had achieved perfection. In reality this never proved to be so. At the same time architects did produce designs which were the basis for masterpieces. The next generation arrived and with it a new style, new trends, new ways to express the needs of human society in buildings.

This will remain so in the future. The progress of architecture cannot be halted.

Bibliography

Groak, Steven (1992) *The Idea of Building: Thought and Action in the Design and Production of Buildings*, E & FN Spon

Index

Index of categories of buildings

Sports stadia

Other buildings, structures, systems, locations

Index of proper names